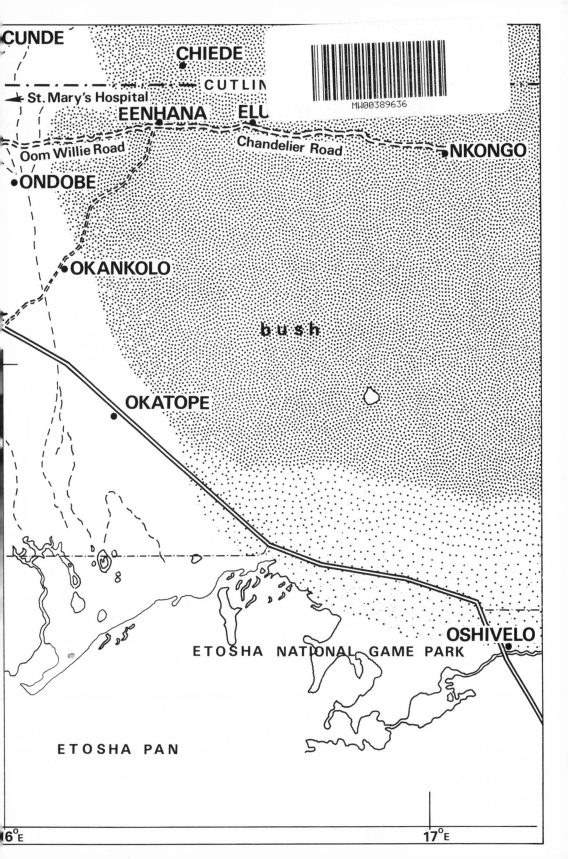

Beneath
the Visiting
Moon

BENEATH THE VISITING MOON

Images of Combat in Southern Africa

by

JIM HOOPER

Lexington Books

D.C. Heath and Company • Lexington, Massachusetts • Toronto

This book is published as part of Lexington Books'
Issues in Low-Intensity Conflict series,
Neil C. Livingstone, consulting editor.

Library of Congress Cataloging-in-Publication Data

Hooper, Jim.
Beneath the visiting moon : images of combat in southern Africa /
Jim Hooper.
p.   cm.
ISBN 0 – 669 – 24637 – 9 (alk. paper)
1. Namibia—Politics and government—1946 –   2. SWAPO.
3.   Atrocities—Namibia.   I.   Title.
DT1645.H66   1990
968.8103—dc20   90 – 36389
CIP

Published simultaneously in Canada
Printed in the United States of America
Casebound International Standard Book Number: 0 – 669 – 24637 – 9
Library of Congress Catalog Card Number: 90 – 36389

The paper used in this publication meets
the minimum requirements of American National Standard
for Information Sciences—Permanence of Paper
for Printed Library Materials, ANSI Z39.48–1984.

Year and number of this printing:

90 91 92 8 7 6 5 4 3 2 1

To BJB
with love and affection
for the good times at the 'Hills;
to HR
for living and suffering through much
of the writing of this; and
to friends who were there when I needed them.

Contents

Preface

THIS is the story of a war in Africa. As with all such tales, it deals with the brutality, fear and sacrifice that have been the fabric of all wars and all sides since man first banded together for mutual protection or aggression. But it is a true story, though told through the eyes of an outsider and foreigner, and that alone must make it suspect to anyone who opens these pages. It is an account of people caught up in a little-understood conflict in an even less-known part of the world, and if my journalistic detachment faded after seeing men I knew—black and white—die next to me, I hope the reader will understand.

Many people have asked how I became the first Western reporter allowed virtually unrestricted access to the secret and vicious bush war in South West Africa/Namibia. And I have to answer that I don't really know, except to suggest that I persevered in pestering those in charge until they decided to unlock the door and allow me in. As to the more pointed question of how I came to be accepted by the deadliest counterinsurgency unit ever to have seen service in Africa, the infamous Koevoet, I can only shrug and point to fate; it was time for someone to be allowed behind the scenes, and I was there.

What I have written will not be popular in some quarters; the line between fashionable and unfashionable truth has been very carefully drawn, and a journalist crossing that line does so at his own peril. But the methods employed by the South West Africa People's Organization (SWAPO) against the Namibian people convinced me that its claims of fighting for "a just society" were no more than rhetoric for the benefit of a naive Western audience.

Since the events described here, much has happened in the old imperial German colony of South West Africa. As a key to proving its commitment to political reform, South Africa finally agreed to the holding of free elections in Namibia under United Nations supervision. In compliance with UN demands, all South African army units were disbanded, while the men I had accompanied were reduced to the role of lightly armed police.

On April 1, 1989, in violation of agreements made by SWAPO President Sam Nujoma, 1,500 heavily armed insurgents crossed from Angola into Namibia to ambush unsuspecting Koevoet patrols. Despite being taken by surprise, the unit lived up to its reputation: in less than two weeks it had broken the back of the invasion, killing over 350 insurgents and sending the balance scurrying over the border to their UN-protected sanctuaries in Angola. Of the 23 Koevoet members, blacks and whites, who died defending the law, I had served with most.

Although Sam Nujoma eventually won the November 1989 elections on the basis of a tribal vote, revelations of atrocities against its own members have clearly demonstrated the brutal and anti-democratic nature of SWAPO. Testimony by Namibian refugees returning from Angola leaves no doubt that Nujoma's liberation movement was responsible for the torture and murder of thousands of its own people in SWAPO concentration camps. Curiously, few of those who railed against alleged South African autrocities and supported SWAPO over the years have yet to voice any criticism, the majority preferring to remain deaf, dumb and blind to the facts. It is perhaps not surprising, therefore, that *Beneath the Visiting Moon* has been judged by those same people as supporting apartheid and the South African occupation of Namibia. Nothing could be further from the truth; nothing I can say here will change that perception if the reader is so inclined.

A SWAPO-majority government in an independent Namibia is now a fact. Whether or not this last unshackled vestige of colonialism follows the pattern of systematic murder and tribal nepotism of other newly independent African countries, only time will tell. One can but pray that the new commitment to democracy and peaceful coexistence now sweeping much of the world will have a profound affect on the future of Namibia.

Acknowledgments

It would have been impossible to write this book without the help of many people. To those who gave unstintingly of their time and positions to open doors normally closed to journalists, I hope I have not embarrassed you too much nor abused your trust. To those people on whom I so rudely imposed by asking that they read various drafts and who offered criticism and suggestions—in particular, Christina Vincent—I am eternally grateful. My thanks must also go to the ever-anonymous Sugar Jones for suggesting the use of my Oshakati letters to her to set the mood in certain chapters. For two others—both journalists of international reputation who profoundly disagreed with South Africa's presence in South West Africa/Namibia, yet believed the story wanted telling—no praise is enough. Lest they be accused of holding heretical views on South Africa (which they certainly do not), they must remain unnamed.

Certainly, without the lobbying efforts of Major Bernie Ley on my behalf, and the unprecedented permission of Major General "Sterk Hans" Dreyer to allow me to accompany his men on combat operations, the book could never have been written. To the surprise of outsiders who knew the unit only by reputation or rumor, at no time was there any mention of censorship; "you have to write what you see," Dreyer told me.

On the sharp end, it was the black and white policemen of Koevoet who showed me a war never before seen by an outsider, and who kept me alive in spite of myself. I suspect I was more often than not a hindrance, forever in the way and underfoot and asking endless and tiresome questions, most of which they bore with rare good humor and not a little stoicism. This story is theirs.

O! wither'd is the garland of war,
The soldier's pole is fall'n; young boys and
girls
Are level now with men; the odds is gone,
And there is nothing left remarkable
Beneath the visiting moon.

—As You Like It, I. i. 64

Beneath
the Visiting
Moon

1

In Search of a War

E VEN now, the memories are sharp as broken glass—a fractured mirror of moments and people. Especially the people.
As though I could step through it and they would all still be
there—if broken glass and shattered bodies could be put back
together again.

It was my war, my beat, in that absurd and proprietary way
journalists have of labeling something which has irrevocably
touched them. Mine also because I'd missed the one great conflict
of my generation, a conflict which shamed me for not having
been there, and sent me in search of its replacement long before
understanding why. The journey took me across the top and
down the side of the African continent, then southward, looking
for my surrogate Vietnam.

In retrospect, the search and the story that emerged were as
cliché ridden as the most hackneyed B movie of the 1940s: the
eager novitiate, innocent beyond his years, who is grudgingly
allowed a brief glimpse of war by a band of warrior brothers. He
goes away but is drawn back to share their lives. He sees men die
and learns fear, receives his red badge of courage, and finally
leaves to tell their story.

Although one hand still complains when the weather turns
cold and wet, and the other cramps now and then to make me
awkwardly self-conscious, I can't deny it was part of the search,
a childish fantasy lurking in mists. But when fantasy became reality I understood it was only luck that mattered. It rode near at
hand and in undeserved abundance, deflecting the ultimate reality; others it deserted entirely. The ultimate cliché: Why me? The
ultimate answer: I don't know.

"But isn't there anything you *regret?*" someone asked not so long ago, eager for my confession and recantation.

"Certainly not," I answered with studied insouciance. "Why should I?"—an answer and attitude guaranteed to draw pinched frowns of disapproval (it was so predictable), but why explain something he couldn't possibly understand? I wish I'd told him to go find out for himself, then come back and ask me again, but I've always been slow on those things. Not that it would have made any difference; he knew better, and that was that.

It wasn't long afterward that a letter arrived from one of the helicopter pilots I'd flown with: "I hope all's well with your injuries, but the funny thing is, it's the ones you can't see that take the longest to sort themselves out." More of the B movie.

My first two years of chasing African wars had led me . . . well, nowhere, I'd confide to friends over a beer or two in the village pub. The search had taken me into Morocco, then on to Chad and Sudan, the last two positively reeking with intrigue and CIA-contract types stumbling over each other. Good, romantic color, if you're inclined that way, which I wasn't. I was looking for stuff with plenty of meat on its bones: "bang-bangs" in the parlance, but so far, I'd only heard them from a distance.

Uganda came next, and that was better, lots better. Crazy, in fact. I was still too stupid about Africa to understand I'd come to the wrong place at the wrong time until the wrong side were lining me up for a quick burst of simple murder. That was when I decided I'd had enough of the Dark Continent and caught the first available flight back to England.

But as luck would have it, an article in the London *Guardian* caught my interest one day. Here was another possibility, I thought, reading the piece filed from Windhoek. I was aware, in a vague sort of way, of the low-intensity bush war taking place along the Namibian-Angolan border, but I'd never managed to keep the details in my head. Just another of those little *contretemps* Africa was famous for; with a couple of dozen going on, who could keep them straight?

As far as this one went, little had appeared in the press beyond brief South African claims of having killed so many

SWAPO insurgents (and who the hell were they?) for the loss of so many of their own forces. Until now, I'd shied away from anything associated with those white pariahs of Africa, but here was a conflict that might be worth considering. The sparseness of the information coming out told me there just might be a story or two in it—provided the Boers would let me in.

Having rarely come across anything resembling official cooperation in those countries I had visited, I expected even less from the South Africans. The picture painted of them by the international news media was grimmer than anything I'd experienced in some of the less pleasant parts of Africa. A country under siege, said screaming headlines and concerned television reporters, flames and rioters dancing in the background. The message was that the repression and brutality I'd seen elsewhere were mild compared with what was happening in the bastion of apartheid.

Rehearsing what I hoped would be a persuasive argument, I arrived at Trafalgar Square in London one winter's day and made my way through the cluster of sullen protesters outside the South African embassy. Inside, I was led upstairs to the office of the defense attaché, Colonel Rob Crowther. After a frosty introduction (it was obvious that Western journalists were the enemy here), I explained what I had in mind to do, then sat back and waited for the customary and curt "No." To my surprise, I was asked to explain in greater detail. Crowther listened stonily. When I'd finished, he asked what I knew of Africa in general and South Africa in particular. I outlined my previous travels through the continent.

"As you probably know," said Crowther, slowly turning a pencil end over end, "foreign journalists are not exactly the flavor of the month in South Africa."

I could see it coming. *Sorry, chum, but no dice.*

"All I can do is forward your request for a working journalist's visa to the Department of Foreign Affairs in Pretoria with my recommendation that it be granted. That's no guarantee that it will come through. They're a little sensitive about allowing more journalists into the country at the moment." The beefy Afrikaner stood to indicate the meeting was over. "We'll let you know," he said noncommittally.

Six weeks later, I received a call confirming Pretoria's approval;

the visa was ready. With qualified relief, I took the train up to London to collect it. Crowther and his tall, immaculately dressed air attaché, Colonel George van Niekerk, rose smoothly as I was escorted into the fifth floor office overlooking Nelson's monument. After a few minutes of compulsory small talk, the stolid army officer asked if I was still serious about covering the bush war in Namibia. My unequivocal "Absolutely" lacked conviction to my ear, but Crowther nodded and promised to flash a message to Defense Force Headquarters in Pretoria. They would begin organizing a tour of the operational area for me.

I asked about censorship.

"As far as clearing whatever you do write on the defense force, for security reasons we would prefer to have a look at it before publication. But we won't insist on it. Obviously, you could write whatever you want anyway once you're outside the country. All we ask is that you tell the story fairly and with a bit of balance."

I had turned to go when Crowther stopped me.

"Don't expect everyone to welcome you on our side. We know we still have serious problems in our country that need to be resolved, but the international media haven't helped the situation. Instead of reporting in a balanced way, they've concentrated almost exclusively on apartheid and violence. They ignore the reforms that have been made, and damned seldom have they made comparisons between human rights in South Africa and other countries in Africa."

"What we're saying," interjected van Niekerk, "is that we don't expect you to write that everything is fine in South Africa. We know better than you that it isn't. So we're not going to throw you out for being critical. All we're asking is that you write honestly about what you see, without distorting the facts or taking situations out of context."

I left England on Zambian Airways a week later for the eleven hour flight to Lusaka. At the Zambian international airport, passengers in transit were directed to a large, glass-fronted lounge. I stood in front of the floor-to-ceiling windows overlooking the airport. A shiny Mercedes-Benz limousine passed below, an East German flag fluttering from one fender. I watched it stop next to a small Soviet-built passenger jet. An entourage of blacks and whites emerged from the car and boarded the aircraft. I snapped a photo of the scene.

"I'd put that away if I were you, friend," someone said softly in a rich Australian accent.

I looked around. The voice came from a fellow traveler who was stretched out on a couch. He lifted his head and stroked a luxurious mustache as he slowly scanned the lounge, then cocked one eye at me.

"They catch you taking pictures, and you're going straight to jail. The least they'll do is confiscate your cameras. They'll bring a nice price for whoever decides you're spying. Around here only spies take pictures of airports and East German tourists."

I nodded my thanks and slipped the camera into its bag.

After an eight-hour layover in the Zambian capital, I connected with a South African Airways flight. ("You mean to tell me that the South African national airline actually flies into Zambia — one of the Frontline States? — on a scheduled basis?" I had asked the travel agent, somewhat nonplussed. "Sure, why not?" she had said.)

Pretoria hardly seemed a city under siege. Contrary to what I had seen on television or read in newspapers, there were not police on every street corner, leashed dogs threateningly in hand. Instead, working-class blacks and whites mingled along the crowded sidewalks, while well-dressed black businessmen strolled shoulder to shoulder with white colleagues and shared tables in expensive restaurants. Where was the open racial hatred the media had told me about?

My initial meeting with Colonel Tim Krynauw at the Media Liaison Section started off a little tensely, underscoring the complaints I'd heard in London.

"We've really gone out of our way in this office to accommodate the press by showing them all sides of the situation here," said Krynauw, "and all they've done is kick us in the teeth by reporting only the negative part. Make no mistake, there's enough of the negative if that's what someone wants to present to the rest of the world as the only truth of South Africa, but it's hard to have any trust in the so-called objectivism of the international media.

"In any case, I believe you want to do some stories about the defense force and what's going on up on the border. That's being organized. But before getting you out to the operational area in South West, which is still pretty quiet, we thought you might first want to spend a little time getting background information on the defense force here. In the meantime, if there's anything you're especially interested in, let me know."

The next few weeks went by in a whirl of side trips and interviews. One of my first excursions was to Messina, near the Zimbabwe border, where I had my initial exposure to a South African Defense Force (SADF) unit.

"We're essentially a quick-reaction counterinsurgency unit," said Commandant (Lieutenant Colonel) Peter Rose as we walked across the compound of the old copper-mining company. All around us, soldiers were hammering, painting and clearing rubbish, as the compound was being converted into a new head-quarters for the black 116 Battalion.

"This is a favorite infiltration area for ANC [African National Congress] terrorists. They've been coming across from Zimbabwe recently to plant land mines along the roads near the border. Their aim is to chase out the white farming families along the Limpopo River. Their first victim was a black farm worker. Since then, they've killed a dozen other people. Practically an entire family was wiped out in one mine incident.

"Because the blacks in this area are North Sothos, we thought an SADF unit composed of the same tribe would be the most effective. So far, it seems to be working. When the local blacks see their own people in uniform and see that they're treated just like any white member of the defense force, it has a very positive effect. Without the support of the local people, terrorists have a far more difficult time of it."

I mentioned that I hadn't realized blacks were conscripted into the South African Defense Force. Rose gave me a quick, patronizing look. "No non-white is conscripted in South Africa. They're all volunteers. And there are enough volunteers that we can be fairly choosy about who we take."

Trying to cover my ignorance, I asked how many of the blacks in 116 Battalion were in positions of authority.

"We're still a fairly new unit, so all our company commanders and platoon leaders are still white. But most of the NCOs are

Sothos, and we've just commissioned our first Sotho lieutenant, who serves as the unit's supply officer. In order to integrate our personnel more effectively, we have language classes every week for the whites. The classes are taught by a Sotho instructor, and I require that all whites in the battalion learn a minimum of five hundred North Sotho words a year. Aside from possibly saving someone's life someday in a contact situation, I believe it's a matter of respect for the people you serve with."

Rose gave me a tour of the buildings under renovation. "The first thing we had to do was build suitable barracks for the men and quarters for our married NCOs," he explained. "You'll find no difference between what we'll have here when it's completed and the facilities for a white unit. These men are members of the SADF. The same standards apply for everyone."

So why doesn't it extend to the rest of South African society? I wondered.

Rose knocked on the back door of a freshly painted bungalow. The door was opened by a black woman with a baby on her hip. Rose introduced her as the wife of one of his senior noncommissioned officers and asked her if I could look through her home. She opened the door and invited us in for a cup of tea. The home would have compared favorably with those supplied to an NCO in any Western army. Sitting at the kitchen table and listening to Rose ask the woman about her house and baby was a scene full of contradictions.

Returning that afternoon to the shabby motel where I was staying, I walked into the bar. The bartender, a large and muscular Afrikaner woman, turned her back as I took a bar stool. Finally she faced me and rudely asked what I "needed."

Setting the drink down with a bang, she snarled in a strong Afrikaans accent, "So why are you here writing shit about South Africa?"

Somewhat taken aback, I said I hadn't written anything as yet about South Africa. She wasn't appeased. "We know your kind here, and we don't want your kind here. Go back where you came from and leave us alone. We know how to deal with our blacks. We don't need you damned *journalists*"—the word dripped with venom—"coming here and making things worse."

Stunned at her obvious hatred of whatever it was I represented, I started to explain that until I had a better idea of what was happening in the country, I wouldn't be writing anything.

She interrupted me: "Listen, I know people who can come over here and take care of you."

Setting down my drink, I politely excused myself and walked out. *Verligte* (enlightened) thinking certainly had not filtered down to some elements of Afrikaner society. I had already heard that the Northern Transvaal was a hotbed of Afrikaner nationalism, with many open supporters of the Ku Klux Klan-like Afrikaner Resistance Movement. The next morning, I wasn't sorry to put Messina and that particular motel behind me.

In Cape Town, a special request to visit the South African Cape Corps (SACC) was granted. One of the oldest units in South Africa (its members claim it is the oldest) the SACC is composed almost exclusively of Colored South Africans. The contradiction of non-whites volunteering for military service to defend a system which at that time denied them a national political voice was something I found difficult to comprehend. From a Western point of view, it defied all logic. Was it some kind of perverse anomaly, or was the apparently easy integration of black and white in the SADF a portent of things to come throughout South Africa? Sitting easily behind his desk, Colonel Graham Jacobs, the second in command of the SACC, clasped hands across a flat, hard belly and explained how far things had progressed within the military.

"Up until the time I was commissioned," he told me, "a white national service *private* could ignore orders from a non-white sergeant or warrant officer. And here I was, about to become a commissioned officer, and it was going to be the same thing. I have to tell you, it wasn't a situation I was looking forward to.

"See, I was part of the first group of Coloreds to be commissioned, and we were definitely planning to make an issue of this. We had gone through the same selection courses white officers were required to complete. And on top of that, we were volunteers, not like the whites, who by law have to serve. We were *asking* to be allowed to defend our country. It wasn't right that a white private should be able to ignore our orders or to actually order us around.

"Fortunately, before we completed our officer's course, the

law was changed. The day I received my commission as a lieutenant in the South African Defense Force from the then minister of defense, P.W. Botha, was the proudest day of my life. And I've never looked back."

I asked Colonel Jacobs if, given the present political situation in South Africa, he had any difficulty in attracting new recruits.

"We've just been authorized by Parliament to form another battalion within the Cape Corps. When the news about this got out to civvie street, we had three times more applications than places available. Even for normal recruitment—finding new kids to replace those who have finished their two-year contract in the SACC—we have them queued up and waiting."

How much racial prejudice did he still find in the defense force?

"Listen, you don't change a man's spots overnight. Of course you still find it, though far less in the military than outside. Some of our young officer cadets have gone through pretty rough times at the infantry school at Oudtshoorn, where they train alongside white cadets. For the good ones, the tough ones, it just makes them that much more determined to succeed.

"And I'm not saying they have problems with all, or even the majority, of white officer cadets. It's actually a minority of them. You know, a few years ago I visited your military academy at West Point, and the American black cadets there said it was the same: a minority of whites who didn't like them just because they were black Americans.

"My own opinion is that integration within the SADF is one of the best things to have happened in this country. When a white troopie up in the operational area in South West Africa finds himself sleeping side by side with a Colored or a black in the bush, eating out of the same mess tin, depending on each other in combat—well, when he comes back, there's bound to be an attitude change. He's been educated in the real world."

2

Colonizers, Revolutionaries and Churchmen

As the flight to Windhoek moaned steadily westward over the Kalahari, I ordered a whiskey and dropped the seat-back tray in front of me. Pulling out the file of material accumulated before leaving England, I settled into reviewing the background of the country I was heading toward.

Hardly unusual in terms of African tribal and political complexities, South West Africa/Namibia was as intriguing as it was little known. Since Diego Cão planted his cross on the barren Skeleton Coast in 1484, parts of this vast and sparsely populated land had seen Portuguese, Dutch, British, German and South African explorers, colonizers and administrators. Over the years they had been allied with, occasionally at war against, often simply ignored by, the indigenous Ovambos, Kavangos, Hereros, Caprivians, Tswanas, Damaras, Namas and Bushmen.

Less than a year after the outbreak of the First World War, South African forces captured German South West Africa and proclaimed it the South West African Protectorate. In 1920 the League of Nations formally confirmed the country as a "C" Mandate to be governed as an integral part of the Union of South Africa, then part of the British Commonwealth.

Following the Second World War, the new United Nations charter ended the mandate system and established an international trusteeship on a voluntary basis. Loath to lose the mineral wealth of its colony, the Union of South Africa refused to surrender South West Africa to the United Nations. The issue was submitted to the International Court of Justice (ICJ), which ruled that South Africa should continue its administration of the territory under the terms of the original mandate.

In 1960 Ethiopia and Liberia instituted proceedings against South Africa over the South West Africa issue at the International Court of Justice. In 1966 the ICJ judged that neither Ethiopia nor Liberia had the necessary legal right or interest in the matter and rejected their claims. In 1971, however, a reconstituted ICJ decided that South Africa was illegally occupying the country. This claim was rejected out of hand by South Africa as being both illegal and illogical.

The liberation movement that was the catalyst for these later events was one of the many that sprang up throughout Africa in the 1950s. Founded first as the Ovambo People's Congress in 1958, the South West Africa People's Organization (SWAPO) officially came into being in 1960. By 1962 SWAPO, under the leadership of Sam Nujoma, began recruiting Ovambos for guerrilla warfare and sabotage. Recruits were sent to the Soviet Union, China, Algeria, Ghana and Tanzania for training.

In 1966 a unit of SWAPO's military wing, the People's Liberation Army of Namibia (PLAN), made its first cross-border infiltration from Angola to establish a base camp in northern Namibia. Information regarding its existence was soon passed by the local Ovambo people to the South African Police, and on August 26, 1966, the first shots of the bush war were fired.

It was not until the Portuguese withdrawal from Angola in 1975 — and the immediate support of the new Marxist government by thousands of Cuban troops — that SWAPO had the opportunity to establish permanent training and operational bases. Taking advantage of Cuban, Soviet and East German instructors and virtually unlimited supplies of East bloc weapons, PLAN began preparations for larger-scale operations. Still, as late as October 1977, South African and South West African security forces referred to the conflict as the "corporals' war," a reference to the highest-ranking member of the standard ten-man border patrols. On October 27 of that year, however, the situation changed when PLAN surprised everyone by sending across a one hundred-man unit. Contact was made shortly after they had crossed the border, and in a three-day running fight sixty-one insurgents were killed for the loss of five members of the SADF.

Although this would not warrant more than a footnote to accounts of larger conflicts, to the security forces the implications were clear: SWAPO was preparing to seriously escalate the bush war. Rather than waiting for them to cross the border, the South Africans decided to hit them deep into Angola, where they trained for and planned their infiltrations. In May 1978 the SADF launched Operation Reindeer, a surgical airborne assault against Cassinga, SWAPO's operational headquarters 150 miles inside Angola. The operation was spectacularly successful, and SWAPO lost many highly experienced PLAN members among the six hundred dead, though SWAPO later claimed that Cassinga was a refugee camp and that the dead and wounded were all noncombatants.

Subsequent punitive and preemptive cross-border operations by SADF and South West Africa Territory Force (SWATF) units followed, all aimed specifically against SWAPO and its People's Liberation Army of Namibia. Each was successful to varying degrees, and substantial quantities of East bloc equipment were captured and returned to Namibia. In the course of one operation in 1981, two Soviet lieutenant colonels were killed and a Soviet warrant officer was captured.

The effect of these well-planned attacks was twofold: not only were relatively large numbers of experienced insurgents killed, but bases and logistical infrastructure so severely disrupted that SWAPO was forced to move to more secure bases farther from the Namibian border. SADF and SWATF units remained in southern Angola to intercept PLAN insurgents on their way south. Although this interdiction strategy was probably less than 50 percent effective, it substantially reduced the number of insurgents reaching Namibia, where specialized counterinsurgency units operating along the border dealt with those who slipped through the net.

The United Nations passed Security Council Resolution (SCR) 435 in 1978, which called for UN-supervised elections in South West Africa. When the UN Security Council refused to allow any party other than SWAPO to have observer status during proceedings on the Namibian question, the South Africans refused to accept the conditions of the resolution. The United Nation's insistence on recognizing only SWAPO and none of the other parties in Namibia convinced Pretoria that there was little probability of free and fair elections ever occurring under UN supervision. The specter of yet another Soviet-backed, anti – South African country along its borders sent Pretoria's political strategists to the drawing boards.

At the end of 1978, South Africa startled outsiders and further complicated the situation in South West Africa/Namibia by initiating its own supervised elections without UN involvement. In spite of South Africa's invitation to SWAPO to participate, the organization chose to boycott the elections. A multi-party conference made up of elected representatives eventually led to the creation of the multiracial Democratic Turnhalle Alliance (DTA), which took control after the elections. This gave a degree of administrative control to the various minority parties as well as to representatives of all the tribal groups in Namibia. The United Nations, still backing SWAPO as the "sole and authentic representative of the Namibian people," refused to recognize the legitimacy of either the elections or the new government.

The first Namibian National Assembly formed from the 1978 elections eventually collapsed as a result of bitter infighting among the eight political parties. It was replaced with a South African administrator general. Before being dissolved, however, the infant government passed sweeping anti-apartheid laws. The government died a premature death, but the new laws survived.

In 1985 Pretoria, eager to take the edge off the demands of the United Nations, allowed a transitional government of black and white Namibians to be seated, but on its own terms. Those political leaders selected in the 1978 elections were installed by the South Africans as ministers and assembly members. One of the new ministers, Andreas Shipanga, previously had been SWAPO's minister of information before being arrested and jailed in Tanzania by SWAPO president Sam Nujoma.

In 1983 SADF and SWATF forces withdrew from Angola back into Namibia. The basis for this decision was an agreement with the Angolan Marxist government that the Angolan army would provide neither logistical nor material support to SWAPO. Within weeks of the withdrawal, however, intelligence sources confirmed that PLAN insurgents were again using Angolan army bases not only as resupply depots, but also as staging points from which to launch infiltrations into Namibia.

Unwilling to expose itself to further international criticism as a result of another major invasion of Angola, South Africa clamped a news blackout on the bush war and reestablished bases in Angola, which were secret in name only. If the Angolan government was unwilling to abide by its agreement to deny support to SWAPO, Pretoria was equally unwilling to wage a limited and strictly defensive counterinsurgency war from inside the Namibian border. Further, those security force units ostensibly tasked with patrolling the Namibian side of the frontier were authorized to cross into Angola in hot pursuit of fleeing insurgents. Although the details of the conflict were little understood by outsiders, it soon became a minor, if somewhat blurred, *cause célèbre* among Western liberals because of the South African connection.

The echoes of those first shots in 1966 were still being heard when I arrived in South West Africa/Namibia on a hot April morning in 1986. As I ducked out of the still-cool airliner and clumped awkwardly down the steps to the blistering tarmac, I had no idea that I was on my way to seeing the bush war more closely than had any other Western journalist in its twenty-year history.

I caught a bus from the airport for the forty-minute drive to Windhoek, where I made my way to army headquarters. A South African sergeant met me at the desk and escorted me upstairs for an introduction to the press liaison officer, Major Zorro Kariko.

Major Kariko was not having a good day. He had lost a German television crew. They were supposed to be at the airport right now for a flight to the operational area. The driver who had been sent to pick them up at the Kalahari Sands Hotel couldn't find them. They'd gone shopping for souvenirs. The driver was on the telephone, saying that he'd looked everywhere and still couldn't find them. The flight crew were calling from the airport to say that they were going to leave without them, they didn't give a damn who they were, they had a schedule to keep . . . .

"What tribe are you from?" I asked, pencil poised.

Kariko's eyes narrowed. "Take the phone!" he shouted to the white officer in the office next to his. He dropped the receiver into its cradle and gave me the look my question deserved.

"Black Namibian," he said slowly. "Next?"

"Well, as a-uh, black Namibian, how do you feel about your country being in the hands of white South Africa?" Incisive; right to the heart of things.

He sighed and looked at the ceiling. I'm sure he didn't roll his eyes; he just looked at the ceiling.

"Look, how much of Africa have you seen?"

"Well, a bit of it," I said.

"Well, so have I. So let me tell you that I'll take the present situation for the time being, rather than see us turned into another Angola or Mozambique." He leaned forward and placed both forearms solidly on his desk. "Of course, I was only born here, so obviously I can't know as much as you media people. You always let us know what's really best for us, don't you?"

Things hadn't started off at all well.

"I understand SWAPO maintains an office here in Windhoek," I said. "I'd like to get their side of the story. Can you give me their address or phone number?"

Kariko cleared his throat and thumbed through his Rolodex file. He scribbled two names and numbers on a slip of paper. "These are the two people who run their office here. Give them a call and see what they have to say. I'll be surprised if they agree to speak with you. Unless you're on their approved list, they're not too eager to give interviews."

I stopped in the lobby of the Kalahari Sands Hotel and rang the first number Kariko had given me. It was answered by Danny Tjongarero. I introduced myself and asked if I might meet him for an interview.

"I don't think so," he said curtly. "I'm quite busy writing a report at the moment. I won't have any time free until next week. You can call my colleague, Mr. Nico Bessinger, and ask him."

Replacing the receiver, I dialed the second number. Bessinger's response was the same: he was too busy working on a financial report to grant an interview. I explained that I would be in Windhoek for the next few days and that I would be happy to cancel any other appointment to meet him.

"Absolutely not," he said. "There is no way I can make any time available for you."

"Mr. Bessinger," I pressed, "I'm trying to get some sort of balanced picture of something I know very little about. I think we can agree that the South Africans aren't going to tell me anything that's against their interests. And I'd prefer not to have to write that while they'll talk to me, you won't."

"If you do that, it will be a lie, an absolute lie. And anyone who knows the true story about the South African racist regime and what it's doing in Namibia will know it's a lie."

"Then would it be possible for us to get together, at your convenience, for a chat and a drink, perhaps? I'll be here for the next three and a half days and I'm more than willing to work my schedule around yours."

"No, I'm sorry, but I'll be entirely too busy for the next week, working on reports for the Council of Churches of Namibia. You can call Mr. Tjongarero, perhaps he will have time for you."

"But I've already called him and he suggested I call you, so ... "

"Sorry, I am too busy. If you will excuse me, good-bye." Click.

Puzzled by the open belligerence of the two men, I walked up the hill to the Tintenpalast (Ink Palace), the old imperial German fort that now served as the country's administrative center. I had an appointment with another SWAPO activist.

Paul Helmuth was the very picture of an elder statesman. Dressed in a somber three-piece suit, he started by telling me of his days as a founding member of the South West Africa People's Organization.

"I suppose my political awakening came after I returned from World War II," he said. "I left Namibia illegally and went to Cape Town in South Africa, where I was able to find work on a ship. At that time, South Africa was rather progressive compared to Namibia."

The winds of change were stirring in a postwar Africa, and Helmuth was profoundly affected by the new spirit of national liberation. By the late 1950s, he was serving the newly formed Ovambo People's Congress as a secret courier between Cape Town and Walvis Bay in South West Africa.

The Ovambo People's Congress became the Ovambo People's Organization and then the South West Africa People's Organization in 1960. The following year, Helmuth was spirited out to the Soviet Union. Sponsored by the United Nations Educational, Scientific, and Cultural Organization (UNESCO), he spent the next four years studying Russian and political science in Moscow and Kiev. More studies followed in Tanzania before he was sent to Sweden. "Twenty-five percent of my time was spent studying and the rest lecturing on the occupation of Namibia by the racist South African regime," he said, "and UNESCO paid for it all."

Helmuth returned to Tanzania in 1969 for a SWAPO conference. "You have to understand that I was a committed nationalist and revolutionary," he said. "I had dedicated fifteen years of my life to the liberation of Namibia for all its people. But I saw things which shocked me. Because of tribal politics, many of our Caprivian brothers in the struggle had been imprisoned by the SWAPO leadership. Not only that, but food and clothing donated by the United Nations were being sold by senior people, while Namibian refugees — our own people who had escaped from South African oppression — were starving and dressed in rags.

"I started asking questions and pressing for an investigation. What I had seen was completely contrary to the principles on which we had founded the liberation movement. Tribal politics was just another word for racism, and that was something we had all sworn to destroy.

"One night a friend told me that I was going to be arrested because of the inquiries I was making. The leadership had secretly denounced me as someone who could no longer be trusted."

Marked for arrest and imprisonment by the very organization he had helped to found, Helmuth escaped and returned to Sweden, where he was granted political asylum. In 1977 with guarantees of immunity from the South Africans, Helmuth accepted an invitation from another disillusioned revolutionary to return to Namibia. In 1986 Paul Helmuth, a black Namibian, was a member of the black-majority National Assembly of the Transitional Government of National Unity (TGNU) in Windhoek.

From the other side of the fence, Helmuth was viewed as a traitor for his involvement with the TGNU. On my return to England, I spoke with Jacob Hannai, SWAPO's deputy chief representative for Western Europe. "Paul Helmuth is among the defeatist elements," Hannai declared. "I cannot finish naming the whole list, but he is among those. And, of course, what he is telling you about is to suit the situation where he is now. Because that institution where they are — the interim administration — was actually established at the expense of South Africa. They are saying they are working against the racist South African regime, but actually they are working for it. You cannot expect much from those cowardized elements."

I asked Hannai about Misheke Muyongo, who had founded the Caprivi Africa National Union (CANU). In 1966 he and his followers left the Caprivi Strip in Namibia and joined SWAPO; Muyongo became vice-president of the movement. In 1985, however, citing tribalism and oppression at the hands of the Ovambo-dominated SWAPO, Muyongo and most of his old CANU members accepted amnesty from the South Africans and returned to Namibia.

"It is the same for Misheke Muyongo as Paul Helmuth and the others," Hannai said. "Muyongo, he had been vice-president of this movement and a member of the Politburo of the Central Committee of SWAPO . . . but eventually, of course, some people like him and like many others . . . became too tired to fight for the cause which SWAPO had been pursuing all these years. They thought they would fight today and they will win independence tomorrow. So they became defeated, demoralized, and went back to Namibia. They preferred to go back and work within the enemy rather than fighting for their cause and win a just solution which will be satisfying to the people of Namibia. So they are defeatists."

Hans-Eric Staby was a white minority member of the National Assembly. Tie loosened and sleeves rolled up, he sat in the office of his architectural firm in Windhoek and stared out the window. "You know, in November 1978 we held our first elections based on one man, one vote. Representatives were elected on a racially proportional basis to sit in a national assembly. But since the United Nations recognized SWAPO as the 'sole and authentic representative of the Namibian people,' the results weren't accepted by the international community. The fact that we invited SWAPO to take part and they refused didn't make any difference."

Some months later in England, I spoke with Dr. Peter Katjavivi, who had been SWAPO's secretary of information and publicity until 1979. Studying in Oxford and still a committed member of SWAPO, Dr. Katjavivi responded by saying, "How can someone invite us to come and partake in the so-called interim

government which is imposed by the government of South
Africa? In other words, we have to participate in something which
is already defined for us. We are rejecting it because it's . . . not
going to enable us to achieve our objective of being truly independent."

When I asked him what sort of political system he envisioned
for Namibia, he explained that "SWAPO is a nationalist movement dedicated to achieving independence for Namibia and
allowing a truly democratic society to take place." He went on to
add: "But if I think a bit more with respect to Namibia, I would
say this: my own view is that I would like to see a one-party state
to come about through a natural process. There's nothing wrong
in having a one-party state, *per se*. It has worked well in other
countries."

The West German-based International Society for Human
Rights—described by SWAPO as "a right-wing element supporting South Africa"—claimed to have evidence of "executions and
the systematic maltreatment of SWAPO opponents in SWAPO
refugee camps in Angola and Zambia." While admitting to
holding "a few traitors," SWAPO at the same time condemned
South Africa for quashing opposition by detention without trial,
but made no apologies for doing the same.

Sitting in the garden of Queen Elizabeth House in Oxford,
Dr. Katjavivi rationalized the contradiction by saying, "We are
operating under abnormal conditions. We are in the neighboring
countries of Angola and Zambia, which culminated in the infiltration of South Africa into Angola and Zambia, aimed not
only against SWAPO but also against our host African countries.
We are a responsible movement. We are sensitive to some of
these issues.

"I don't think SWAPO rejoices over holding a few traitors
without trial. This is a hard decision. These are the lessons of the
kind of struggle we have reached. I think none of us when we
studied the armed struggle in 1965—from the writings of Ho Chi
Minh, for example—anticipated to have to deal with these kind
of cases."

In Windhoek a group calling itself the Parents Committee
began investigating allegations of torture and executions in

SWAPO-run refugee camps. Erika Beukes, a dedicated SWAPO activist for many years, was a founding member of the committee.

"For the past year," she told me, "we've been meeting with Namibian refugees who had escaped from the camps and they told us stories so terrible we could hardly believe it." A letter she showed me from a Namibian living in Zambia read in part:

> *The leadership should tell or bring about the group of young Namibians who were forcefully rounded up from the Boroma concentration camp in Kabwe ... amongst those killed are Jackson Hamupembe, Teodor Shongola, Halleluya Ambunde, Limpumbu Shongola, Vilho Komemaya ... and many, many others ... It is rumored that Shilonga Ilya Shilonga was seen in one of the prison camps in Zambia, especially in Kabwe, and had one eye.*

"Many of us had long been members of SWAPO," said Beukes. "We still support the goal of an independent Namibia, free of South Africa, so we were careful to keep our inquiries out of the press. We didn't want to damage the movement many of us had belonged to for many years. All we wanted to know was what happened to our children and relatives. I was desperate to find out about my brother, who had disappeared. I had talked him into joining SWAPO, and I felt responsible."

When their requests for information went unanswered, the Parents Committee approached the Council of Churches of Namibia (CCN), where Beukes worked as a secretary. "It soon became clear," she told me, "that the Council of Churches had no intention of investigating the allegations. The president of the council told me that they couldn't act on 'rumors.' "

The general secretary of the Council of Churches of Namibia, Dr. Abisai Sheyavali, at first declined to comment on alleged SWAPO atrocities when I reached him by telephone.

"Dr. Sheyavali, all I'm asking for is the CCN's position on the accusations being made by the Parents Committee. Can't you just give me a simple statement on these allegations against SWAPO?"

"Well, of course, we cannot imagine them doing anything like what's been suggested."

"But have you investigated the allegations?"

"No, we have not asked officially about the situation."

In 1987 at the European Parliament in Strasbourg, France, members of the Parents Committee confronted SWAPO President Sam Nujoma, asking him about the fate of Namibian children in SWAPO camps in Angola and Zambia. According to the London *Daily Telegraph,* Nujoma, defender of freedom, slapped one of the members and told her, "You will die."

3

White "South West,"
Black Namibia

OVER breakfast one morning, I was introduced to Henk
Rheeder, a gangly South West Africa Territory Force sergeant. Henk would escort me north to the operational area. A
white South African and former journalist, he had come west two
years earlier.

"I may go back to the States someday," said Henk, using the
popular term for South Africa, "but I kind of prefer the way of
life here in 'South West.' Things are a lot more relaxed here than
back in the States." It was a refrain I would hear over and over
from transplanted South Africans.

The night before we were to start driving north, Henk took
me on a pub crawl. Our first stop was the NCO mess, where we
bellied up to the bar side by side with black and white members
of the SWATF. A steady stream of American country and western
music twanged in the background. As an American journalist, I
came under close scrutiny. Willi, a black sergeant on the bar stool
next to me, bought my first beer and asked the usual first question
about how I liked Namibia.

I admitted that I had seen only Windhoek and really not much
of that, since most of my time had been spent on interviews. The
white bartender, three horizontal stripes of a SWATF sergeant on
his sleeves, leaned on the polished surface.

"I tell you, this is a good country. God's country. I'm South
African, but I don't want to go back there to live." I asked him
why.

"No, it is just easier here, the whole situation between blacks and whites. Genuine.[a] I tell you, I am an Afrikaner, brought up on a farm in the Northern Transvaal, believed in apartheid. I didn't dislike blacks, I just believed you didn't socialize with them. I came out here five years ago with the South African Defense Force, and when it was time to go back to the States, I transferred into the SWATF." He pronounced it, like everyone else, *Swatee-eff*. "I tell you . . . excuse, I'll be back just now." He straightened up and turned to serve some newcomers.

The heavy-set black sergeant on my right grinned and nodded toward the bartender. "Gysbert, he is okay, but he talk a lot," he said good naturedly, feeling his way through English. Afrikaans was the *lingua franca* of both the SADF and SWATF, and for many of the soldiers, English was a little-used second or third language.

The bartender returned and took up his former position after a reflective swipe at the bartop with a towel. "Yeah, I tell you, South West is a good place. I live in a neighborhood with blacks, we have braais [barbecues] together, it's not a problem. We don't have apartheid here. Genuine."

He pointed toward Henk, who was talking with a group of black and white NCOs at the other end of the bar. "Henk there, he's got a black boss, Zorro Kariko, and he doesn't seem bothered by it. If a man can do the job, what's the difference whether he's black or white?

"Willi here," he indicated the sergeant on the bar stool next to me, "he and I couldn't have had a drink together on civvie street five years ago in the States. Even if I wanted to. In the sergeants' mess, yeah, okay, but not outside on civvie street. It's a lot better now, back there, but they still have a long way to go to catch up with South West. No, I became a Southwester when I joined the SWATF. This is my country now."

I asked him to set up another round. Willi shook a finger in my face with mock severity. "It is against the regulations. You're civvie. Can't buy unless you a. . . ," he looked at Gysbert. "Hoe sê jy '*lid*' in Engels?"

---

[a] *Genuine* is the South African equivalent of "really" or "honestly." In casual conversation it is invariably pronounced *jenyin*.

"Member," Gysbert translated.

"You can't buy here unless a *member*," and pushed a bill across the bar, scribing a circle with his finger to indicate a new round for the three of us. We lifted our beers and drank in unison.

"Look," said Gysbert, "if you're in a restaurant and a black sits at the table next to you, and he's not bothering anyone, what's the problem? You know what I mean? If you get up and leave because he's there, who's the fool? That's what I found out here in South West. Genuine."

He poured out three brandies. "This is on me." We drank. "Anyway, that's what I found out."

Willi shook his head. "He's okay, he just talk too much."

Henk walked over. "Let's go over to Eros—the airfield—and see what's going on at the air force club."

I gave my hand to Gysbert and Willi.

"See you," said Willi.

"See you," said Gysbert. "Hope you get the stories you are after up in the operational area. Not much happening right now. Rains are late." Willi shook his head again at how much some people talked. I followed Henk a little unsteadily out the door.

When we entered the air force club, the *There I was, thought I was gonna die* flying story stage had already been reached. The speaker, a tall air force commandant, was deep into flying his helicopter through heavy ground fire during one of the big operations against SWAPO in Angola. About thirty seconds after we walked in, he crashed. The accompanying hand movements and sound effects depicting his last moments in the air were impressive. It called for a drink.

He noticed me at the bar. "How's it?"[b] he asked. I'd sat in on a briefing he'd given to a foreign television crew a couple of days earlier. "You getting the information you wanted?"

I rocked my hand back and forth. "More or less," I said. "Lot of things I didn't know, I have to admit, but it sounds pretty much like the standard sort of stuff put together for wandering journalists. Nothing exactly earth-shattering."

"Yeah," he said, "but there's not a lot happening right now.

[b] *How's it?* is the English-Afrikaans corruption of *Hoe gaan dit?*—literally *"How goes it?"*

And there's not much infiltration going on up north. Rains are late. But the Russians and Cubans have been pretty active."

"Yeah? Like what?" I noticed that among air force personnel, the first language seemed to be English rather than Afrikaans.

"No, they just brought in a few more MiG-23s, along with a number of instructor pilots with lots of experience in Afghanistan. We think those are just the first ones, that they'll have some more there before too long."

"Sounds like they might be expecting trouble. You guys ever penetrate Angolan airspace?"

There was a tiny pause. "Certainly not."

"Then what about that South African C-130 they claimed to have shot down last month? That was quite a way up in Angola."

"Well, I'll tell you, after the first couple of press releases out of Angola, everything suddenly went real quiet. Seems someone got confused and shot down a civilian Hercules that had been leased from an American company. Dangerous flying in Angola. That's why we wouldn't think of it." He drained the last of his brandy and Coke, swirled the ice around, and ordered another.

I looked around the bar. Unlike the army canteen, there were no blacks here. "Does the air force have any black pilots?" I asked him.

"Not yet, but we will sooner or later. It's a tough selection course, but as long as they meet the same standards, I certainly wouldn't mind flying with a black pilot. There may be some who wouldn't—in fact, I know there are some who wouldn't want to. But things are changing. Maybe faster than some people want, but things are definitely changing."

Apparently, I didn't look too convinced.

"Look," he said, "how many non-white officers have you seen in the defense force?" I said I had seen a few.

"And have you seen any evidence of apartheid in the officers' mess? Were they sitting at separate tables in the corner?" I allowed that they were sitting with white officers.

"And have you noticed white troopies not saluting them?" I admitted that the non-white officers I'd seen were afforded the same military courtesy as white officers.

"You know," he continued a little testily, "you Americans tend to forget that until the Korean War, blacks in the U.S. military were only in segregated units. It was Eisenhower who pushed through reforms by ordering that blacks be integrated into white units. The same thing's happening here. The color barriers are falling fast in the military. They have to."

"Okay, look," I said, "I accept that all that is happening. And maybe that it will have a major effect on the future of race relations in South Africa. But if it's happening so easily in the military, why can't the same thing happen at the same time outside — in civilian life? Is it so different?"

"Of course it's different. Ours is a pretty rigid society. That old Dutch Calvinist thinking is a major part of our heritage. Whites, blacks, Coloreds, Asians, they've all been neatly categorized by our old *voortrekker* ancestors' interpretation of the Old Testament. In the military, though, new concepts are appearing out of basic necessity, and there's more than a subtle difference. Suddenly you have all colors in the same uniform, eating the same food, sharing the same barracks, living under the same rules. When that happens, it's inevitable that attitudes are going to be changed. It's a practical starting point for change."

"But how long's it going to take for that thinking to spill over into the Afrikaner society back in South Africa?"

"Well, it's not all going to happen overnight. It can't, not with our history and the way we've lived. But if non-whites are going to volunteer to defend South Africa — and they are all volunteers, you know, only whites are conscripted — then they're going to have to get the same respect as a white in and out of the military. The only apartheid in the defense force," he intoned, repeating a line I'd already heard, "is based solely on rank. How about a drink?"

A couple of hours and too many beers later, Henk dropped me off. Climbing out of the car in the dark, I stepped straight into a hole and fell flat on my face. Something crunched in my ankle. Hobbling into my room, I could see the ankle was already swelling. Wrapping it in an ice-filled towel, I spent what was left of the night watching the ankle swell and turn fascinating shades of black and blue. After months of preparation and planning, I had just knocked myself out of directly covering the bush war.

You stupid, stupid son of a bitch, I thought. *You get this far and blow it!* That no one had suggested I would be allowed to join the security forces on operations made no difference; I knew—somehow—that I would, in spite of their basic distrust of Western journalists.

Until now. Now I had ruined everything.

4

Apartheid, Propaganda and Tribalism

L OOKING decidedly delicate, Henk picked me up at my room early the next morning. Our first stop was the hospital. Henk asked for a few aspirin, and I asked for an X-ray plus a few aspirin. The X-ray showed a hairline fracture, and for the first time in my life, I found myself modeling a cast. Henk asked if I still wanted to go. Nothing, I told him, throwing some painkillers down my throat, was going to stop me from covering the scene along the border. It was the whole purpose of the trip.

Having started the drive four hours late, we didn't reach our first scheduled stop at Otavi until shortly before dusk. Henk drove unerringly along the dirt streets to the local army canteen. A couple of beers down the hatch to cut the dust, and we wandered into town for a meal.

The restaurant and bar of the Old West-style hotel were still quiet when we walked in. There was a pause in the plank-floored room as heads turned, and a half-dozen pairs of eyes took in the scene, watching curiously until we settled at a table in the corner. I leaned the unfamiliar crutches against the wall and propped the cast on an adjacent chair. Two pool players carefully chalked their cues and went back to their game. The regulars sitting at the bar picked up their conversations again. The whole room seemed to shift slightly and heave a quiet, collective sigh before returning to whatever they were doing or saying before we came in.

Between posters of Marlboro cowboys and others extolling the virtues of Lion, Castle or Windhoek Lager beer, the walls were hung haphazardly with spears, bows and arrows, knobkerries and curiously shaped drinking gourds. An old fan turned slowly overhead, thin strips of blue plastic trailing weakly from the blades. Whitney Houston crooned from the jukebox.

The owner, a young, modishly dressed Greek, came over to take our orders. I mentioned to Henk that given the heat in the room, perhaps we could sit outside. I had noticed an outdoor terrace just off the bar as we came in. Henk and the Greek exchanged looks.

"The mosquitoes are pretty bad out there tonight," offered the owner.

Henk nodded, adding, "I think we'd be more comfortable in here."

I leaned back to look out onto the terrace. Then I understood: everyone sitting on the dimly lit terrace was black. Legalized apartheid might not exist in Namibia, but, like most places around the world, it was alive and well on a *de facto* basis. It was also a scene that I remembered from my boyhood in rural towns in the American Deep South.

I was nineteen years old, riding a Greyhound bus from Tampa toward Detroit that Christmas season in 1963. The bus stopped after midnight in Macon, Georgia, where I had to change. Moths fluttered around the bare light bulb over the screen door that squeaked open and banged shut behind me as I walked into the waiting room. I stopped. There was something wrong here, and I didn't know what it was at first. Then I understood. I had walked into the "colored" waiting room. Everyone in the shabby, dimly lit room was black.

I had never seen it before, never come into contact with enforced segregation. I started backing up, then turned to go. My hand was on the door handle when I was stopped by a voice. A wizened little black woman—her prune-wrinkled face set off by white hair and gentle eyes—had risen from a scarred bench behind me. She put her hand on my forearm.

"You don' hafta leave, chile, ain' nobody in here gonna hurt you."

I stared at her for a moment and mumbled, "I—I'm sorry."

I turned and fled, the screen door banging shut behind me. From outside I saw the faded sign: Colored. It matched the one over the drinking fountain and a third pointing toward hidden toilets. To the left were the others, all crisply lettered: Whites Only. Ashamed of my cowardice, I stood alone on the loading platform and shivered in the cold Georgia night until my next bus arrived.

By midmorning we'd reached Oshivelo and the military checkpoint on the "red line," the southern border of the operational area. While Henk handed over his identification to the guard and signed the required forms, I hobbled out of the car to read and photograph the sign that greeted everyone entering Ovamboland.

1. Due to the possibility of
    mines or ambushes being
    laid along the road to
    Ondangwa by SWAPO with the
    intention of injuring or
    killing innocent civilians,
    the road is patrolled by the
    Defense Force each morning at
    06h30. The gate opens at
    07h30 and closes again at
    18h00 in terms of the curfew
    announced by proclamation
    of A.G.8
2. Try to travel in groups of
    not less than four vehicles.

"We haven't had any problems this far south for a few years," Henk assured me as he floored the throttle of the sedan. Accelerating past the speed limit, he gave me a smile: "But you can still drive as fast as you want from here up to Ondangwa. If there are any terrs around, the faster you go, the more difficult it is for them to hit you." He reached under his legs, then straightened up and placed a pistol on the seat between us.

Approaching Ondangwa, the first town of any size in Ovamboland, I was struck by the number of blacks in uniform. White soldiers were definitely in the minority. Brown, open-topped Casspir and Buffel armored personnel carriers full of black troops in brown army uniforms moved in both directions along the road. Ratel and Eland armored cars mounting 20-mm or 90-mm guns further emphasized a serious military presence.

Occasionally, Casspirs in green camouflage paint passed us. "Those are Koevoet," said Henk.

"Koofoot?" I asked.

"Yeah, that's the police counterinsurgency people. Animals."

"Oh," seeing another Casspir go by and dismissing it as irrelevant.

On the northern edge of the town was Ondangwa South African Air Force Base. A four-engined C-130 Hercules was in a steep spiral high above the base. Two helicopters chattered low over the flat, sparsely bushed ground outside the flight pattern.

"The choppers are up just in case there's a terr out there with a SAM-7 rocket. Keeps their heads down," said Henk. A bulldozed berm of sandy dirt topped with razor wire and punctuated with guard towers surrounded the base. "All the casevacs[a] — wounded — are flown into the hospital there before sending them down to the States."

Watching the base drop behind us, I nodded in answer. That within a year I would come to know that hospital with more intimacy than I wanted was the furthest thing from my mind. At the moment, there was something else demanding my attention.

Henk looked over at me. "What the hell are you doing?" I was struggling to cut the cast off my leg. "Don't you think you should keep that on for a few more days at least?"

"Just don't mention it to anyone, okay?" I grunted as the point of the knife found my calf. "Look, if I show up wearing this thing, there's no way they're going to even consider letting me go on

---

[a]Casualty evacuations.

ops. And that's where the story is, Henk. So be a buddy and don't say anything about it, okay?"

"But they're not going to let you do that anyway. It's not part of your program."

"Well, at least I can ask 'em, and the worst they can do is say no." I peeled the fiberglass shell away. Tossing the cast and cotton wadding out of the window, I rewrapped the ankle with an elastic bandage, propped the foot on the dash, and returned to watching the passing landscape.

Tall makalani palm trees growing from the flat terrain slipped by the window. Massive, gray anthills jutted above the sparse scrub that clung tenaciously to the thin, sandy earth. Long-horned African cattle grazed placidly along the unfenced road-side and wandered at will across the road. Henk stopped and swore regularly as they ambled nonchalantly in front of us.

Scattered along the sides of the road were literally dozens of Ovambo-owned bars, auto-parts businesses and markets. The names of the drinking establishments competed with each other for exotic flavor. There was the Beverly Hills Bottle Store, and OJ's Mississippi Satisfaction, the Los Angeles Inn and California Auto Spares and Bottle Store. The Jamaica Inn wasn't far from the Picadilly Circus Bar. Namibian nationalists might frequent the Namib Inn, while those with budding relationships could head for the Famous Lovers Bar. And depending on one's frame of mind, there was always a choice between the Happy Bar and the Sorry Bar.

Perhaps it was the proliferation of drinking establishments that naturally led to at least an equal number of auto repair shops. Many of the Ovambo soldiers — most having grown up tending cattle at their fathers' traditional *kraals* in the middle of the bush — had been able to buy cars with their army pay. Their lack of driving experience, compounded by beverages with more punch than sorghum beer, apparently made these repair shops particularly lucrative.

The Continental Hotel, Bottle Store, Auto Parts and Super-market, owned by an Ovambo entrepreneur reputed to be the wealthiest man in Namibia, included a service station and Datsun dealership. Whites shopped alongside blacks here for what couldn't be found at the SADFI (commissary) on base. Smaller markets and open air butchers—the fresh meat hanging from hooks in the heat—were tucked among the other businesses along the road. It was obvious that war had brought a degree of prosperity to Ovamboland.

Thirty minutes north of Ondangwa, we rolled through the gates of Oshakati Base and drove directly to SADF headquarters, where my first briefing was already scheduled. Like most I'd received, it was the standard fare for journalists arriving in Sector 10. A well-rehearsed team of briefers had all the facts, figures, graphs and answers to anticipated questions at their fingertips. The emphasis was on Communications Operations (COMOPS), a sophisticated hearts-and-minds program designed to draw the rural Ovambo population away from SWAPO.

According to a short, bespectacled major, the war for hearts and minds was essentially won. "If we had elections today, I can promise you SWAPO would lose," he declared adamantly, waiting for the logical question.

I decided to play along. "Then why haven't there been new elections?"

"Some people aren't as sure as we are," he answered with a certain annoying smugness. "Or maybe they're afraid of losing their soft jobs," he suggested in a transparent reference to members of the transitional government.

Before departing on a tour of the operational area, an introduction to Brigadier Jakes Swart, Commanding Officer of Sector 10, gave me the opportunity to present my case on getting into the bush. I emphasized the importance of my seeing the war firsthand.

"It's really the only way I can report on it with any authority or credibility," I said as earnestly as I knew how. He listened courteously, but was noncommittal. After a few minutes of polite conversation, Henk and I took our leave.

"I told you it wasn't going to get you anywhere," said Henk when we found ourselves outside again. "It's not on your program."

"Old American proverb, Henk: The worst he can do is say no. No one ever gets anywhere without trying."

Three days in Oshakati went by in a blur of briefings. The

next move was east. Henk and I thumbed a ride with an air force brigadier who was making an inspection tour of his bases along the border. We climbed off his aircraft at Rundu, headquarters for Sector 20.

"Hope you get the stories you're after," he said as we thanked him for the ride. "If there's anything I can help you with, give me a call in Windhoek."

We were whisked away by a major who had been waiting for our arrival. He drove us directly to headquarters and another prepared briefing. I had to give the South African marks for efficiency.

"SWAPO infiltration into the Kavango began in 1980," said the briefing officer, standing in front of a map of the operational area. He had given the rundown to so many hacks that he was starting to sound like a tape recorder. I also had the feeling that he wasn't crazy about Western journalists.

"It peaked in 1983," he droned, "by which time insurgent activity had extended 80 kilometers to the east of Rundu. This was an unacceptable situation. We realized that a strictly military solution was not the answer, so efforts were concentrated in instituting a COMOPS program built around the specific needs of the local Kavango population."

A tall, solidly built officer walked into the room and leaned against the wall. Colonel Dion Ferreira had spent much of his career in counterinsurgency operations. His camouflage beret marked him as the Ferreira who had commanded the elite 32 Battalion, the Portuguese-speaking unit made up of ex-FNLA Angolan soldiers.

"Hell, it's too easy to forget the basics of revolutionary warfare," he interrupted, still leaning against the wall next to me. "Mao Tse-Tung wrote the book on it, you know. One of his most famous quotes was, 'The peaceful population is the sea the guerrilla swims in.'" He reversed a chair next to me and sat down, his arms resting on the back.

"It was the local population here—whether because of intimidation or inclination—who were making it possible for the terrs to operate. The terrs can't operate independently—they need food, shelter and information if they're going to be successful. And the only place they can get all that is from the local pops.

"The only answer, then, was to go to the people. So with our Kavango soldiers from 202 Battalion, we showed and proved to the rural Kavangos that we had more to offer them than SWAPO. We built schools, sent medical teams to the kraals, drilled boreholes, held meetings and generally managed to discredit SWAPO by openly inviting them to participate in these projects.

"We knew we were winning when the locals started informing on the terrorists. We knew we had won when we heard that a local headman had stood up to a group of SWAPO and told them to leave his kraal—that they weren't good for his people. When they threatened to kill him, he told them to go ahead but promised that his clan would kill them as soon as he was dead.

"Of course, one of the advantages that we had was that SWAPO is basically an Ovambo organization with very few Kavangos in it, and the two dozen terrs operating here were all Ovambos. Tribalism worked against them. By the middle of 1985, we had cleared all of Sector 20 of insurgent activity, and we've kept it cleared. I can promise you that this is one of the safest areas in the country."

Following South Africa's determination to Namibianize the war, 202 Battalion had been formed with locally recruited Kavango tribesmen. When I arrived on my tour, the leadership element of 202, previously all white, was gradually being replaced by South African-trained Kavango officers and NCOs.

Captain Alois Gende, 202 Battalion's operations officer, settled in the chair across from me, favoring the leg he'd recently broken playing rugby. He carefully propped the cast on another chair.

"I was the first Kavango selected for officer training. I started with the black 21 Battalion in South Africa and came back here as a corporal when 202 was being formed. Before then, all the officers in 202 were white and most of the NCOs. Now 80 percent of our senior NCOs are Kavangos, and by the end of 1987, we'll have at least ten new lieutenants—Kavangos—serving as platoon commanders. Things are progressing."

As if to emphasize how safe the Kavango was, we traveled by pickup truck to our next stop in Sector 20. The four-hour drive in an unarmored and unescorted vehicle was ample proof of Ferreira's claim that this part of Namibia was safe from insurgent activity. I was content that the SADF wasn't going to risk having a foreign journalist blown up by a land mine or ambushed by infiltrating SWAPO insurgents.

Our overnight stop was the strikingly beautiful Omega Base near the neck of the Caprivi Strip. This was the home of the 201 Bushman Battalion. Still commanded by white officers, 201 was manned by Vasekela Bushmen forced out of Angola, as well as by Barangwena Bushmen indigenous to the Kavango and Western Caprivi.

The Vasekelas were essentially refugees. Their once-peaceful existence in Angola had been threatened in the late 1960s when Soviet and Chinese-backed insurgents fighting the Portuguese began crossing the border from Zambia. Many of the Vasekelas were abducted and forced into military training at the hands of their traditional black enemies.[b]

Faced with the choice of fighting alongside or against these groups, the Bushmen began joining Portuguese units. The 1974 military coup in Portugal and the subsequent abandonment of Angola by the Portuguese Communist junta left the former Bushman soldiers unprotected. In late 1975 they crossed the border into Namibia and asked the South Africans for asylum. The local Barangwena Bushman tribe eventually gathered in the same area, and 201 Battalion was formed.

Commandant Johann Jooste had commanded the unit for two years. "These are some of the finest men I've ever worked with," he told me over dinner in the heavily masculine, open-air officers' mess. "They are capable, quick—even eager—to learn, and their loyalty is unquestioned."

If Sector 20 was free of insurgent activity, I asked, what was the function of 201 Battalion?

"Trackers," said Jooste. "Half the unit is on operations at any given time, working alongside SADF or other SWATF units based in Ovambo. In their own environment, they may be the best trackers in the world, and their endurance and stamina are unbelievable."

---

[b]The Bushmen, one of the most ancient ethnic groups of southern Africa, are a non-Bantu people. With their small stature, coppery-colored skin and narrow, almost Oriental eyes, they are distinctly different from blacks.

I wondered if it wasn't a pity that such an essentially happy and, well, simple people—by Western standards—should be made into soldiers.

"These people aren't simple. Unsophisticated, perhaps, by some standards, but I don't know any white whose knowledge of the bush is as complete as the Bushman. He's highly sophisticated in his own environment. And as far as making them into soldiers, they're volunteers. We haven't forced them into anything. They can leave any time they want. They're paid well, given education, medical care and housing. And that extends to their families as well. We're lucky to have them."

Our final stop on my tour of the operational area was Katima Mulilo, headquarters for Sector 70. Located at the eastern tip of the Caprivi Strip, Katima was a sleepy border town spoken of with nostalgia by those who had served there.

"About the only excitement we get around here," admitted Commandant Frans Verfuss, "is when Old Gertie wanders out of the bush into town." Old Gertie was a one-tusked rogue elephant who enjoyed nibbling at well-maintained gardens.

"I couldn't get to work one morning last week because she was standing in front of my garage picking flowers off a vine! And I couldn't shoo her away. She wouldn't budge. Last year the game department chaps were going to shoot her until almost everyone in Katima signed a petition protesting against it. Wouldn't be the same in Katima without the old girl."

Although one of the early Namibian liberation movements, the Caprivi African National Union, emerged here, Sector 70 had been free of overt insurgent activity since 1978, when SWAPO launched a standoff mortar and rocket attack from Zambia. Ten South African soldiers were killed when a 122-mm rocket hit their barracks.

The predictable South African response was a major cross-border punitive operation into Zambia against SWAPO. This not only neutralized the immediate threat, but also encouraged Zambia to henceforth deny SWAPO the use of Zambian soil for launching further attacks against bases in the Eastern Caprivi.

(There is a story about the determined Zambian border guard who halted the invading column of grim-faced South Africans with up-raised palm and a demand to see their passports. His style—if not his common sense—was so admired by the South African commander, the story goes, that he was picked up and removed to the side of the road under guard while the column rumbled past.)

The two indigenous tribes of the Caprivi, the Mafwe and less populous Masubia, were among the least aggressive and politically radical peoples of South West Africa/Namibia. Their major points of contention harked back to the late nineteenth century when the German administrator of the Caprivi arbitrarily appointed chiefs and demarcated tribal boundaries, giving the Mafwe ascendancy over the Masubia. Complicated intertribal disputes based on decisions made by an obscure imperial German officer a hundred years earlier were still causing problems.

Verfuss leaned back in his chair with a private smile as he prepared to brief me on the political situation in the Caprivi.

"The recent political scene here is a little complicated, so I'll just give you the bare outlines. Feel free to interrupt if there's anything you don't understand.

"As you know, there are two tribes in this area, the Mafwe and Masubia, each tracing its background in different directions and each a little contemptuous of the other. Well, not long after SWAPO was formed, the Caprivi African National Union— CANU—was founded as a Masubia-based organization. In 1966 its membership—something like 250 or 300—left the Caprivi to join SWAPO in Zambia and Angola.

"As you also probably know, CANU President Misheke Muyongo became vice-president of SWAPO. Ovambo dominance of SWAPO, however, led to a lot of tribal problems, and quite a few of the CANU members were falsely accused of being South African spies—the standard charge against anyone not agreeing with Nujoma—and imprisoned by SWAPO.

"We took advantage of the split by offering amnesty to any CANU member who wanted to return to his home in the Caprivi. The only condition was that if they had committed crimes against the civilian population, we would prosecute them. If they had carried out attacks only against the security forces, there wouldn't be a problem. Over 125—mostly Masubias—returned. Right away, they started to reform CANU as a legitimate political party.

"In June 1985 Muyongo—who's a hereditary chief of the Mafwe, by the way—accepted amnesty. He returned and immediately involved himself in politics, attempting to consolidate the older Caprivi Alliance Party—the CAP—and the newly reformed CANU under one banner.

"His two old CANU lieutenants in SWAPO, both Masubias, also accepted the amnesty offer and followed about a month later to prevent Muyongo from cornering the political marketplace in the Caprivi. Muyongo succeeded, however, in merging CAP and CANU into the United Democratic Party [UDP] of which he became president. Right after that, he affiliated his UDP with the Democratic Turnhalle Alliance in Windhoek. Okay so far?

"His old lieutenants in the armed struggle weren't very happy with his dominance and the fact that most of the United Democratic Party's senior members were Mafwes, so they decided to continue an independent CANU.

"Then the previous Caprivi Alliance Party representative in the transitional government in Windhoek also fell out with Muyongo and continued the CAP as a separate, independent party. The next move was to start planning a Masubia CAP-CANU alliance to counter ex-CANU president and ex-SWAPO vice-president Muyongo's United Democratic Party, which had been the Mafwe CAP-CANU alliance."

"Listen," I said to Commandant Verfuss, "would you mind running all that by me at least one more time? I think I'm confused."

In an area of 500,000 square miles, more than half of Namibia's population of 1.2 million was represented by the Ovambo people, who lived within the 30,000 square miles of Ovamboland. If the Kavango and Caprivi were free of armed infiltration, this traditional tribal area certainly was not. It was here that the winds of change era gave rise to the South West Africa People's Organization, *née* Ovambo People's Congress.

With over 200 miles of open, heavily bushed border with Angola and a population generally sympathetic to the insurgents, Ovamboland was the scene of regular SWAPO incursions. The number of insurgents south of the border at any given time seldom exceeded 100, but their presence demanded a disproportional counterinsurgency response from the South Africans.

In spite of wildly exaggerated claims of success, however, SWAPO had little to boast about militarily. Its victories had been limited to sabotaging telephone and electric poles, occasional standoff mortar and rocket attacks against Oshakati and remote bases, and the rare ambush against patrolling security force units. According to the SADF, over 12,000 insurgents had been killed or captured since the beginning of the war. Security force deaths for the same period were less than 450.

Jacob Hannai, SWAPO's representative in London, vehemently disagreed with these figures when I'd returned to England.

"It's what you always hear being mentioned because the South Africans are in control of the media," he said angrily. "But I can tell you that the People's Liberation Army of Namibia have been very much successful. This year alone, they have eliminated quite a lot of racist troops. They have destroyed enemy bases at Eenhana, Ongwelume, Ruacana, Okahana, Tsandi, and Oshakati." (I forbore mentioning that I'd just returned from Namibia and that the places he mentioned were standing unscathed.)

According to Hannai, "The South African Defense Force have—among more than 100,000[c] racist troops in Namibia—a number of specialized military units who are, in fact, instructed to carry out what they call counterinsurgency operations. They have a unit which is known as Koevoet, and this Koevoet consists of some members of the South African Defense Force and all those elements who have been defeated in the war for liberation in Zimbabwe, and they are committing all types of atrocities.

"As I said, this Koevoet . . . in 1982 they have wiped out a village at a place called Oshikuku, and all these years they have been kidnapping people, they have been killing people in cold blood, and they have destroyed crops. Most of the civilian population in the rural areas have been complaining about their crops being destroyed by the racist army running over their fields. And the Koevoet specialize in specifically to eliminate the supporters and members of our organization, SWAPO."

When asked about charges that many Namibian civilians had died from driving over SWAPO-laid land mines and that SWAPO had committed its own share of atrocities against the civilian population, Hannai dismissed it out-of-hand. "That is what one

---

[c]20,000 – 25,000 was the actual figure in the operational area.

is made to believe. I could not see a situation where the freedom fighters of our movement . . . can indulge in planting land mines. But what I'm telling you is that those who have been involved in the atrocities against our people are the South African defense forces. I've already told you that the Koevoet have indulged in a number of campaigns in order to discredit SWAPO. Sometimes [they] have been planting land mines, sometimes [they] have been killing people, sometimes [they] have been committing all types of atrocities against [the people], and immediately after the acts have been committed, then they say it is SWAPO. It is a systematic campaign to discredit the movement.

"We are not committing atrocities. We don't see any situation why we have to go and kill our own mothers, brothers, and sisters, because we are fighting for them. Because these South African defense forces, the way they are doing that is to suppress the will of the people, and they really do it all expenses."

In spite of Hannai's claims, SWAPO's losses were appalling, but their amateurish efforts were forcing South Africa to maintain a counterinsurgency presence along the Angolan border at a cost of over $3 million each day.

"We really can't afford it," a South African officer told me, "but we don't have much choice. We're not going to risk having another Marxist country along our borders. No way."

Wherever I went during my introduction to the operational area, my questions were answered straightforwardly, occasionally off the record, but always with a frankness I had not anticipated. Unfortunately, most of the information for the record had already been beaten to death by other journalists who'd been given the same tour.

After eight days of touring bases in the Kavango and Caprivi, Henk and I caught a flight back to Ondangwa Air Force Base. When we landed, the army lieutenant meeting us shook his head gravely.

"Authorization just came through an hour ago; you leave tomorrow for a week in the bush with Koevoet." The look on his face indicated what he thought of the idea. The look on Henk's face was pure astonishment. I would have needled him about it "not being part of my program," but I was too annoyed to say anything.

Koevoet? But weren't they the police unit I'd heard about? I tried to hide my frustration, deciding that I'd been stuck with them as a sop to a pushy, wandering journalist. Police? How the hell was I going to do a firsthand account of counterinsurgency operations by hanging out with a bunch of cops? It was proper soldiers who were fighting this war—like 101 Battalion, which I'd heard plenty about—not some knuckle-dragging, off-the-wall police unit. I couldn't decline, not after the effort to accommodate me, but *cops*?

That night over a few beers at Driehoek, the SADF guest quarters in Oshakati, I was given a few facts about this outfit I'd be spending the next week with. Koevoet, pronounced *koo-foot,* was Afrikaans for "crowbar," though the official designation was the South West African Police Counterinsurgency (SWAPOL COIN) unit. Of its operational personnel, 90 percent were black, most of them locally recruited Ovambos. The whites were either South African Police seconded to the South West African Police (SWAPOL), or "Southwesters" already in SWAPOL. Although they comprised barely 10 percent of the total security force presence in the operational area, it emerged that they accounted for well over 70 percent of the contacts (combats) with SWAPO. It was a grudging admission from one of the people sitting around the table.

"But, man, those guys are animals. No discipline, long hair, all they do is drink and get into fights with the army and make problems for our COMOPS people. Okay, maybe they shoot a lot of terrs, but they're a real headache in Oshakati, I can promise you. Genuine. And a lot of them have been brought up on charges."

"What sort of charges?"

"Oh, you know, minor stuff like murder, torture, rape."

"And what's been the outcome of these trials?" I asked.

"Most of them have ended with not-guilty verdicts, but I think a couple of their people were convicted for murder. I'm not sure if they swung or not."

"You're kidding. You mean . . . *hanged?*"

"Like I said, I'm not sure. Ask them about it."

"Have you heard the joke about them?" asked an army major. I shook my head.

"No, it seems there was this man-eating crocodile up on the Cunene River that was a real problem, see, eating a lot of the local population, so General Meiring, the army general for South West, tells his chief of staff to sort it out, that he's got ten days to take care of this croc. Well, after an all-night planning session, they start the operation. First the air force sends in the photo-reconnaissance Mirages; the intelligence analysts look at the picture and find out where this croc is hanging out. Next, the reconnaissance commandos go in and do a complete recce [recon] of the area and come back with all the gen about where he suns himself, where he eats and sleeps. So then a major operation is jacked up, with the airborne making a big drop, artillery moving in, infantry, everything—and on the end of the tenth day, the defense force delivers the crocodile to General Meiring.

"Well, next day, info comes down that there's another man-eating croc causing big problems along the Cunene. The defense force has used up all their assets, so the general tells Koevoet they've got ten days to sort this crocodile out. Well, they sit down and drink for nine days. On the morning of the tenth day, they jump in their Casspirs and start racing for the Cunene. About two miles out of Oshakati, they see this lizard, and all of them come to a screeching stop. They all jump out of their Casspirs, run over and grab this lizard, see, and then beat the shit out of him until he admits he's a crocodile."

There was a hearty round of laughter and knowing nods. It was obviously a favorite army joke about the police. "Man, that's the way those people operate," said the major. "Genuine."

The surprising part was that no Western journalist had ever been authorized to accompany them on a week-long deployment into the bush. "But all they're going to do is run you around in the quietest area they can find," a visiting journalist from Windhoek said. "There's no way they'll take you into an area where there's any risk of a contact happening. You actually think they'd take a chance on getting a foreign journalist killed? No way." Not knowing whether to be relieved or disappointed, I finally wandered off to bed.

I awoke suddenly at two in the morning. Outside the tent-topped guest hut, rain, lightning and thunder battered Oshakati. The dream had been terrifyingly surreal. I had found myself at the door to a tan, tiled room. Floor, walls and ceiling all the same. A faceless attendant stood next to the door. As I entered the room, I asked him, "Are you going to drown me?"

"You already are," he answered.

My feet suddenly slipped from under me, and I hit the floor hard, not feeling anything, and immediately began sliding over the level tiled floor as though it were sloping steeply downhill. My feet came to the far wall, and instead of stopping, I went through *the wall and into a softly lit void of silence and peace. I was still flowing through comfortable nothingness when I snapped awake.*

Lying under the mosquito net, I lit a cigarette and listened to the storm. In spite of the drop in temperature and the cold spray being driven through the windows, my chest and back were soaked with sweat. I flinched at the crackling hiss of lightning and simultaneous explosion of thunder. Was it a premonition? No, just a bad and strange dream. Was this really what I should be doing tomorrow? No, it was today already; today I was going out. No, just a bad dream. But it was a long time before I fell asleep again.

5

Koevoet: An Introduction

L UGGAGE in hand, I waited outside the dew-covered guest quarters, nervously watching the sky lighten. A battered, mustard-colored pickup truck with one white and two black policemen in camouflage uniforms shuddered to a stop on the washboard road. One of the men climbed out to throw my bags into the back and motioned me to take his place in front. My small talk was met with stony silence.

A short drive across the Oshakati base brought us to the sprawling headquarters of the South West African Police Counterinsurgency unit. Feeling distinctly self-conscious in the crisp, new bush uniform I'd been given, I wandered into the green maze of modular structures. Clusters of dirt-encrusted men in stained olive drab, obviously just returned from the bush, lounged along the shaded central walkway, speaking animatedly to cleanly washed and attired colleagues. From the guttural and incomprehensible Afrikaans of the speakers, I caught the words "contact," "terrs" and "kills" repeated with disconcerting regularity.

Unsure of where I was supposed to go, I paused alongside a group to ask the way. Conversation came to a halt as suspicious eyes examined me from head to foot. The initial suspicion changed to barely concealed smirks at the sight of my cameras and baggage. Following the directions of one amused giant with a jagged scar across his face, I limped down the passageway and knocked at the door of Captain Bernie Ley's office. There was a growled, "Yeah, come in," from the other side. Stocky and bearded with a quick-moving energy, Ley was already up to his eyebrows in paperwork when I entered. I was subjected to another slow scan before: "So you're the one the army pushed on us, eh?"

"Well, yeah, I guess so," clearing my throat.

"Terrific."

Frowning at the interruption, he shoved the pile of official forms to one side, brusquely introduced himself and immediately got down to business. "Blood group? Next of kin? Your group leader will issue you with a weapon. Ever fired an R5? You understand that neither the South West African Police nor the government of South West Africa can be held responsible for any injury you may sustain while accompanying this unit on counterinsurgency operations? Got that? Good, sign this."

Damn, I thought, leaning forward to scrawl my name across the bottom of the sheet of paper Ley slapped down in front of me.

After I'd answered the rest of his rapid-fire questions, I mentioned what I'd been told the night before about being kept away from any area where there might be a contact. "Look," I said, rather full of myself and still dismayed at being pushed off on a bunch of heavy-handed cops, "I appreciate the opportunity to see how you guys operate, but I really don't want to go out on some Boy Scout camping trip."

Ley fixed me with an exasperated look. His cheeks swelled, and a sharply expelled sigh escaped his lips. "Listen, pal, we're sending you out for the next week with one of our best groups. That's four Casspirs, a Blesbok, almost fifty men and a helluva lot of experience. Our job is to stop the terrs. If you think we're going to waste that resource on a media-relations exercise just for you, you're crazy." I'd just made my first mistake.

"Oh," *sotto voce.* Then, brightly: "Do I need to take any identification?"

As I was asking, Captain Roelf Maritz, who, I would learn, enjoyed the reputation of being shot more times and carrying more shrapnel than the rest of Koevoet combined, walked through the door. I caught a quick, private look pass between him and Ley. *Another journalist,* it said.

"I don't think any terr's going to be too impressed with your press cards, pal," said Maritz, raising an eyebrow. I could tell I was making a real hit here.

"Right," I said. "By the way, is it okay if I take a picture of the map?" One wall of Ley's office was covered by a detailed map showing all police and army bases across the operational area of northern Namibia.

"No."

This is getting better and better, I thought. *Well, they're South African cops, aren't they? What did you expect?* "Is there some place I can leave my suitcase and typewriter?"

Ley jerked a peremptory thumb in the direction of a standing metal locker in the corner of his office. Shoving all my worldly goods into it, I goggled. The interior was already filled with captured East bloc weapons: assault rifles, rocket-propelled grenades, a portable surface-to-air missile, anti-personnel mines, pistols, and a wealth of other normal day-to-day items. Just the sort of things one naturally expected to find in an office locker.

"By the way, you ever been in a contact?" he stared, scratching the thick growth on his face.

"Sure. Lots," I smiled weakly.

"Okay, come on," said Ley impatiently, "let me introduce you to the boss." I obediently tagged along in his burly wake. Across the open-air passage was Brigadier Johannes G. Dreyer's office. We found him standing outside his door, hands on hips and chatting easily with some of his men who had just returned from the bush. Ley made the introductions and charged back to his office, shaking his head at the kind of people he had to deal wtih.

As the brigadier and I exchanged pleasantries, I had the feeling that this graying, lean man with the bristling mustache was assessing me closely. There was a charisma and strength of character about him that was difficult to ignore. Everything about him—his directness, his obvious self-assurance, even his fluid, almost insolent posture—bespoke a man accustomed to taking command and getting what he wanted. Even the army referred to him by his nickname of "Sterk Hans" (Strong Hans). It was rumored that he would already have been commissioner of the South African Police had he been willing to accept an assignment away from this legendary, infamous unit he had founded eight years earlier. Dreyer's devotion to Koevoet was legend—and by all accounts reciprocated with worshipful awe by its black and white members.

"I believe you're going out with Zulu Alpha this morning. That's one of the most experienced groups we have. Marius Brand, the group leader, is one of our best operators. I think you should find it interesting. If there's anything you need, please let me know."

Seeing I had interrupted the black and white policemen who were waiting for us to finish, I excused myself and wandered outside where the armored personnel carriers and supply vehicles were being loaded for the week's deployment. The cars' machine guns, which had been removed when the groups had returned from the bush the week before, were being remounted. Into the cars was going a formidable collection of South African-manufactured and captured Soviet-manufactured weapons. The amount of ammunition being stowed in the APCs suggested a serious intent. A steady stream of men moved from storerooms to cars, carrying personal weapons, grenade launchers, medical kits, hydraulic jacks, crates of ration packs, tools and spare parts.

"Maximum firepower," said a voice behind me. I looked around. It was Warrant Officer Marius Brand. "You can have too little, but you can't ever have too much." For the next week my life would be in this man's hands. Tall and lanky, Brand moved with the loose-jointed swagger of a western gunslinger. Above a thin beard were two of the coldest eyes I had ever seen. "In a contact, you gotta overwhelm the terrs, break them up and kill 'em now-now. Especially in an ambush—you drive straight into them with maximum firepower." He smiled, but the eyes stayed as cold as the snake's on Zulu Alpha's group insignia.

Brand took my rucksack and heaved it into the back of the Blesbok supply vehicle. We walked to his command car, ZA-1, and he showed me where to stow my camera bag. "You can take that seat across from Otto," he indicated, introducing me to a young Ovambo with warrant officer insignia on his sleeves. The young man shook my hand in the black African style—hand grip, thumb grip, and hand grip again while his left fingertips touched his right forearm. He returned to supervising the final loading of the car.

Nine other Ovambos, all special constables, crowded into the Casspir. Each inserted a magazine into his short R5 assault rifle and wedged the weapon tightly next to his seat. After stowing personal gear, they hoisted themselves to sit on the rim of the open-topped vehicle, their legs dangling inside. By eleven o'clock, we were pulling out of Oshakati, the men laughing and waving to friends along the dusty road.

Settling into my assigned place, I carefully examined the

interior of this South African war machine that figured so prominently in television news coverage of South Africa. Along each side were five molded rubber seats and backrests, each separated by small, spring-loaded gun ports. Over the gun ports was a row of thick, bullet-proof windows. Above the green-tinted glass, the armored body sloped sharply inward on both sides, leaving a rectangular view of the sky that stopped two feet short of the doors at the rear and one foot short of the forward-most seats. Gun ports and two smaller windows were set into the outward-opening hydraulic doors at the back. A narrow aisle ran forward from the doors to the driver's and co-driver's seats. Between the open section above me and the enclosed cab was a separate hatch occupied by Brand. Over the driver's position directly in front of him was a forward-shielded turret mounting two machine guns, the handles of the weapons within easy reach. Because of the exposed position, different car commanders devised various means of additional protection. In addition to the standard square hatch cover raised behind them, some of the men slipped thin armor plates or bullet-proof glass into custom-made brackets on either side of the hatch. But they were still dangerously exposed to small arms fire. Brand, I noted, disdained the use of any extra protection other than the hatch cover at his back.

My sense of being totally out of place was magnified by my being the only person still occupying a seat inside the weapons-littered car. From the rectangular coaming above, ten pairs of feet swayed around me as the Casspir rolled along the road. Plucking up my courage, I finally followed suit and lifted myself to the rim of the open well, holding on to the back plate behind Brand. Sitting across from me, eyes narrowed against the wind, was Special Warrant Officer Otto Shivute, whom Brand had introduced me to earlier. Just twenty-three years old, he had been with Koevoet for six years. When we stopped for a minute to wait for one of the Casspirs to catch up, I asked him through Brand how many contacts with SWAPO he had experienced. He smiled shyly, shrugged and said simply, "Baie." A lot.

"Hoeveel?" I pressed, trying out a little Afrikaans from the dictionary I had brought with me. How many?

Shivute spoke quickly to Brand. "He thinks it's around 100 or 120. He hasn't kept count," Brand translated. I looked at Shivute with a new appreciation. This pleasant-looking young man with the pistol riding easily on his hip was a highly experienced combat veteran.

"Why did he join the police?"

There was a brief conference between the two. "No, he says he had relatives killed by SWAPO because they refused to support them. After that, he knew that the terrs didn't believe in all the things they claimed they were fighting for. Killing people because they disagree is not freedom or democracy. He also says he likes the work. Perhaps someday he'll have the chance to find the terrs who killed his relatives."

"Otto's good. Damned good," Brand would tell me later with undisguised pride and respect. "Wait till you see him on the spoor,"[a] he added, for whom all his geese were swans.

Once back on the road, Brand noted, "We're killing the terrs faster than they can be replaced. They're having to kidnap recruits and train them against their will." I listened without comment. It was a story I'd heard in at least two briefings I'd received on SWAPO. I had already discounted it as one of those propaganda standards used by both sides and something almost impossible to verify.

We headed southeast to Ondangwa, then turned north on the tarred road leading to the Oshikango border post. Ten miles south of the Angolan border, we were forced to divert off the macadam to avoid a culvert that SWAPO insurgents had blown up two nights earlier. A civilian pickup truck followed in our wake. Its driver waved at some of the Ovambo policemen he knew, pointing and laughing at the destroyed culvert.

"When they got back to Namakunde they probably told their detachment commander they'd destroyed half a dozen Casspirs with that," Brand laughed as we rolled up the shallow bank and regained the road on the other side of the damaged section. "When you see the claims SWAPO makes, you wonder what they were smoking when they came up with them. The terrs exaggerate the hell out of what they've done down here just to make them-

---

[a] Spoor — The Dutch-Afrikaans word for "tracks," in this case those left by SWAPO insurgents.

selves look good to their detachment commanders when they get back to Angola. And SWAPO is happy to believe them. Sounds good in their press releases."

Ten minutes later, we turned off the road and into the bush where every civilian became a possible source of information. At our first stop, I followed the black constables out of the rear door of the Casspir and into a typical Ovambo kraal. Surrounded by a palisade of crooked tree trunks driven into the ground, it was entered through a secret gate of two logs, which were moved to one side. Inside, similar walls twisted haphazardly in confusing patterns. I would learn that each kraal had its own unique layout, a tradition followed from earlier days when the inhabitants needed time to gather their spears and clubs in response to raiders from another tribe.

In one area were the thatched and wattle huts of the young men, in another those for girls who had reached puberty. The senior wife had her own hut, while another accommodated younger wives—if the head of the family was wealthy enough to afford them. He had his own hut and adjacent fenced rectangle— always oriented toward the east—where he could drink his sorghum beer with other men or meditate undisturbed by women. Horned skulls of cattle slaughtered for special occasions were tied one above the other to the kraal fence by tough strips of bark.

Large, conical baskets of tightly woven bark and topped with round, thatched roofs were propped upright above the ground. Lined with clay as a barrier to ants and termites, they held stores of *mohango,* the staple crop of grain sorghum. Mohango fields sometimes extended for 100 meters or more around a kraal. Brand explained that because the security forces were forbidden to drive through the fields, SWAPO often used them for hiding places. His anger at the regulation showed. "I can promise you that if the boys find spoor going into the mohango, I'm not going to let them go in alone without fire support from the cars. We'll drive through those fields with them, and to hell with COMOPS."

"What about the people around here? Do they support SWAPO?" I asked.

"Depends on the area," he said. "Around here, which is where you find the heaviest infiltration, a lot of them are pro-SWAPO. The further you go west or east, the less support you find. There

are certain kraals we know where the PBs[b] help them, but there
are others that are definitely anti-SWAPO. That's where we get
most of our info, from the local pops. They might not like us, but
a lot of them like the terrs even less."

As we entered through the fence, a family of a dozen men,
women and children emerged from their various huts. Their faces
showed neither fear nor welcome, rather a stoical resignation. All
were dressed in shabby, Western-style clothes set off by traditional bead necklaces and bracelets. Taking individual family
members by the hand, the constables separated them to question
each privately about the presence of any SWAPO insurgents in
the area. To my surprise, Shivute came back with reports that
three insurgents had been seen or heard about in the last two
days. In spite of the blown-up culvert and the weapons everyone
carried, I still had difficulty believing that there was a real war
going on here. Everything seemed so quiet and peaceful. My surprise must have been evident.

"I can promise you there are ten to fifteen terrs within ten
klicks [kilometers] of here," said Brand, answering my unasked
question. "The bad thing is that if they hear we're in the area, they
sit tight or get the hell out. They're really scared of us."

We pulled into a tiny, "modern" village of corrugated tin shacks,
where the men quickly disembarked and spread out to check identity cards. The atmosphere here was noticeably different. A group
of flashily dressed young men stared toughly at us. Their open
hostility drew the constables' immediate attention. After separating them, two or more policemen pressed closely around each
one, questioning in loud, harsh tones as identity documents were
demanded and closely examined. The obvious intimidation quickly
cowed even the most belligerent. Eyes dropped and heads shook
meekly. *Terrific public relations,* I thought, dismayed and embarrassed at what I was observing. Still, I'd seen far worse in other
parts of Africa. However distasteful this is, it hardly compared
with what I'd seen in Uganda. Why was it unremarkable for the
police of a black-ruled country to commit systematic murder, yet
unacceptable for these South African-led blacks to indulge in
verbal bullying?

---

[b] PB — *Plaaslike bevolking,* Afrikaans for "local population."

When it appeared there were no insurgents, the policemen crowded into a dirt-floored, single-roomed *Cuca*[c] shop to buy tins of warm soft drinks. I shouldered my way inside and scanned the plank shelves of beer, soft drinks, cheap whiskey, soap and candy. Brand and Shivute shared a liter bottle of warm Coke while discussing where to go from there.

After working the area until late afternoon, it was obvious the three insurgents we'd heard about were keeping a very low profile. Information from the civilian population placed the three here within the last two or three days; where they were now, no one seemed to know.

Brand conferred at length with someone on the radio. "We'll RV [rendezvous] with Zulu Mike and go north," he explained. "Maybe we'll have better luck up there."

I nodded. North took us toward the border, and the nearer we were to SWAPO's sanctuary, obviously the greater the chance of something happening. With the afternoon sun on our left, we turned off the dirt road and entered thick bush. A few miles on, I caught sight of an armored personnel carrier waiting in the shade of a large tree. Nearby were three more of the big Wolf Turbos. How we had managed to find them in the featureless terrain completely baffled me. Brand and Shivute dismounted to join Zulu Mike's group leader around a map. Heads nodded in agreement as they stood, brushed sand from knees and reboarded the cars.

Crashing through heavy undergrowth, we burst onto a wide clearing that ran as far as I could see to the east and west. The column of green APCs paralleled the southern edge of the strip until Brand shouted a command to the driver and we turned to drive across. Shivute, one hand on the raised hatch behind Brand and another on the rim of the coaming, motioned with his chin toward the approaching treeline.

"Angola," he said softly.

Angola? Did he say Angola? We reentered the bush, and I looked at the others, all of whom were gazing steadily at the ground. Surely not. I must have misunderstood. Besides, in my briefings it

---

[c] The name was derived from a once famous but no longer available Portuguese-Angolan beer.

was said that the security forces crossed the border only in hot pursuit of fleeing insurgents. I pulled the small dictionary from my pocket and thumbed through it. Finding the word I wanted, I leaned forward and tapped Shivute on the leg.

"Wragtag?" (Really?) I asked, pointing around us. "Angola?"

He lifted his eyes from their examination of the passing ground and nodded indifferently. "Ja."

So what was all this about "hot pursuit?" Unless I was grossly mistaken, we weren't chasing anyone. Which meant we'd just invaded another country *looking* for someone to chase. I suddenly understood why everyone's eyes were fixed on the sandy surface to either side of us: they were searching for footprints — spoor — of SWAPO guerrillas who, by permission of the Angolan government, had every legal right to be here. By extension, we were breaking every international law in the book by our armed incursion across a sovereign nation's border. And that very much included me.

The deeper we drove, the more tracks of heavy vehicles I saw, tracks — I turned to look behind us — identical to those we were making. And they were everywhere. It was obvious the South Africans not only entered Angola at will, but with complete impunity. This was certainly more than some Boy Scout camping trip. I shook my head in wonder as a slight shiver of excitement went up my back. *Damn.*

Just before sunset and almost 30 miles inside Angola, a suitable location for a temporary base (TB) was found deep in the bush near three deep, hand-dug wells. Crude but effective winches of well-worn tree trunks perched atop the branch-lined holes. Buckets of sweet, cool water were drawn to top off the cars' tanks. From one well, a bucket came up containing a long-dead rat. The contents were nonchalantly emptied to one side and the bucket sent back down. I coughed and hurriedly left the scene, not wanting to know which car's tank had received its resupply from that particular source.

With the Casspirs and Wolf Turbos set around the TB, guns facing outward, food and bedding were unloaded. As the camp was being organized, I turned to inspect the cars. Both types were similar in design philosophy, though the Wolf was wider, higher, four tons heavier and powered by an engine with three times the horsepower of that in the older Casspir.

With their V-shaped hulls, blunt, angular surfaces and externally mounted running gear, no one could describe them as anything but brutally ugly. The purpose behind the design was to deflect the blast of land mines and at the same time offer a measure of protection against small-arms fire. An exploding land mine would blow away the wheel that detonated it, but the people inside would be reasonably safe. There were stories of cars rolling over as many as three mines stacked one on top of the other, the blast lifting a Casspir's dozen tons of steel and men ten feet or more off the ground. Yet, no one had ever been killed, and the worst injuries amounted to occasional broken arms or legs. Having decided there was probably a greater chance of hitting an anti-tank mine than running into a firefight, I welcomed the protection.

By the time I completed my inspection, a dozen cooking fires were already going. Feeling uncomfortably dirty under a day-old layer of sweat and dust, I wet the corner of a towel and made an attempt to wipe off the accumulated grime. Sergeant Dean Viljoen, Zulu Mike's group leader, laughed at my efforts. The trim, blond Afrikaner shook his head with good-humored disapproval.

"It's something you get used to. We usually don't bother. You won't believe just how good a hot shower feels at the end of a week in the bush." Looking enviously at the Ovambos who were washing from mess tins, their faces and torsos lathered with soap, I thought it would feel pretty good after only one day.

Shivute and Sandak, Zulu Alpha's second Ovambo warrant officer, hunkered down with Brand and discussed the next day's movements before going off to check on their men. When they had walked away, Brand explained that Sandak was a hereditary clan headman (chief) with a price on his head. SWAPO had tried more than once to kill him. He'd had two pickup trucks blown up by mines or hit by SWAPO gunfire. He had also been seriously wounded once by an anti-personnel mine.

Viljoen walked over to where we were sitting and asked to have a look at my cameras. Porky, one of Viljoen's car commanders, followed diffidently in his path. Photo equipment, I would come to learn, was always a particular point of interest among the men and often an easy way to get a conversation started.

"Porky wants to know what cameras and lenses you're using," Dean explained, introducing his gangly partner. A white Namibian—a Southwester—Porky's English was marginal, which seemed only to compound his natural shyness. Tall, painfully thin and quiet, this gawky, beardless eighteen-year-old with the quarter-inch haircut and jug ears looked like he should be back in high school. He was the sort you imagined spending long hours after school on the basketball court practicing his hook shots, not driving through the bush behind two machine guns, looking for Communist insurgents.

He went back to his car and returned with a new 35-mm camera. He'd saved for a year to buy it, he explained, holding it proudly. I answered his questions about films, lenses and filters and offered what advice I could while Dean helped with the language barrier.

The other whites, almost as shy and quiet as Porky, kept to themselves. Apie,[d] big, dark and bearded, busied himself with preparing a *potjiekos* for the evening's meal. Like almost every South African I would meet, he had his own secret recipe for this traditional Afrikaner stew—even, such as now, when available ingredients were limited.

Picking through the ration packs, Apie opened and emptied cans into a blackened cast-iron pot that sat on the fire. Tasting the bubbling mixture critically, he wrinkled his nose and added a good measure of Tabasco sauce. Stirring his creation with the air of an artist, he raised the spoon once more to his mouth. Frowning, he emptied what was left of the hot sauce into the pot. His expression after another delicate taste suggested he had outdone himself. Eyes watering, he made a quick grab for a canvas water bag. A superb, if somewhat lively, *pièce de résistance.* Christo, even taller and more gangly than Porky, sat quietly with a cup of coffee, watching Apie's sudden contortions with silent engrossment. Getting half a dozen words out of him was like pulling teeth.

Being in the middle of Indian Country with fires blazing seemed a touch unorthodox, I thought, but Brand explained that the SWAPO insurgents were too frightened of Koevoet to even *think* about hitting us, worse luck. But if they did, then by God they'd leave spoor we could follow in the morning and get some

---

[d] A not uncommon nickname, it translates to "little ape."

kills. I stared at him for a minute and laughed. "Oh, well, yeah," with unconvincing cool, wondering if he was all there. The lights might be on, but there wasn't anyone at home, I decided. Bonkers.

Shortly after midnight, I was awakened by a hand on my shoulder. I started and raised myself on an elbow, thinking confusedly that it was already time to get up. Brand and Shivute were kneeling next to me. Otto held his R5 assault rifle and stared across the camp into the dark.

"The boys just told Otto there are some people out there in the bush," Brand whispered. "They think they are just some of the local population trying to steal some things. We're going to scare them off. Stay where you are and don't move," and he disappeared in the direction of his car.

A few seconds later there was the hollow *thunk* of a mortar tube and then a distinct *pop* as the illumination round burst high overhead. The magnesium flare, descending on its small parachute, threw a harsh, blue-white light over the camp. I heard the unmistakable sound of a machine gun being charged and cocked, immediately followed by a series of bursts, the tracers arcing high overhead from the Casspir to disappear into the night. I cringed and fought the impulse to roll off the stretcher and burrow into the ground. The firing ended when the flare burned itself out, followed by the sounds of people running panic-stricken through the darkened bush. Immediately, there were hoots and laughter from around the camp. Silence returned—except for someone snoring.

Apie had slept through it all.

Back in Namibia two days later, we were raising dust down the Oom Willie laterite road that led to the army base at Eenhana. On either side was thick, heavy cover. I had been told that more than a couple of Koevoet groups had been ambushed along this stretch. Otto Shivute was thumbing through an Oshivambo-Afrikaans— English dictionary. Finding and writing down the words he wanted, he showed them to Brand, who laughed and nodded.

The young Ovambo turned to me with a smile and read them carefully in Afrikaans-accented English. "If we lucky, ambush!" I glanced toward Brand who was concentrating on the dense bush to each side. He had already cocked the .50 caliber machine gun and pulled the locking pin from the gun mount. I looked back at Shivute, nodded in feigned agreement, and immediately started wondering if this was really the crowd I should be hanging out with. It was obvious no one here was thinking on all cylinders.

From sunup to sundown, the radios in the cars were constantly in use, screeching and crackling at full volume to be heard over the engines and crash of trees falling under the blunt noses of the Casspirs. Groups operating from Opuwa in the west to Rundu in the east kept Zulu Base[e] and each other advised of their progress and situations. Brand kept me abreast of the Afrikaans transmissions, especially when a group was on a follow-up—chasing spoor.

Everyone would be particularly attentive to the radio as a group reported closing on a "hot" spoor and a contact appeared imminent. When we heard that helicopter gunships had been scrambled to act as airborne spotters, we knew that the trackers estimated the spoor to be no more than fifteen minutes old. Sometimes the attention-grabbing "Contact!" would come through unexpectedly, leaving everyone hanging until the outcome was relayed.

The worst calls were for a casevac chopper to take out their own wounded. When Brand passed the information to Shivute, who in turn told the Ovambo policemen, the faces of blacks and whites alike took on expressions of concern and expectancy. Who? How bad? Ops K was a close, tightly knit family, and a call for a casevac would keep everyone holding his breath till the extent of the injuries was known.

It soon became obvious that stealth wasn't part of the tactics. A Koevoet group on the prowl could be heard for hundreds of meters around. There wasn't only the noise of the radios, but the incomprehensible chatter of the Ovambo special constables, the sound of engines and drive trains, the scraping of tree branches and low bush over and around the car, ammunition belts for the machine guns clacking back and forth in their metal boxes and the rattle of whatever was loose in the cars. It was a blurred and constant sea of noise that became a normal part of the environment. We certainly weren't going to sneak up on anyone.

---

[e] Koevoet's operations room at the unit's headquarters in Oshakati.

One afternoon I noticed Brand listening intently to the radio. He finally took the handset away from his ear, spoke to Shivute, then turned to me. "One of Zulu Five's[f] groups have three spoor about 50 klicks west of here. Terrs came across last night, grabbed ten kids and headed back towards Angola. Zulu Five says the spoor's about eight hours old, but with all those kids, the gooks aren't going to be able to move very fast."

The first good spoor Zulu Alpha's trackers found was soon lost on hard ground, found, lost, then found again. Side by side with Zulu Mike, we followed it most of the day. Although it had already been described to me time and time again, I was amazed at the aggressiveness the trackers displayed.

Cars flanking them, the black policeman moved at a dead run, often outstripping the APCs, which couldn't keep pace through the thick bush. They would go until winded, drop back to the Casspirs, and their places taken by others who jumped off the sides of the rolling cars and took the tracks.

Remembering Brand's comment, I watched Shivute running easily, the R5 held on the end of its sling under his arm. Occasionally, he came to a stop, dropped his chin and carefully examined the tracks. Without raising his head, the eyes slowly lifted to scan the bush ahead. Satisfied with whatever he was looking for, he would hunch his shoulders as his body tensed, and then he was off again, sprinting almost effortlessly through the deep sand.

On hard ground where the spoor became indistinct, the cars would stop and everyone disembark, fanning out in an attempt to pick it up. What the men could tell from an imprint I could barely see was astonishing. "This one old man — short steps," they'd say, or "This woman carrying baby," or "This one SWAPO — man with gun walks proud. You see?" they would ask me through Viljoen, pointing to a spot on the ground.

"Ah, yes, mm-hmm," I'd answer, not seeing a thing that I could even remotely identify as a footprint.

We stopped frequently in thick bush to clean leaves and twigs from the front of the radiators and allow over-heated engines to cool. We stopped almost as frequently to change tires punctured by heavy thorns or stumps. I was busy with my notepad during

---

[f]The western-most Koevoet base at Opuwa.

a tire change when Brand squatted down next to me with a cup of coffee.

"You know those kids I told you about—the ones the terrs took?"

"Yeah?"

"I just heard that four of them have been found. Apparently they couldn't move fast enough, so they were left behind. The Zulu Five group thinks they're only a couple of hours behind the others now.

"By the way," he asked out of the blue, "ever fired an RPG-7?" I stopped my writing and shook my head. The only ones I had even seen before this trip were in photographs. "We have a few extra rockets if you'd like to shoot one off," he continued innocently, one eyebrow raised.

I slipped the notepad into a breast pocket. "Yeah, that might be interesting," I said. "But what would I shoot at? There might be someone wandering around in the bush."

Brand shrugged and waved a hand. "Just shoot it into the air. If it doesn't hit something, it'll automatically explode about 500 meters after you fire it."

I looked toward his Casspir and was surprised to see Apie coming toward us with an RPG launcher in one hand and the rocket-propelled grenade in the other. It seemed that the two of them had already planned it. Setting the flared bottom of the Soviet-manufactured weapon on the ground, Apie screwed the long, bright-green booster to the bottom of the warhead and slid the booster down the muzzle. The bulbous, armor-piercing warhead on the business end of the launcher made it appear unbalanced.

He lifted the loaded weapon and settled it on my shoulder. My hands found the closely spaced handles. After I received a brief explanation from Brand, Apie cocked the hammer and quickly backed away, a deadpan expression on his face. I looked to my left and noticed a group of Ovambo constables with hunched shoulders, grins on their faces and fingers in their ears. A glance to the other side showed Brand, Apie and Shivute in the same pose. It seemed there was a joke here that I wasn't getting.

"I just aim it into the sky and pull the trigger, right?" I asked a little nervously, looking toward Brand. When I looked at him, my torso twisted and the launcher balanced across my shoulder swung with it. The groups on either side of me quickly shifted to remain at right angles to the weapon.

"Right," answered Brand, fingers coming out of his ears for a second, "but not too high or the back blast will burn your legs." I swung back. The two groups of men shifted again.

"What if Dean sees it?" I asked, looking at Brand again. Everyone moved with me. "Won't he think something is happening?"

"No, no, I've already called him to let him know."

"Oh, okay," I said, swinging back. Out of the corners of my eyes I saw the men move again, fingers still in their ears. "Okay, here goes!" I centered the cross hairs of the optical sight on a cloud, took a deep breath and squeezed the trigger. Immediately, there was the loudest, sharpest and most physically painful *bang!* I had ever heard in my life, leaving me in a cloud of gray smoke with my ears ringing. Grass and dirt blown up by the back blast settled over me. Looking through the smoke and debris, I saw the warhead explode a few seconds later in the air.

Unlimbering the empty launcher from my shoulder, I worked my jaw in an attempt to clear my ears. To my left, the group of Ovambo constables were laughing and slapping their thighs. Their laughter sounded exceedingly faint. I looked to the other side. Brand and Shivute were fighting grins. Brand's mouth was working.

"What?" I asked, my own voice sounding hollow and dim through the ringing. I was still moving my jaw back and forth and pressing my ears in an effort to clear them.

Loud, isn't it? I read his lips. The words were distorted by his laughing.

I'd been had.

Working steadily eastward, we stopped one afternoon outside the bulldozed berm of dirt and sand that surrounded the army base at Elundu. We climbed down, and the Casspirs drove off to the fuel depot to rebunker with diesel. Half a dozen of us walked through the gate, the dirt-caked policemen swaggering imperiously. A fresh-faced army private quickly raised the red and white striped pole and averted his eyes under the contemptuous looks from Brand and the others. I squared my shoulders, affected a grimace and started working on my own swagger.

We entered the sandbagged canteen and settled on padded bar stools made from steel shipping containers for 155-mm artillery shells. Through an archway was the officer and NCO mess, where a few lieutenants, sergeants and corporals were relaxing over their supper. The hum of conversation died as we crowded into the tiny canteen. There were quick, sidelong glances toward us as meals were hurriedly finished, and the diners left through a door on the opposite side.

A young soldier, the downy fuzz of a first mustache blurring his upper lip, squeezed behind the rough-sawn bar top and deferentially dispensed cold cans of beer from the cooler. There was a short symphony of pops and hisses as the beers were opened, followed by an *adagio* of sighs and smacking lips when the first swallows hit bottom. Two freshly showered corporals in starched army browns came through the front entrance. The two stopped abruptly and did a double take when they saw the green Koevoet uniforms and filthy faces. Eyes turned toward them and narrowed. There was a tangled about-face as they jammed the door in their eagerness to leave.

"What's the matter with these guys?" I asked Brand. Here was a perfect opportunity to talk with disciplined army professionals who had to know more about bush warfare than some small police unit. The only problem was that they didn't want to join us.

"I don't know," he said innocently, tilting his head back and blowing cigarette smoke toward the ceiling. I saw the others smirking at each other. "The army doesn't like us too much," volunteered Viljoen with an air of undeserved injury.

"Why's that?"

"Well, we just don't get along with them too good," said someone else.

"Why?"

"Well, there was this fight a while back . . . " His voice trailed off. I waited expectantly. " . . . but no one was killed."

"Killed?"

"No, genuine; no one was killed. I mean, after they started it in the canteen at Eenhana they were getting the worst of it. So when they went for their Casspirs, we had to go for ours. You know," he said, shrugging as though it was only natural.

"I don't understand," I admitted.

"You know, when they started using the guns on *their* Casspirs we sort of had to defend ourselves . . . "

"Hold on. You were *shooting* at each other? With *machine* guns?"

"Yeah, but no one was *killed.*"

"But why?"

"No, well, I guess because it was dark and everyone was pretty drunk."

"Oh."

"Fucking army," someone else spat. "Make no mistake, man, we get most of the kills and they get the credit for it. All you see in the press releases is 'the security forces killed so many terrs.' Everyone back in the States thinks it's the army getting the kills. That's bullshit, man!"

"But aren't you all on the same side?" I asked. The pause that followed confirmed they bloody well weren't on the same side at all. I felt a pall of suspicion settle over me at the very suggestion.

Further diatribes were interrupted by the base commander, who appeared at the doorway. As if to show they were the innocent parties, the policemen generously waved the lieutenant into his own canteen and handed him a beer. One of them made a show of standing and offering him his bar stool, checking sidelong to see that I noticed. Moments later the medical officer peeked round the door and was greeted with rare *bonhomie.* He stepped in cautiously and another bar stool was immediately vacated for him. *See what good guys we are?* A beer was placed in front of him, and I was introduced.

For the next two hours, Brand and his cohorts told each other stories of contacts and kills, all obviously for the benefit of myself and the two other outsiders. The policemen would occasionally stop to politely answer questions from the two army officers. As I listened to the stories and watched the rapt faces of the base commander and his medical officer, I began to understand that maybe these people I was with were something more than just cops.

After much handshaking and thanks for hospitality, we finally made our exit. Walking out through the gate, which lifted smartly for us, one of our number cleared his throat. "No, we get along fine with the army. It's them who start the shit every time. But those guys were okay; they didn't try to start anything."

"Yeah," someone sighed disappointedly in the dark.

On the fifth morning, word came over the radio that a small outpost near the border had been mortared — "revved" — in the middle of the night. Quickly breaking camp, we jumped into the waiting Casspirs and headed for the scene of the crime. When we pulled up an hour later, three other Koevoet groups were already there. Walking over the area, I noted that half the mortar rounds had failed to detonate, their tail fins protruding at an angle from the hard ground. The aim wasn't very good, either. All had impacted at least 100 meters short of the intended target, "Charlie tower," an elevated concrete reservoir guarded by a squad from the South African Cape Corps. A message had been scrawled in the sand where the mortar tubes had been set up: "Boer dogs. If you are looking for us, we will be in Namakunde."

The spoor of thirty to forty insurgents was found, and all the groups fanned out, racing off in a cloud of dust to pick it up further ahead. The dust came to an abrupt end as we ran into a series of *oshonas,* low marshy areas with a foot or more of water. The cars slowed to a crawl.

Struggling through the 'shonas, the groups accepted that the insurgents probably were already far across the border, heading for safe haven at Namakunde, the Angolan army base eight miles inside Angola. An official policy of hot pursuit meant that the fighting groups were allowed to cross the border and chase them to within five miles of the base. A terse radio call from Brigadier Dreyer gave a stern reminder to go no closer. I wondered if the strict adherence to the rules of engagement was normal or more the result of my presence. As it soon turned out, the question was immaterial.

By late afternoon and a little over a mile inside Angola, it was obvious Koevoet had lost this round. Not only that, but the four Casspirs of Zulu Alpha were stuck fast in the middle of a particularly soft-bottomed 'shona. Branches were cut from trees growing in the calf-deep water and jammed into the mud under the tires. Shoulders were put to the cars. The wheels only spun on the slippery bottom, spraying the pushers with mud, and settled a little deeper. Occasionally, the tires would gain a sort of purchase and begin to move to the cheers of the men — only to bog down again within a few feet.

Before the cars had muddied the water, we had clearly seen

the soft imprints left by dozens of feet walking north. The original excitement of following such clearly defined spoor soon turned to impotent rage at being locked in the 'shona. Zulu Base eventually radioed to say that intelligence sources confirmed fifty-eight SWAPO insurgents had crossed the border and were now in the Namakunde base. The unwelcome news elicited explosive oaths of anger and frustration. This was in direct contravention of agreements between Angola and South Africa that FAPLA would in no way support SWAPO. Brand swore furiously, but it was all academic—the insurgents had made good their escape.

Brand explained our predicament to Viljoen over the radio, then fired a "thousand footer" flare to mark our position for him. A few seconds later, we saw an answering flare streak into the air far to the southeast. Viljoen radioed to say that he would try to reach us before dark, but at the moment he was having his own problems getting around the 'shonas. It wouldn't do for both groups to get stuck.

As sunset approached, the Ovambo special constables began to unload bedrolls and weapons, wading to a dry spot in the middle of the stagnant water. When I saw them setting up mortars and positioning machine guns, it finally hit me that we were there for the night. At first mildly amused by the situation, I slipped on a sweater against the drop in temperature and curled up on the still-warm hood of the Casspir. The things one went through for a story, I thought with a wry and private shake of my head.

The sun disappeared into silence. As if on cue, the quiet was broken by the bass burps of frogs declaring their undying love for each other. I shifted uneasily on my hard perch. *What a dumb place to be.* I sat up and leaned back against the windshield, whistling tunelessly. A furred and feathered orchestra of unseen creatures began their accompaniment to the warty cacophony. *Tweet, burp, chk-chk-chk, burp.* I suddenly had a vivid mental image of loinclothed Apaches slipping silently into position around the cavalry. *"It's quiet—too quiet," the sergeant whispered to the scout, who nodded knowingly.* What B grade movie did that come from, I wondered, slightly bug-eyed from trying to penetrate the gathering night. I smirked at myself—totally without conviction—and crossed my arms protectively.

Viljoen radioed again to say that it was too dark for him to continue and that they were stopping for the night. He fired a last thousand footer for us. It blazed into the blue-black sky, reaching its zenith, then slowly descended and dimmed before winking out. The finality of it brought our predicament into unwelcome perspective. We were stuck. In Angola. And it was very dark. No other group was near enough to get to us that night and render assistance. Not all that far away were at least fifty-eight armed-to-the-teeth SWAPO insurgents holed up in a FAPLA base. And with the FAPLA border post at Oshikango less than three miles to the east, they had to know exactly where we were. The flares fired to mark our position for Viljoen and Group Zulu Mike—who had given up trying to reach us—had also marked our position for anyone else in the area who might be interested.

Dear Mom,

You just wouldn't believe where I'm writing this letter from. . . .

Trying to be nonchalant, I stood, climbed over the machine gun mount and down into the Casspir. Clearing my throat respectfully, I mentioned these minor points to Brand, wondering what the plan was if those fifty-eight chaps slipped on down tonight and laid into us with some serious pyrotechnics. A few mortars. Maybe an RPG or two. Not that I was worried or anything like that. Not a hardened war correspondent like myself. No, just *curious,* was all. I mean, I naturally reckoned he already had everything worked out: some *brilliant* piece of police work which would handle any eventuality.

He eyed me for a moment, then slapped at a mosquito. "Fuck 'em," he said through a yawn, "they can't hit shit anyway."

I stared silently at him for a moment. There was a lengthening pause neither of us saw fit to interrupt. I sat down on one of the molded rubber seats and tried to see Brand's expression inside the totally darkened Casspir. *Oh.* Stretching out across the seats, I zipped up the sleeping bag he tossed at me and tried to fluff up a rock-hard ammo vest for a pillow. *You were right: these people must have been brain-damaged at birth. They're totally out of touch with reality.* The night passed without incident, though it was a bleary-eyed and much-relieved noncombatant who saw the eastern sky finally touched by dawn.

Late in the morning, Viljoen and his Wolf Turbos appeared through the bush and stopped at the edge of the 'shona. Two of them backed into the water, being careful to stay on reasonably hard bottom. The second pair remained on dry ground, positioning themselves, like the first two, in tandem. Cables were run between the four Wolf Turbos and then to the nearest Casspir. Zulu Alpha's Casspirs, bogged down in a neat line, were similarly attached to each other until all eight APCs were hooked together. To the bellowing roars of exhaust-belching diesel engines, the chain of cars slowly dragged themselves one by one from the clinging mud until the last had emerged.

Back on solid ground, we stopped to brew coffee and dry socks and canvas boots over the fire. I was digging a thorn out of my foot when Brand squatted next to the fire. He spoke angrily to the others in Afrikaans before turning to me. "I just heard on the radio that they finally rescued those kids. The terrs left them and started running when the group got too close. Didn't help them. Floored all three of the bastards."

"So what's wrong?" I asked.

"No, the oldest kid, a fifteen-year-old girl who's a real little SWAPO sympathizer—when they took the kids back to their village—she told everyone that *our* people had kidnapped her and the others. Shit!"

On my last morning with Zulu Alpha, we responded to the scene of another mortar attack. Again, spoor was found, this time from eight insurgents, but lost on hard ground, found again—just as before. At least this time we had no 'shonas to wade through.

In the middle of a field of rumbling cars, Brand asked if I'd like to ride with the "Brig," who had come out for the hunt. He pointed to a Wolf Turbo sporting the letters *BD*. Grabbing my camera bag, I hopped out and ran to the spotlessly maintained Wolf. Climbing through the rear doors which hissed open for me, I thought I had entered the wrong car; there was no sign of Brigadier Dreyer. Then I caught sight of a familiar figure in the driver's seat.

"If he has the time, you can't keep him out of the field," one of his staff volunteered with a barely suppressed grin.

The week with Zulu Alpha came to an end. SWAPO, through fortune or skill, had managed to keep out of the group's way. Groups working other areas of Ovamboland's 30,000 square miles found what they were looking for. Seven SWAPO insurgents had fallen to Koevoet's guns.

After more than 600 miles of patrolling, it was a much sobered journalist who returned through the gates of Oshakati at the end of the week's deployment. I hadn't experienced a contact, but it wasn't for want of trying on Zulu Alpha's part as far as I could see. The one large group of insurgents we'd chased had cleverly used the terrain to their advantage, knowing the marshy 'shonas would slow us long enough for them to return to safety. Although their attack had been totally ineffectual, I had to give them credit for good escape and evasion tactics.

As we pulled into headquarters, I already had my lines well rehearsed. I'd be just as happy if they said no, I decided. Home and hearth and a girlfriend were beckoning. But I was here and it would be foolish not to try pushing my luck just a little further for a decent article. Without some bang-bangs, the story was interesting, but basically flat and no different from what other journos had already written.

Limping into Captain Ley's office in my diesel, dirt and sweat-stained clothes, face and arms as filthy as the clothes and criss-crossed with scratches from battling the bush, I took a deep breath and asked if I could sign on for another week. Ley surveyed my disheveled state with an amused air, put down his pen and leaned back, hands behind his head.

"I think it can probably be arranged," he allowed, trying to keep from laughing outright at my appearance. "Take a seat and I'll go ask the boss."

Oh, shit, I thought, slumping exhaustedly into a chair. *Me and my big mouth.*

6

The Sound of Guns

T HE next morning, I rolled out of Oshakati with Group
Zulu November. At the last minute, Sergeant Jim Durand
had been assigned to ride with me. I immediately felt guilty when
he explained that this was his last week with Ops K, but as my car
commander spoke no English, Dreyer wanted someone along
who could translate.

Hardly the image of a killer, Durand was almost baby faced
in spite of the beard he sported. A touch over six feet tall, his soft,
well-spoken English was at odds with the jarring Afrikaans-
accented English of most of the unit. As was the tattered copy of
Plato's *Gorgias* in the patch pocket on his trouser leg: "Something
to read when things are quiet," he said a little embarrassedly. Outward appearances belied a reputation for aggressiveness and
quick thinking under fire which had made him one of the legends
of the unit. Brand had already related a campfire story or two
about him.

After six years with Koevoet and over 120 contacts, Durand
was heading back to South Africa with his wife and new baby to
take up somewhat quieter police duties. When he laughingly
mentioned that guys always seemed to get hurt or killed just when
they were ready to leave, I began feeling uncomfortably responsible. What if something should happen to him simply because I
wanted a story? And that terrifying question if we did have a contact: What if I did something to cause it?

"No, no, it's okay," he assured me easily. "If I wasn't doing this,
I'd be out setting up night ambushes anyway."

The group leader of Zulu November was stocky, taciturn and

barrel-chested Boesman (Warrant Officer Stephanus Pretorius in real life, but no one in the unit called him anything but "Bushman.") Another legend within Koevoet, Boesman was also in his sixth year of counterinsurgency operations and led Koevoet's highest-scoring fighting group of the year. In February 1986 the group had been leading a follow-up when they hit a forty-man SWAPO detachment lying in ambush. In the swirling confusion of the contact, thirty-five of the insurgents were killed for only five wounded on Zulu November's side. As we rolled out of Zulu Base in Oshakati, Boesman's tally for the first four months of 1986 already stood at 47.

My car commander for this second week with Koevoet was Warrant Officer Lukas Kilino, who had started soldiering at age fourteen against the Portuguese with Holden Roberto's FNLA liberation movement in Angola. Big and powerfully built, he had attended officer's school in Kenya, then spent two years in the People's Republic of China being taught the finer points of both insurgency and conventional warfare. He had become airborne qualified, making fifteen parachute jumps, learned to use explosives, and was intimately familiar with both Western and East-bloc weapons. The two-year course had been so difficult, he remembered, and the winters so cold that a number of fellow Angolans had died during the insurgency training.

When the Soviet-backed MPLA seized power in Angola, Kilino, a senior officer in the Chinese-supported and CIA-backed FNLA, became a marked man. Evading his erstwhile allies against Portuguese colonialism, he made his way south and joined South Africa's little-publicized 32 Battalion. After years of harrowing, deep-penetration operations into Angola against SWAPO, he transferred to Koevoet. His eyes, like Dreyer's, seemed to miss nothing. It wasn't difficult to spot him as a professional.

Boesman's sixth sense took us into an area where the trackers picked up fresh spoor almost immediately. At one point, they figured it no more than two hours old, and Boesman radioed the air force to put the helicopter gunships on standby. Within a minute, the air force called back to say that they could be overhead within twelve minutes of getting the word to scramble.

Although a contact appeared imminent, this particular group

of insurgents "bombshelled," each taking off in a different direction, and "anti-tracked," backing up on their own spoor, staying on hard ground wherever possible and moving from one tuft of tough grass to another; anything and everything to make their tracks indistinguishable. The trackers admitted these were some "old SWAPO" who knew how to survive.

Setting up camp that night, I listened to an inexhaustible repertoire of contact stories. Durand told of the time his group was following the spoor of a half-dozen insurgents. The bush was thick, reducing the visibility to only a few meters. He was behind the gun mount of his Casspir when suddenly he was looking down at a SWAPO insurgent holding an RPG-7. The man was just starting to raise the launcher to his shoulder when Durand depressed the gun and pulled the trigger, only to discover the weapon had jammed. "Man, I thought it was all over." The insurgent looked up at the 20-mm pointing at him, looked down at the RPG in his hands, then dropped the deadly weapon at his feet, raising his hands high overhead.

(Actually, I had heard the story a week earlier from Marius Brand, who added, "And *then* that crazy bastard Durand casually told him to pick up the RPG and bring it to the car!")

Kilino sat down next to Boesman and talked of his days with the FNLA and his time in China. There was an intimacy between these two men, black and white, brought about by great mutual respect and sharing extreme danger. The conversation turned to me, and Kilino asked about America, and especially the "negroes" there, curious to know if they served with whites in the army and police. His Chinese political instructors, he said, stressed that blacks in America were still essentially slaves and kept in poverty and subjugation with no political rights. "And you call them 'niggers'—like *kaffir*," he observed. I squirmed and tried to explain that such had been the case once—and not so long ago—but that things had changed enormously in the last twenty years.

Through Durand, he told me about his brother, who also had left Angola to join 32 Battalion. He arrived after Kilino had left, believing Lukas had been killed in the aftermath of the revolution. He served five years as a medic with the highly secret unit, yet never heard his brother's name mentioned. Tiring of the two- to three-month-long missions, he also eventually transferred to

Koevoet, where he found Lukas. The reunion of the two in Osha-kati—each thinking the other dead for the last ten years—was, he told me, like seeing ghosts come alive. Before going to sleep, Kilino pointed at me and spoke earnestly in Afrikaans to Boesman.

"Lukas wants me to tell you," Boesman translated, "that the Communists are no friends of black Africans. He says the Communists think all blacks are stupid and use them only for their own purposes. He wants to make sure you understand that." As a black African who had been trained by them to fight the Portuguese, chances were he knew what he was talking about. I motioned I understood. Kilino nodded and without another word went to sleep.[a]

Mornings at a temporary base started before dawn, when the first sleepy risers stirred last night's coals into life, sending sparks into the cold dark. There was the lonely sound of a cough here and there; the small ruby glow of a first cigarette punctuated the awakening camp. Sweaters were pulled on against the chill, while simply silhouetted figures slowly began to cluster around the fire, palms toward the warmth.

As thin light began to filter through the bush, more figures slipped from brown, dew-covered sleeping bags, some moving to the perimeter to urinate, others washing from mess tins. Before the sun had made its appearance, there was the smell of coffee in the crisp air. Sleeping bags were rolled up, and everything loaded into the idling, warming cars. I had just tossed my rucksack up to the policemen at the back of the Blesbok when I noticed Boesman at the edge of the camp. Deeply religious and private, he had un-wrapped a small Bible from a piece of oilskin and was sitting alone under a tree, reading a passage. I watched quietly until he finished and carefully rewrapped the Word of God. I wondered which passage it had been.

When the sun was full born on the horizon, we moved out, another long and dusty day ahead of us. On this morning, a full moon still hung in the western sky. The morning followed the pattern of all the others: stopping at kraals and questioning the

---

[a]Kilino was later promoted to the rank of inspector-lieutenant. A battery of psychological examinations, which every potential officer must take, showed an I.Q. in the genius range.

locals, advancing through the bush to the next kraal, everyone scanning the ground for spoor. Breakfast was a normal mid-morning affair, eaten on the move out of ration pack cans.

We were sitting under a mopane tree during a noontime coffee break when without preamble came that attention-grabbing word over the radio: "Contact!" Behind the word, gunfire was heard. Coffee cups stopped at lips and were slowly lowered as ears strained to pull more from the air. Then the call came for a casevac chopper.

Silent looks passed between the men sitting cross-legged on the ground. One man went to stand nearer the car, as though it would force more from the radio. Finally, the story crackled through the speaker. A group had hit an ambush. Three insurgents had been killed, but one car commander was seriously wounded. The impact of the bullet fired at close range from heavy cover had knocked him completely out of the car. Within minutes, a helicopter pilot taking off from Eenhana confirmed that he was airborne and gave his estimated flight time to their position. Nothing more was heard.

Flicking what was left of the coffee aside, we climbed into the Casspirs. The mood was camouflaged with thin jokes. Diesels rumbled, clutches were engaged and we moved out. The routine continued. Later, with two hours of daylight left, we turned west toward the Security Branch base at Ohangwena. Durand and I were sitting opposite each other, our eyelids heavy and heads nodding to the sway of the car. The interior of the Casspir brightened as we crashed out of the bush onto a grassy pan dominated by a water hole and spotted with a few stunted trees. It was then that Boesman saw them and shouted into this microphone:

"CONTACT!"

I snapped back from wherever I was, my eyes opening wide and meeting Jim's for one of those interminable half seconds. Durand held my surprised stare for the same split-second before spitting "Contact!" and swiveling to snatch his R5 from its vertical rack. The Casspir's engine bellowed, and ahead I heard the guns of at least one car already firing. Then our car was veering hard left, the car ahead breaking to the right, all four cars fanning out across the pan. Totally unprepared for the violence of the maneuver, I was almost flung from the seat as I fumbled with the record switch on my cassette recorder and scrabbled with the other hand for my camera bag.

Around me, the first infusion of adrenaline had already dissolved the lethargy of a second earlier. There was a blur of hands grabbing for weapons and the arrhythmic ripple of *shh-klacks* as bolts came back and fell on chambered rounds. Muzzles were jammed brutally through the spring-loaded gun ports of the Casspirs, and the firepower of a Koevoet group exploded like a bursting water main. At that moment, only Boesman's car had a positive target. But with no one else knowing the strength or location of it, everyone began laying down maximum suppressive fire to all sides.

The high-pitched chatters of assault rifles on full automatic mingled with the deep-throated *thudthudthud-thudthud* of the .50 caliber Brownings; everyone shouting, firing, looking left-right for targets, some standing and firing over the edge of the Casspir, others through the gun ports below the windows. There was the sudden burn of hot brass on bare skin, and I heard the steady, hollow *whunk!* of a grenade launcher firing to my left. The tracker to my right jammed the short barrel of his R5 through the gun port just as the eleven-ton car bounced hard over a rut. The muzzle came back inside on full automatic, spattering those around him with hot splinters of bullets shattering against the inside of the car.

I jerked my stung legs away with a sharply expelled *"Jeezus!"* and was trampled over by the grenadier diving toward the rear of the car for more ammunition. I was bowled over again as he came back through the throng of unsteady legs, everyone trying to hold on and fire from the shaking, twisting Casspir as it careered left and right to present as difficult a target as possible for an RPG rocket or "heatstrim,"[b] either of which could take out the car, wounding or killing the people inside.

I was trying to take photos of the chaos inside, the air seeming solid with the firing, shouting, thin smoke, hot brass, bursts of excited Afrikaans and Oshivambo over the radio, engine racing

---

[b]High-explosive, anti-tank rifle-launched grenade capable of penetrating six inches of armor.

and drive train screaming in protest as the driver jammed up, down and through the gears. I yelled stupidly at Durand, "HOW MANY ARE THERE? WHERE ARE THEY?"

"WHEN YOU DRIVE INTO THEM LIKE THIS THERE'S NOTHING ELSE YOU CAN DO!" he yelled back.

I tried twice to stand to get shots of what was happening outside, only to be slammed down into my seat by one of Kilino's huge hands. Looking through the window, I saw the ground erupting zipper-like under the impact of the .50 caliber bullets racing toward the water hole, splintering tree limbs. I stood again, ducking under Kilino's hand. In the brief moment before Lukas yanked me down again, I saw Boesman's car angling away from us, pouring fire into the bush near the water hole at the edge of the pan. We raced in behind him, turning to hit the suspected position from the opposite side. Above the roar, I heard Durand yelling, "STOP! STOP! UNDER THE BUSH! THERE'S ONE UNDER THE BUSH!"

We shuddered to a stop as the hydraulically operated doors hissed open. I jumped out with my cameras and ran behind the trackers, who half-mooned around a clump of low-hanging thicket, their weapons spitting bursts of high-velocity bullets and erupting streams of empty cartridge cases. Durand was next to me, yelling, "THERE'S ONE IN THERE!" and I suddenly wondered what the hell I was doing outside the car. When the men moved forward, I followed them under the branches, expecting a body, but seeing only webbing and leather pouches, a gourd half filled with homemade mohango beer. I realized the firing had stopped, replaced by hard, gasping laughter and the high-pitched giggles of fear and excitement.

"The bodies are over here," I heard Durand say behind me. Following him, I saw the first one lying face up on a pile of dead branches next to the water hole. Further on, at the base of a tree, was the second, face down. The trunk of the tree bore the bright wounds of heavy .50 caliber bullets. Both bodies had the limp heaviness of new death. One of the Ovambo trackers yanked the second body onto its back. He reached inside the camouflage shirt and pulled a tan, checked collar into view. "Civvie clothes, see?" he hissed, contemptuous of the attempted deceit. An AK-47 lay alongside, the ballistic launcher for the nearby heatstrim rifle grenade shot cleanly off the muzzle. The dead insurgents were stripped of equipment, and the dangerous rifle grenades tossed underhand into the pond.

"Hey!"

I looked up at the shout and saw two of the trackers raise their weapons toward the nearest mohango field. A waving white shirt was followed by an old man emerging cautiously from the tall stalks. The trackers motioned him forward, and he shuffled on aged legs to the first body, then to the second, staring dumbly.

"What will you do with the bodies?" I asked Durand, watching the timid arrival from the corner of my eye.

"We'll leave them for the locals to bury," he said unconcernedly. I looked at the old man, his white hair and cotton-like tufts of beard contrasting against his black, lined face. The natural human fascination with violent death, or the father of one? I wondered.

Boesman shouted for everyone to return to the cars. The sun was dropping rapidly, and he wanted to reach Ohangwena before dark. As we walked toward the cars, the tracker ahead of me suddenly hawked, twisted abruptly sideways and spat hard in the face of the open-eyed body atop the branches. The flies buzzed angrily and quickly resettled, oblivious to the old man who stood nearby, head bowed as though in prayer. I prayed it wasn't his son who lay at his feet.

Back at the cars, Boesman explained that when we came out of the bush, the two insurgents had broken from their hiding place next to the water hole. Had they stayed hidden, they could easily have taken out one or more of the Casspirs, or gone entirely unnoticed.

(Two days later, another group working the area picked up information that the two had been part of a five-man team. The other three had been gathering food a mile away when they heard the firing and escaped—until the end of the week, when they fell to the guns of another Koevoet group.)

Jim Durand called the contact "A last one just for old times' sake." Daubing at a blood smear on his leg, he admitted it was the worst injury he had taken in his six years with Koevoet. I breathed a private sigh of relief.

That night around the fire at Ohangwena, a full moon hang-

ing in the African sky, the contact was relived over and over
again. The tape I'd made of it brought everyone gathered round
to hear, asking that it be rewound and listening again, recognizing each other's voices amid the fury of the firing. Some reen-
acted Kilino shoving me down when I tried to stand. Others
howled with laughter as they pantomimed the grenadier running
over me once, then a second time. In the middle of it all, Lukas
caught my eye. He nodded and pointed at me, then raised a huge
black fist, thumb up. I ducked my head and actually blushed, ter-
rifically pleased with myself and the accolade. I hadn't screwed
up.

The morning after returning to Oshakati, I was scheduled on a
flight back to Pretoria. On the way to Ondangwa Air Force Base,
I asked the army lieutenant to make a short detour. It was Wednesday, the beginning of a new week for half of Ops K. Around
the long, corrugated stores next to headquarters, teams were
loading up for another seven days in the bush, a week spent in
base. There was Marius Brand, ever the slouching gunslinger, hol-
ster tied low on his thigh; and there were Shivute, Apie and Sand-
sak, Viljoen, Porky and the others whose names I could never
remember, just as I had seen them that first day two weeks before.
Shaking hands, saying the good-byes, I was struck with the un-
canny feeling that some part of my destiny lay here.

   As the car pulled away, I turned to look back, watching until
they disappeared from view. *You crazy bastards,* I thought. *Go safely.*

7

Ovamboland Return

BACK in England, I dove headfirst into my work. The stories I wrote about Koevoet and the Namibian bush war sold well; I could go on to other things now. Story finished. But sitting at my desk overlooking the quiet Hampshire countryside, I couldn't shake the feeling of needing to return.

Memories of the place, the unit, continued to haunt me. Every full moon over the South Downs would take me there as I thought of the people I had met and wondered how they were faring. Were they in the bush at that very moment? Were they okay? Had any of them been hurt? The story wasn't complete; what I had written was no more than a thumbnail sketch. There was a book to be written about this obscure conflict, and the people—especially the people—and I wanted to be the one to do it.

I finally knew I had to go back. Writing to Sterk Hans Dreyer and Bernie Ley, I asked if I could return to do the book that was taking shape in my mind. Then I waited. And waited. Fate had cracked open a door to a war that no other foreign journalist had ever been allowed to see in detail. Not that I had seen all that much of it; more like a quick peek through a door left intentionally—perhaps accidentally—ajar. Was there a chance of the South Africans allowing me all the way through that door in spite of their profound distrust of Western journalists? The story needed telling. Maybe it wasn't earth-shattering, but it was one that hadn't yet been put to paper from firsthand experience. What was the answer going to be? All I could do was cross my fingers and hope.

Three months later, the call came. The connection was terrible, snapping and crackling. I pressed the receiver against my ear, jamming a finger in the other.

"Jim, I have some bad news for you," shouted down the line.

My shoulders slumped. I wasn't getting the authorization. They didn't want a foreigner snooping around; it was all off. Bloody South Africans. What did they have to hide? *Damn.* "What is it?" I shouted back with all the *savoir faire* I could manage.

"Hate to tell you this, pal, but it doesn't look like you're going to have a white Christmas."

"What?"

"I said, you're not going to have a white . . . "

You son of a bitch, I thought fondly, replacing the receiver. I'd done it; I was going back.

Knowing the conditions I would be facing, I began organizing everything I'd need for a stay of up to six months in the operational area. Trading in my old, heavy 35-mm cameras, I selected lightweight models that could be trusted to take over the functions of f-stops and shutter speeds in a fast-moving situation. I ordered a stock of film, filters, cans of compressed air, lens cleaners and batteries. Although I laid no claim to being much of a photographer, the opportunity to record the bush war was too good not to make the investment in equipment.

Taking a trip to Bristol, I sat down with my old friend Nigel Gifford of Camera Care Systems, and together we redesigned one of his firm's standard camera vests. The final version held two cameras in Velcro-closed pockets on my chest. With the camera slings around my neck and the vest cinched tightly against my chest, I would have both hands free to hold on while riding on the rim of a Casspir or Wolf Turbo. A third camera would go in a pouch on my belt. Not entirely trusting these new-fangled electronic cameras, I would take along a trustworthy old Nikkormat as backup.

A few days before my departure, Sugar Jones, my best girl and blue-blooded English lady, invited me up to London. As a special treat, she took me for oysters and Guinness at a place she knew just off Regent Street, where she tried—as so often before—to understand why I was making this trip.

"You will write, just to let me know you're okay?"

"Every chance I get."

There was a long pause. Our attention centered on the barman who was making a production of drawing the dark Guinness into pewter mugs. He placed them on cardboard mats in front of us and turned to open the oysters.

"You could get shot, you know," running her finger around the rim of the mug. "It's hardly worth it."

"That's where you're wrong, Jones; it is worth it. It's a unique chance to tell a story that hasn't been told before. I'd be crazy just to throw it away. And it's what I've been working towards since I sold my home in Florida and started kicking around Africa. It's something I've wanted to do ever since I was a kid. I joined the army for Vietnam, and they sent me to Berlin, instead. In the army's infinite wisdom, every request I made for reassignment was disapproved. Well, this is going to be my war, the war no one else has covered from the inside. Call it a fantasy, a dream, whatever. There aren't many people in this world who have the chance to do that."

"But there are so many other things to write about that have nothing to do with violence. Why can't you find something else?"

"Because for the moment this is what I need."

"Why?"

"Maybe to find out if I can do it."

"But you already have. What about all those other places you've been to?"

"Peripheral. Coming under fire doesn't mean you really know what's going on. The only way to understand any conflict and write about it with any insight is to live it with the people involved."

"I wish I could understand this attraction war has for you. I really don't like it at all. Why do you do it?"

"I don't know—it's always been something that fascinated me. Not war so much as what draws people to it, myself included. It's a part of man. A very basic part. It always has been, and I think it probably always will."

"I can't believe that. If it was true, then we haven't advanced at all. And there will always be wars. It's an appalling thought."

"Sure, but that's never stopped it. It's been modern and fashionable and socially correct for centuries to say, 'I hate war.' Just as we're supposed to say, 'I hate pornography.' The fact is, neither would exist if there weren't enough people secretly titillated by one or the other. And nothing I could write would ever change that."

"But just writing about war glorifies it. Don't you see that?"

"No, I don't, though I'll grant you that it depends on *how* someone writes about it. If you want to change attitudes, you can't just ignore it, you have to describe it as honestly as you can. If man is intrinsically against everything war represents—as you believe— then a true account of the horrors can only help prevent it by making it even more repugnant."

"But you like it."

"War? No. The risk? Yes. To that I plead guilty. It's my drug. Maybe it's a perversion. I don't know. And maybe it's immoral to use war as my vehicle for risk-taking. In the eyes of some people, I guess it is. But I need it. I wish I could describe it, but for anyone who doesn't need it, it wouldn't make sense."

"Try me."

"The thrill. Maybe that sounds superficial, but the thrill of standing on the edge and coming out alive is overwhelmingly exciting. It's putting it all on the table for the big one when you have no idea what the other side is holding, only that he wants to take everything you have. I could never do that with money, but doing it with my life is easy."

"Then why not simply shoot yourself? Or take a handful of pills? Or jump off a bridge? It's the same thing."

"It's not the same thing at all. In the first place, I'd have complete control. There's no risk; it's predictably final. And in the second place, I don't want to die."

But you just said . . . "

"I said I enjoy the thrill of being where it's possible and coming out the winner. If I *knew* that I wouldn't come out I wouldn't do it."

"Then you're being a slave to your own passions. You're looking for cheap thrills like a common slut."

"Even sluts can be nice people. Or so I've been told, m'lady. Though I think sluttishness might be a matter of perspective."

"Touché, you creep," she laughed. "You're right. Whatever would dear mummy say? Another Guinness, kind sir?"

Later that night, she reached over me to switch on the lamp

and propped her chin on my chest. I yawned and peered at my watch. "Do you know what time it is?"

"I do wish you weren't going. What if you should be killed? Or worse, crippled? I'm not terribly keen on the idea of bringing flowers and reading to a bedridden ex-lover."

"I shall surely do my very best not to get killed, Sugar," I said sleepily, ignoring the other. "I'll be okay."

"How can you be so sure?"

"I am. Don't worry. I'll be fine."

"But . . ."

"Come on, Jones. It's okay. Everything's going to be fine." Remembering the dream suddenly, I wasn't entirely sure.

A week in Pretoria allowed me to renew contacts, find a professional photo lab to develop the film I'd be sending back and sort out my travel arrangements to Oshakati. There was no great rush; the rains were still late.

At the end of the week, I caught a South African Airways flight to Windhoek. Seated next to me was a young South African geology student who would be spending the next few months with a mining company in Namibia. The conversation came around to the bush war in Ovambo. He had spent a year of his national service "up on the border" and had no fond memories of the experience. When I mentioned that I was planning to spend six months there, he stopped me.

"You mean to say," he interrupted, "that you're spending six months in the operational area—and you don't *have* to?"

"Journalist," I offered a little self-consciously. "Writing a book." He examined me closely for a moment before turning to gaze at the Kalahari Desert sliding by 30,000 feet below. He'd certainly heard some peculiar things in his life, but . . .

Early the next morning, I boarded a Namibair twin-engined Cessna and talked my way into the copilot's seat for the last leg of the trip. There was a brief stop for fuel in the picturesque mining town of Tsumeb, and then we were off again. Over the Etosha Pan, we descended until less than 100 feet separated us from the salt flats flashing beneath the belly of the blue and white plane.

"Just in case there might be a terr down there with a SAM-7," the pilot said with a shrug.

The pilot eased us even lower as we flew alongside the tarred road I had traveled with Henk seven months earlier during my first introduction to Ovambo. A delicate pull on the control yoke lifted us enough to clear a tall tree. Black and white soldiers patrolling the road grinned widely and waved from their open-topped Buffels and Casspirs.

Thirty minutes later, we banked sharply on to final approach for the long runway at Ondangwa Air Force Base. Ahead of us, a Puma helicopter had just landed. As we taxied up to the flight line, I noticed a brace of stretcher bearers carrying a wounded soldier from the chopper, and remembered Henk explaining that the primary trauma center was just beyond the flight line. As I stepped down to the sun-softened tarmac, Bernie Ley and his wife Marga were there to meet me.

"Welcome back," Bernie said. "How's it?"

"Great," I said, my head turning to follow the stretcher-bearers. I looked back at Bernie and shook hands. "Great."

In four months, I would be walking across the same spot under entirely different circumstances.

8

Letter from Fort Apache, Namibia

December 9, 1986

Dear Sugar Jones,

A quiet morning inside the Oshakati base. The temperature has climbed past 80 degrees, en route to 100 plus. Your itinerant scribbler pecks away on his scarred and trusty Olivetti in the shade of a crimson-topped flame tree. Along the dirt street fronting the yard, a bewildering array of armored cars and APCs — Buffels, Casspirs, Wolf Turbos, Ratels and Elands — rumble in both directions, raising plumes of dust. Across the road in a sports field, mixed black and white teams in shorts and broad-striped jerseys are making serious attempts to kill each other at rugby.

Oshakati is something out of the Wild West, a Fort Apache set in a modern war zone. Armor-plated cavalry patrols roll out of the gates and head into the bush, returning a week or two later, some of the men carrying wounds taken in the bush war, all of them filthy and exhausted. As they return, others, fresh and clean, pass them on their way out.

Yet life seems to function as casually and complacently as anywhere else. People — most of them in uniform — go to work in the morning and come home at quitting time. They laugh and cry, argue and love, worry about their bank balances, tinker with cars, watch videos, drink, have their scandals, go to church, and paddle their kids like people everywhere. Dirt roads cut through the blocks of cheaply built prefab homes, and bits of jealously tended grass struggle for survival under the few trees.

There are some things that set it apart, however. At various times during the night, "fire plans" go into effect with tower-mounted machine guns firing into "no-go" areas lit by mortar-fired parachute flares. Conversation barely falters at the coughing sound of a heavy machine gun, and children babble excitedly at the sight of the slowly descending magnesium flares. Sandbagged bunkers squat as naturally in front yards as children's swing sets and everyone knows how to reach the nearest one by the quickest route. The base has been hit twice this year by stand off mortar and rocket attacks. The house occupied by one Koevoet officer and his family was demolished by a rocket in the first attack. They were given new quarters a mile from the first, and during the second attack, a mortar round landed squarely on top of it. Neither he nor any of his family were injured, having already taken shelter in the nearest bunker. It's rumored that when he moved to his third house, his neighbors began looking for new quarters themselves. The only casualties in either of the attacks occurred elsewhere on the base, where a mother and unborn child were hit by a sliver of shrapnel. The mother lived.

Returned a couple of days ago from my first week in the veld, encrusted with dust and dried sweat. (None-too-subtle hints and slurs by my mentors at the very suggestion of a wash in the bush persuaded me to follow suit and return to base looking closely akin to a coal miner after a hard day's work underground.) There are some drawbacks to this thing of following local tradition, I must say. The Ovambos wash every day. Among the whites, however, it's considered bad form to divest oneself of the topsoil whilst in the bush. Very uncool. Very bloody unpleasant as well.

Depending on whom you talk to, the rains are either early or late, though certainly sporadic, which means the infiltration is still in its seasonal pre-infancy. Radio reports from groups working across Ovamboland told of a Casspir detonating a land mine (the worst injury a ruptured spleen), four "terrs" captured, another killed, weapons caches discovered—all in all a quiet period. Another month, six weeks, they tell me, and things will really start happening, with February and March being the peak infiltration period. The Summer Games, it's called here with nonchalant bravado. Which means that barring a chance Encounter of the Serious Kind I can look forward to weeks of grinding through the bush and eating lots of dirt in pursuit of this story.

That this war is little understood—or even known about—in the outside world is hardly surprising; it is remote, there are no fixed battles, it involves few but a local population caught tragically in the middle and the sons of South Africa and SWA/Namibia serving here "up on the border." It is a hazy side issue to the big South African picture, and dimly seen as through a mirage.

As far as the international community is concerned, South Africa illegally occupies this country. As far as the South African government is concerned, it claims it's protecting—or preventing—this place from becoming another Russian-dominated country on its border until genuinely free elections can be held. Which means that they're unlikely to allow elections until they can be assured of a pro-Pretoria—or at least tame—government being voted in. Or until they can no longer afford either the economic drain on their resources or the political price of international condemnation.

Of course, SWAPO's claim (backed to the hilt by the United Nations) that it is "the sole and authentic voice of the Namibian people" is no less one-sided and intransigent. While there are obviously SWAPO supporters among the various ethnic groups, the hard fact is that SWAPO is an Ovambo-based movement, and representatives of other tribes within the organization are relatively few. Disillusioned members who have returned to Namibia continue to tell stories of almost inconceivably brutal treatment at the hands of SWAPO's predominantly Ovambo hierarchy. (Stories, by the way, which are ignored or vehemently denied by SWAPO's supporters here and overseas.)

Should elections ever come to pass for whatever reason, it must be borne in mind that 55 percent of Namibia's population is made up of the seven tribes of the Ovambo people. And given that SWAPO is predominantly Ovambo, the inescapable conclusion is that the open elections demanded by the United Nations would result in SWAPO being voted into power by a majority of the people. How much of that would be due to SWAPO intimidation of a politically unsophisticated rural people, or to the same people's desire to see "scientific socialism" at work, or to outright tribalism is open to conjecture. Africa watchers, political scientists and sociologists could argue it till the cows come home and likely still be no closer to the truth.

Am only now beginning to appreciate that in terms of combat efficiency, these guys I'm with are probably as good as their reputation, which is considerable. They very much fit the mold and psychological profile of other elite special warfare units I've seen: loners, reasonably intelligent, extremely aggressive, and thriving on adrenalin highs. If they're not fighting insurgents, they're not above getting into punch-ups with the army or amongst themselves. Whatever their rationale for being here—protecting Namibia, South Africa, or simply the lot of a policeman (and I have no doubt they deeply believe whatever reason they give)—the fact is that most of them love and need the constant stimulation of combat. As I think I told you, none receive unsolicited assignment to Koevoet; all are volunteers, and *many tend to extend their service far beyond the two years they're expected to stay with the unit.*

What I find disturbing is a general belief among many people, both overseas and in South Africa, that Koevoet is manned exclusively by social misfits and psychopaths whose brutality toward the civilian population is reminiscent of Nazi death squads. Aside from being witness to a teenage Ovambo boy being cuffed sharply on the ear by one of the Ovambo special constables, I haven't yet seen any evidence of physical intimidation. And yes, you're right: I'd have to be naive not to think that my presence keeps them on their best behavior. And, like you, I've also wondered if the reason I've been allowed to return is because someone saw the possibility of using an outsider to paint them lily white. Am I being co-opted as "a tool of the South African security forces?" I'd like to say certainly not, but in all honesty, I don't really know. If these people are as neanderthalic and brutal as SWAPO, the anti-apartheid movement, the Council of Churches in Namibia, and even some South African newspapers say they are, then I will undoubtedly see some evidence of it over the next few months. To maintain their effectiveness, they'll not be able to alter tactics or personalities just for me once the infiltration arrives. Their entire raison d'être *is killing "terrs," and their record on that is unmatched in the operational area and one in which they take great pride.*

It's slowly starting to penetrate this thick skull of mine that it's all for real, no Hollywood or Pinewood Studio production where after "That's a wrap!" the extras and stuntmen pick themselves up, brush themselves off and start all over again. Of course, etiquette, bravado and a youthful sense of immortality preclude any serious mention of possible death. Their successes against the opposition, however, that's something else again. Discussion revolves around the latest contacts and how many koppe *(heads — their slang term for kills) they've tallied since the beginning of the year. In between their week-long trips into the bush, these 19 to 25-ish year-olds drink heavily, play hard and tell the most extraordinary stories with all the aplomb of suburban commuters on the train home.*

The pieces I wrote on them earlier this year appear to have gone down well. I am afforded a measure of shy respect for having told their story with a degree of straightforwardness that has been notoriously absent in articles about them. Which is personally gratifying, if not a little disconcerting. Reputations here don't rest on the ol' laurels; to maintain them, they have to be built on. I think I'm more concerned with doing something stupid in front of them than being hurt. And the chances of the former are certainly far greater than the latter, I can assure you.

There's so much I don't know. What is second nature to these people is a whole new world to me, and they—particularly the whites—seem to think I'm either old enough or wise enough or experienced enough to take it all in stride, do the right thing at the right time. Sometimes, though, I don't know enough to even know if I'm doing something wrong. Curiously, it is the blacks who appear the most concerned about showing me the ropes, treating me like some sort of respected, but not very bright, elder. They keep a close eye on me, you'll be pleased to know.

It's quickly becoming apparent that one of the major difficulties I'll face here is the language. Although most of the whites speak English, very few of the Ovambos have ever had the need of any language but their own and, to a lesser degree, Afrikaans. There is a wealth of stories that will remain sadly untapped simply because I can't talk with them directly. Many of these black policemen have seen a hundred times the combat experienced by most of the young SADF national servicemen who spend their obligatory year in the operational area. The story I hope to tell will be the poorer for the omission of their experiences.

Quite unexpectedly, I have received permission from the commander of Koevoet to be here for as long as six months. As far as I have been able to determine, it's totally without precedent: I've been told that no other journalist, whether foreign or South African, has ever spent more than a week on operations with these guys. But the good Lord willin' an' the creek don't rise (a genuine American ruralism), I won't need that much time. With luck, the end of March or April should see the project in the can.

I return to the veld tomorrow for a week, am back here for one night, then out again for another week. It's unlikely you'll hear anything from me until well after Christmas (let's hope it's from and not about), given these next two weeks in the bush. So lift a cup of good cheer for me. Miss you.

9

Kaffir Boetie
and Murder Most Foul

J ACKIE, Bennie and I stood on the berm surrounding the security branch base at Okatope. Jackie, dark complexioned, with
straight, black hair and the deceptively powerful build of a rugby
player, was, in the words of one Ops K officer, "certifiable." "Genuine," he added seriously.

"Jackie?" someone else mused. "Man, Jackie's crazy," shaking
his head. "Man, did you hear about that last thing he did on the
other side?"

No, I said, I hadn't heard, what was it? But he just shook his
head again, smiling in the private way people have of conferring
special status for being certifiable.

But I never saw that part, only heard about it second- and
third-hand; snippets of stories which had already taken their place
in a private compendium of Koevoet mythology and folklore.
Exploits and derring-do that on the surface were risks for the
sake of risk, yet on more sober analysis indicated a natural
tactical genius for bush warfare. They enjoyed talking about his
craziness in the bush, his practical jokes out of the bush. What no
one ever mentioned was his rare humanity.

For me, Jackie was warm, intelligent, incisive, funny; qualities
which overlapped like medieval armor a complex and intense
character of infinite contradictions. A doting father with a shy
and breathtakingly beautiful young wife (who agonized over his
trips into the bush), he was as much — or perhaps more — respected
and loved by the Ovambos in the unit than any of the other whites

I met. But it was a love and respect he earned, and returned measure for measure.

"This really is their country," he told me once. "We're only here temporarily to help them. The blacks in my group, they'd be killed if SWAPO ever took over. They've already told me that if the terrs took over, they'd go into the bush and fight their own war against them. We have to make sure they don't have to do that."

It had been another long, hot day. Spoor found and lost the day before had been picked up again this morning. The three insurgents being chased knew their anti-tracking, making it slow, hard work for the Ovambo policemen. At one point, the indistinct spoor completely disappeared near an isolated kraal. As we approached the primitive enclosure, the Ovambo farmer watched us suspiciously from within his domain. When we pulled up next to the crude wall, he lifted two termite-eaten logs from the entrance and stepped outside, helpless resignation etched across his deeply creased face. As the Koevoet trackers of the group I was accompanying began to question him, he shook his head determinedly. Voices were raised, and I watched as he was backed up against the log barricade.

One of the men had begun prodding the farmer's chest with a forefinger when I saw the Casspirs of Jackie's group emerge from the bush and stop in the shade of a large tree near the kraal wall. Eight gun-laden APCs and almost ninety armed men were enough to cow anyone, I realized with acute sympathy for the farmer.

Jackie climbed over his gun mount and on to the car's hood. He stepped down to the massive steel bumper, jumped solidly to the bare ground and walked toward the interrogation scene as one of the special constables raised a hand. Benjamin, a huge, squint-eyed Ovambo who was Jackie's right-hand man, followed menacingly from his own vehicle to take over the interrogation. The farmer lifted his arm to ward off a threatened blow and continued shaking his head and talking rapidly. I focused a camera on the scene and waited. Benjamin turned, spat and spoke angrily to Jackie in Afrikaans. I left my vantage point in the Casspir and joined them. Jackie ignored me and continued listening.

"What's he saying?" I finally asked.

"No," Jackie said wearily, "this old guy just told Bennie to go ahead and hit him. He said we can hit him all we want to, but he knows we won't kill him. He says if he tells us what we want to know and SWAPO hears about it, then they'll come back here and kill him for sure." Jackie and Benjamin turned on their heels and returned to their Casspirs. The frustrated trackers fanned out around the kraal to try finding the spoor left by the humane freedom fighters the old man had never seen.

The group I'd been with had worked alongside Jackie's group until personality conflicts got in the way and we separated. I was wishing now that I'd accepted Jackie's invitation to go with him. I found myself sharing Jackie's dislike for the man whose car I shared. A sneering, taut little bully whose attitude toward his men was directly opposite to Jackie's, he would prove to be one of the few members of Koevoet whom I could abide neither in nor out of the bush.

"Nothing but a bunch of fucking coons," he sneered, waving a hand toward the men around us, men his life depended on in combat. "I have to work with them, but I don't have to kiss them. Parasites. Make no mistake, I'm no *kaffir boetie*[a] like your friend Jackie."

By the time we broke away from Jackie, this person I'd made the mistake of accompanying reckoned the insurgents had made good their escape. Our ears pricked up a few hours later when Jackie reported over the radio that they'd found the body of a civilian, apparently killed by the three insurgents. There was no obvious motive other than their suspicion that he might report their presence to the pursuing Koevoet groups.

Sometime in the midafternoon, word came over the radio: the chase had ended in a sharp, abbreviated contact. The bodies of the three SWAPO insurgents now lay where they had fallen in the bush.

Not long after the contact, the trackers found a POM-Z antipersonnel mine the insurgents had set alongside a bush trail. The green, pineapple-sectioned bomb had been hidden behind a tree, the thin, almost invisible trip wire stretched across the path. The

----

[a] "*Kaffir* brother," the Afrikaans equivalent of "nigger lover."

pin to the detonator had been withdrawn most of the way. The slightest pressure would have allowed it to drop out, followed by an almost instantaneous explosion of deadly shrapnel.

One of the car commanders later described how Jackie had squatted in front of the booby trap and studied it for a moment, then moved around and knelt on the far side of the tree. To Benjamin's frowning disapproval, he reached around the trunk and carefully seated the pin before disarming the device. A slip, and the resulting explosion would have torn away both arms. When I saw Jackie, I asked him why he'd taken the risk, why not just leave the damn thing? He looked at me steadily.

"What happens when one of the PBs comes along and trips it? Can't just *leave* it there. Jesus. These are people, not animals. We couldn't just drive off and forget about it. They have it bad enough already without us leaving things like that for them." He turned to Benjamin and translated my question. Bennie's mouth twisted into a sneer.

Unwilling to meet their eyes, I stared over Jackie's shoulder at one of the Casspirs, feeling chastened and embarrassed by my own stupidity. It was another reminder of how little I knew, how much I still had to learn.

On this end of day at Okatope, the sun casting long shadows, Jackie stood, hands in his pockets and leaning backward in a characteristic pose that identified him 100 meters away. A head taller
and proportionately wider, Benjamin slouched next to him, scowling and squinting in two directions at once. I joined them atop the bulldozed berm of sand around the base where, tired and dirty, we tried to make some sense of the war.

"This is my area, the south," Jackie said, his eyes on the horizon. "This is where I like to work." We were 30 miles south of Oshakati. Unlike the north-central and eastern areas of Ovamboland, the bush here was sparse and scattered, the kraals more numerous and closer together. If SWAPO insurgents were reported "in the south," Jackie would be the first on the scene to dig them out. The network of friends he had cultivated among the local population was unique and invaluable. "Most of the Ovambos around here trust me," he admitted, taking the cold beer from his lips and wiping his mustache. "If there are any terrs around, I hear about it sooner or later."

I thought it must be a damned dangerous exercise, being an informer; an Ovambo farmer in his remote kraal seemed an easy target for SWAPO. Jackie nodded. "That's why no one but me and Bennie here know who they are. But most of the people around here are too afraid of the gooks to say anything. And you really can't blame them. Most of them just wish everyone would go away and leave them alone. Us, the army, SWAPO. These are good people here. Genuine. Pretty unsophisticated, no real politics. All they want to do is grow their mohango, raise their cattle and goats, make babies, drink beer. Whatever. They're just caught in the middle with no way out. I feel sorry as hell for them.

"But the gooks come along and tell them they have to give them food and maybe hide them. They can't say no. The terrs have the guns and they don't. Then we come along and tell them they have to tell us where the terrs are or where they've gone. Sure, we try to scare them into telling us sometimes. Poor bastards. The gooks fuck with them, then we come along and fuck with them. We're trying to protect them, but it's a crazy way of having to do it.

"Okay, so we intimidate them, maybe push them around a little sometimes. I guess the difference is that we don't threaten to kill them. That's how the terrs get what they want — how some of the locals get forced into helping the terrs. Who are you going to listen to the most, someone who looks mean and yells at you, or the terr you know is going to use his bayonet if you don't do what he tells you? I know who I'd listen to the most if I was in their place. That civvie today, the one those three terrs killed, he'll make a stronger example to the PBs than I'll ever be able to." He took a long, last pull at his beer before throwing the can aside. I could feel his anger and frustration, a story that was struggling to get out.

"We were working not far from here one day when this woman comes running from her kraal to stop us. She was crying and screaming that SWAPO had killed her husband. We followed her back to the kraal, and she showed us where he was buried. We had to dig up the body to confirm what had happened and write a report. It wasn't very pretty."

Bennie interrupted to speak briefly, then stalked off toward the cars, beer in hand. Jackie paused, shifted, and reached down to pull a tough grass stem growing from the berm. He chewed on the end, looking out over the flat, sandy vista punctuated here and there with low clumps of bush between the scattered kraals.

"She told us five terrs came to their kraal a couple days before and accused her husband of being an informer for the security forces. They tied him up, then gathered fifteen or sixteen Ovambos from other kraals to watch. When they had everyone there, they popped his eyes out with the point of a bayonet so his eyes were hanging down on his cheeks. They tied a rope around his waist, held one end, and made him run around in a circle at the other end of it. While he was going around on the end of the rope, they made him sing a little ditty they made up for him. The thing he had to sing was: 'If you see SWAPO, call the security forces, if you see SWAPO call the security forces.' His wife said the gooks thought it was very funny, because of the eyes bouncing around on his cheeks.

"After they got tired of that, they made each of the PBs — the locals they'd rounded up to watch — they made each one of them stab him with the bayonet on the end of an SKS rifle. After that, they cut his head off, stuck it on a stake, and tied his body to the kraal fence. Just as an example and warning to other informers."

Jackie paused again. Beyond the barbed-wire fence around the Okatope base, the angular, menacing outlines of the Casspirs stood sharply defined against the darkening, clear sky. The Ovambo special constables stood or squatted around cooking fires, their laughter incongruous and somehow indecent after what I had just heard.

Jackie took the grass stem from his mouth, examined it briefly and dropped it. He put his hands in his pockets, leaned back and looked at me. He shook his head. "The funny thing," he said, his arm going up at the beckoning wave from Benjamin, "is that they were wrong. We questioned him a few times, but he never told us anything about the Swaps."

Jackie started to move away, then stopped and looked back at me. "You know the only thing he ever told us that was worth repeating?"

I shook my head.

"He said all he really wanted was for everyone to just leave him alone."

10

Birth of a Legend

W EDNESDAY mornings at the team storerooms next to Koevoet headquarters were always a scene of mild chaos.
Dozens of Casspir and Wolf Turbo armored personnel carriers
and their Blesbok and Strandwolf support vehicles were parked
in jumbled and haphazard disarray across the parade ground and
between the long, parallel sheds. For half the unit, it was the first
day of another week's deployment to the bush; for the other half,
it was the first day back in base after a week on operations. It
wasn't difficult to see which was which.

Unconcealed enthusiasm and excitement marked the teams
heading out that morning after a week of report writing, vehicle
repair and heavy drinking. A steady stream of men moved
between cars and the corrugated, iron-sided stores. Into the four
Casspirs or Wolf Turbos of each team went weapons, enough
ammunition to handle a major contact, medical kits and the day's
ration ("rat") packs. The Blesboks and Strandwolfs were loaded
with bedding, cases of rat packs, extra ammunition, tools, spare
parts, and drums of diesel and jet fuel, the latter for refueling the
helicopters far from their base. Cars moved in dust-raising relays
to Zulu Twelve, the garage, to have their internal fuel and water
tanks topped off.

For the returning teams, there was a slower-moving and quiet
relief after a long week of long, hot days crashing through the
bush of Ovamboland in search of SWAPO insurgents, eating on
the move out of ration packs, wearing a permanent layer of topsoil and sleeping on the ground. Cars were being unloaded and
washed, weapons stripped and cleaned, punctured tires patched.
Vehicle damage suffered in combat with SWAPO or, more often,

with the terrain was assessed, and the cars taken to Zulu Twelve for repair. Malfunctioning radios would go to the "White House" to have their circuits checked and faults rectified by the electronics wizards. ("Jam stealers," they were known as, along with mechanics, cooks and anyone else in the unit who wore the uniform but never deployed to the veld.)

Inside each group's dark storeroom inventories were being taken to see that all weapons had been returned and—if the group had had a contact—how much fresh ammunition would have to be drawn. These men were looking forward to long, hot showers, real beds and some hard drinking. "Getting ambushed" was the popular term, and an ambush in the canteen usually resulted in more casualties than one with SWAPO. On the mornings after a "serious ambush," more than one sour-mouthed, head-bursting Koevoet cop had wished he were dead.

Next door at Zulu Three, Koevoet's investigative center, the deploying group leaders and senior Ovambo NCOs listened to a situation report from one of the unit's operations officers. Intelligence pooled from all the security force units in the operational area pinpointed suspected SWAPO infiltrations, force strengths, where seen by members of the local population and last-known directions of movement. Group leaders jotted down the information in small green notebooks.

If the army had something cooking, an intelligence officer from Koevoet's archrival, 101 Battalion, would be on hand for an additional briefing. Although a Koevoet group would happily chase spoor into an area where 101 was working, by tacit agreement they tended to avoid each other in the bush. Interservice rivalry was not an unknown phenomenon among the security forces, and serious disagreements had occasionally arisen when a short-tempered, long-armed Koevoet group leader thought a 101 Battalion Romeo Mike[a] team was trying to poach *his* spoor. Of course, as I was often reminded, it was always the army which started the fights, the bastards.

This long-standing rivalry was not reserved for the bush alone, nor the outcome guaranteed. One evening in the

[a]NATO phonetic alphabet designator for *Reaksiemag*-Afrikaans for "Reaction Force."

hotel and bar in Oshakati, two of the Ops K lads were already well into their cups when a young, strapping lieutenant from 101 Battalion took a seat at the other end of the bar. The two cast four hooded eyes in his direction and began discussing the unsavory ancestry of army officers in general and this one in particular. When the lieutenant failed to respond to their taunts, they were obliged to speak to him directly. His manner was to keep his own counsel and elbows on the bar. This they took as a direct affront, the smaller of the two allowing he was going to teach the army some manners. His friend agreed, saying he would help. The smaller one shook his head angrily. "This is my fight."

"But I want to help."

"No way, man, this one's all mine. I'm going to show the bloody army some manners."

"So what do I have to do—just watch? Come on, man, you had the last one. It's not fair."

"Too bad. This is my fight." He slipped off his stool and swaggered down the bar to the lieutenant, who sat his beer peacefully on the bartop and held his palms out.

"Look, man, I really don't want to fight, okay?"

"Whatsamatter, afraid? All you army bastards are afraid. No good at killing terrs and can't take care of yourselves in the bar, either. Well, this is it, pal. Come on!"

"Don't just talk to him, hit the son of a bitch!" shouted his friend from the other end of the bar. He jumped off his stool and strode angrily up behind his partner. "Let me at him," he demanded, reaching over the broad back.

"I already told you, this was my fight," the smaller one said, placing the flat of his hand against his partner's chest and giving him a steady look. Turning back with a smile, he unleashed a sudden blow. The lieutenant neatly sidestepped the roundhouse, dropped his shoulders and with a professional left-right combination, laid the policeman full-length on the floor.

The standing cop focused a bleary eye on his prostrate partner. "You're right," he said, sitting down at the bar and picking up his beer, "it's your fight."

Occasionally, an intelligence officer from the Reconnaissance Commandos[b] would also drop in to pass on information. If the "recces" were operating south of the cutline, it was pointed out on a map as a no-go area until they had withdrawn. An unexpected confrontation could have disastrous results. (A story passed round the campfire—perhaps apocryphal—told of two Koevoet groups chasing spoor for days, only to eventually have a white recce, stripped naked and his black makeup scrubbed off, step out of the bush with arms raised. Given that the Reconnaissance Commandos were the elite of the security forces, the story was related with more than a degree of relish. Part of the mythology.)

Meteorology was a subject of particular interest. Until the annual rains began in earnest, Koevoet's work was slow, boring and exasperating. Without rain, there was little cover on the trees and little groundwater, the presence of which were prerequisites to SWAPO's annual infiltration. Bare trees made the insurgents too vulnerable to detection from both the ground and air; a lack of widespread water for drinking limited how far they could travel with only canteens. And what few year-round water holes did exist were closely patrolled by the army. Normally by now, early December, the rains would have started. But they were late, the skies an unvarying pale blue. No rains, no infiltration.

"Fucking weather," someone muttered from the back of the briefing room.

After the briefing the men wandered across the parade ground to headquarters, where breakfast was being laid out atop green-painted, concrete picnic tables on a tree-shaded patio. The men gathered around the tables, heaping pap (South African version of grits), sauce, fried eggs, fried fish and tomatoes on their plates. In between mouthfuls, those who had just returned from the bush added the *minutiae* which had been missing from the formal briefing: who in particular among the PBs had good "info," suspicions about which kraals were being used by SWAPO, hunches where the insurgents were likely to be operating. But even between friends, some information was always held back. The unit was split down the middle into two basic sections. When

---

[b]South African special forces whose specialty is long-range reconnaissance patrols far behind enemy lines. Although they operated primarily in Angola, occasional special missions saw them in Namibia.

Alpha Group's fourteen teams were deployed in the bush, all of Bravo Group's fourteen would be back in base. Neither was prepared to help the other *too* much for fear of the rivals accumulating more contacts at the end of the year. Friendship and unity of purpose went only so far.

By eleven o'clock, the last teams were rolling out of Oshakati. Two hours later, they had fanned out into the bush, where the search pattern began. Typically, two combat groups of four armored personnel carriers each worked together, leapfrogging ahead of one another. One group stopped at a remote kraal, while the other passed through the bush to the next one, where the trackers debussed to question the local population. Had they seen any SWAPO? When did they pass? How many were they? What direction were they moving?

More often than not, the locals would have seen nothing, since the insurgents avoided most kraals, stopping only at those where the inhabitants were known to be sympathetic and trustworthy. But even if they had not seen SWAPO, the "bush telegraph"—gossip passed back and forth while gathering firewood, fetching water, herding cattle—often gave them potentially valuable information.

"Yes, we heard that three SWAPO passed near here last week, moving south."

"Who told you this?"

"So-and-so," they would say, pointing and snapping their fingers in the direction of the place where so-and-so lived.

The trackers would board their cars and drive on to that kraal. If the information there was no more specific or fresh, the group settled down to long hours of police detective work: stopping, questioning and looking for physical evidence: the tracks of infiltrating insurgents. Days might be spent following up on the vaguest of information. Like police work around the world, it was grinding, often frustrating and generally unglamorous, but part of what made Koevoet one of the most dramatically successful units in the history of counterinsurgency warfare.

In December along the Angolan border, the summer temperatures can reach well past the 100 degree mark. And it is dry, the rains still a month or more away. Dust billowed behind the Casspirs and Wolf Turbos as they worked their way through the dense undergrowth, the trackers scanning the ground for spoor. By late morning, the heat inside the cars was stifling; sweat beaded and trickled down foreheads and faces, streaking the layers of dust and dirt already there. The backs of shirts became darkly wet. The only relief was to stand or sit on the rim of the car's open well and hope to catch a hint of breeze, and even that hope was more often than not frustrating; while there, the dust added yet another layer to damp arms and faces.

In the really thick bush, there was no option but to sit on the molded rubber seats inside to escape the slapping branches and thorn trees. There, an unavoidable and constant rain of detritus and crawling creatures dropped through the open top of the car: twigs, rotten branches, leaves, bugs—Lord, the bugs! Especially the spiders—spiders of every conceivable color, size and shape, dozens of them—and even more varieties and numbers of ants; hairy and smooth caterpillars, beetles and hoppers and moths, and sometimes even a snake, which was guaranteed to liven things up considerably (not even an unexpected contact could trigger such impressively quick reflexes). The floor of the car was gradually covered with debris. The bugs brushed from bare arms and legs scurried to disappear into cracks and crevices inside the car, some crawling thing inevitably leaving a swelling white lump somewhere on the skin.

The eyes and senses soon became used to the sight and feel of latent firepower. Atop the cab was the main armament of two light machine guns or, more commonly, a .50 caliber Browning with two of the lighter guns. Some cars, particularly the Wolf Turbos, carried an additional .30 caliber Browning in a swivel ball mount through the co-driver's bullet-proof windshield. Inside, at least ten assault rifles were propped against the hull. Somewhere there would be a single-shot grenade launcher or one of the new six-shot models. In addition to their short-barreled assault rifles with fifty-round magazines, some of the trackers carried pistols in holsters or simply shoved behind their web belts. At least one car per group carried a light mortar, its crew adept at firing it out the open top while racing full tilt through the bush.

Captured weapons also found their way into the cars. An AK-47 might be seen in a corner. A rocket launcher lay on the floor, warheads and bright green boosters jammed somewhere convenient. A former insurgent now working with Koevoet cradled a Soviet light machine gun, a favorite from his days with SWAPO. Taking the concept of maximum firepower seriously, some car commanders included three or four medium machine guns, usually Soviet made, positioned to be fired through the spring-loaded gun ports below the windows. The term "bristling" didn't even begin to describe it. Each car was a self-contained, rolling arsenal.

But hardware and firepower were only as good as the people using them. Each man, whether white or black, was a volunteer. The majority of the blacks—who made up 90 percent of the operational personnel—were local Ovambos, the same tribe which made up the majority of SWAPO. They were not only on intimate terms with the terrain, language and culture of their fellow tribesmen, but had earned the reputation of being aggressive and deadly bush fighters.

They were also some of the most expert trackers in the world. The majority of them had been born and raised in traditional kraals in the middle of the bush. Their first childhood responsibilities were those of herd boys, minding their fathers' cattle and goats, which represented the wealth of the family. If one of the animals strayed from the herd into the bush, the boy was responsible for finding it. By the time he reached adolescence, he could pick out, identify and follow the faintest spoor. This skill was easily transferred to tracking down SWAPO insurgents.

Because of this, new SWAPO conscripts were taught anti-tracking to hide their tracks—keeping to hard ground, stepping from fallen branch to fallen branch or moving through shallow 'shonas during the rainy season. The techniques had saved more insurgent lives than the Soviet-supplied weapons they carried. A Koevoet group leader would move heaven and earth to recruit a team of Ovambos good enough to spot the traces left by "heavy anti-tracking."

One day, a group leader pointed toward one of the black policemen, a young, almost effeminate-looking Ovambo, who was slowly but steadily picking out the almost invisible trail left by two insurgents. "See that one?" he said, lifting his chin toward the totally absorbed youth. "We caught him about four years ago. His anti-tracking was so goddamn good we decided we had to try to capture him alive. I won't tell you how we did it, but it took a week of our best people trying to stay on his spoor. When we finally got him, it turned out that he'd taught anti-tracking at SWAPO's training camp at Lubango. After we showed him that the situation here in South West wasn't what he'd been told by SWAPO—I mean, he couldn't believe all the Ovambo business and how many Ovambos had cars, that they could travel and live wherever they wanted—he decided to join us. Guy is good. Takes a terr who's bloody good to throw him off the spoor."

I glanced uneasily at the Soviet-made RPD light machine gun balanced over the young man's shoulder. "You're kidding. You've got an ex-SWAPO armed and working for you?"

He seemed surprised at my question. "Sure, Why not? Oh, some of the ones we capture are totally committed to SWAPO, but most of them have a major change of attitude after they see what's really happening on this side of the border. If they decide they want to work with us, we're happy to take them. They're paid reasonably well, given uniforms, fed; any service-related injuries are treated by our doctors or medics. The conditions are 1,000 percent better than what they ever had with SWAPO. Hell, I guess we have forty or fifty ex-terrs in Koevoet right now, and not one has ever deserted and run back to SWAPO."

Most of the Ovambo policemen were in their late teens or early twenties and immensely proud of being part of Koevoet. Although many other young Ovambos dressed in army browns and served with the SWATF 101 Battalion, Koevoet's olive green uniform immediately set these men apart. Each fighting group had its own T-shirt and totem—an elephant, lion, badger or scorpion, a lynx, cobra, crocodile or other creature considered dangerous or disagreeable. The group T-shirts invariably showed a SWAPO insurgent being attacked by the adopted totem. The insurgent's AK-47 would be depicted as broken in half, just as in simpler days a defeated warrior's spear would have been broken to show defeat.

Like members of any elite unit, they reveled in their reputation as swift and efficient killers. The scathing anti-Koevoet propaganda taken from the bodies of the insurgents only reinforced the image they had of themselves. And their swaggering cockiness told the casual observer just how good they believed themselves to be.

Among the whites, none had come to Koevoet without previous experience in either the South African Police or South West African Police. They first had to complete a counterinsurgency course before being provisionally accepted by Ops K, where they were then subjected to an intensive selection course under as realistic conditions as possible. It was not unknown for new members to hit contacts during this selection period. Once accepted, they were expected to stay with the unit for at least two years. More often, they would stay longer. At least one group leader had spent eight years with the unit. Another had fourteen years of police work on the border, with three of those years in Koevoet. Group leaders and car commanders with four to six years in Ops K were not unusual.

It was this unique melding of experience, dedication, aggressiveness and cross-cultural partnership between white Africans and black Africans which had made Koevoet a legend in counterinsurgency warfare. And all of this could be laid at the feet of one man, whose unconventional ideas on counterinsurgency operations had given birth to Ops K.

Johannes "Sterk Hans" Dreyer was as much a legend as the unit he commanded. A rangy grandfather with a bristling mustache and the same aggressive spirit he expected of his men, Dreyer seemed the archetypal fighting general, ready to dive into his personal Wolf Turbo and head into the bush alongside the men who revered him.

"I was sent up here in 1978 to see what role the police could play against terrorism," said Dreyer, relaxing in his paneled office decorated with Koevoet memorabilia. Drawing on experience gained with the South African Police in Rhodesia, he first envisioned a Selous Scout-type unit, employing local blacks as pseudo-SWAPO.[c]

"I learned in Rhodesia that you must use the local population

---

[c]Between 1967 and 1975, the South African Police were drawn in to work alongside Rhodesian units during the counterinsurgency war in what is today Zimbabwe.

because of their knowledge of the customs, terrain and language. An all white force would really be ineffective in this kind of war."

Dreyer approached a senior Ovambo headman and discussed his ideas. The headman was taken with the concept, and at Dreyer's request, recruited sixty Ovambos skilled in tracking and weapons handling.

"We operated on a shoestring budget back then," Dreyer recalled. "I was allowed to bring four officers with me and recruit two more here. We were given two bakkies [pickup trucks] and two cars. That we never hit a land mine is a miracle."

Viewed with much skepticism and not a little suspicion by Higher Up, the first few months of Ops K's existence were spent on training, developing tactics and scrounging equipment wherever it could be found or stolen. Those in charge were still not ready to spend money on what seemed a harebrained idea.

"Our first major success came during the '79 SWAPO infiltration, when twelve terrs managed to reach the white farming area east of the Etosha Game Reserve." Dreyer stood and circled an area on a wall map with his index finger. "On one farm here, they killed an old man; on another not far away"—his finger tapped the map an inch from the first spot—"they killed a grandmother and her two grandchildren, ages two and four. They were bayoneted to death.

"The army had moved into the area, but weren't having much luck. I finally convinced them to give us a try." Twenty-three Ovambo trackers and one white were flown to the scene. They picked up the spoor and followed it for the next seven days. In the ensuing contact, two insurgents and the white group leader were killed. Even so, "Everyone was amazed that we could follow spoor for that long," said Dreyer. "Except us, that is," he added with transparent smugness. Dreyer's concept of using skilled trackers to bring the enemy to bay had worked. "I knew then I had something golden. It wasn't long before we were killing fifty to eighty terrs a month, the equivalent of a SWAPO company."

For the first three years, the existence of the unit was kept a closely guarded secret. Although its reputation grew rapidly among those who were closely involved with counterinsurgency operations, no mention of it appeared in the press or any official document. Still, in spite of its growing success rate, Ops K remained the bastard stepchild of the operational area. The men worked on foot with outdated equipment, little support, and even less recognition from police headquarters.

"Of course, we did manage to 'borrow' a few things from the army," one old hand allowed with a rueful grin. "Getting past guards, through barbed wire and into army supply depots taught us a few things about infiltration ourselves."

With statistics in hand, then-Colonel Dreyer flew to Pretoria to argue his case. He was rather coolly received, not least for his attitude. "I was pretty aggressive," he admitted, "but I knew what I was talking about and they didn't." Still, Dreyer and his numbers were impressive enough to convince headquarters that the fledgling unit should be expanded. Money and equipment were soon on their way, including three Hippo APCs, the gasoline-engined and completely enclosed forerunner of the Casspir.

Until the Hippo armored personnel carriers arrived, all the work was done on foot. "Those were the days when groups of sixty or eighty—hell, sometimes even a hundred—terrs were coming across," reminisced an old-timer. "Those were some serious contacts. There were a lot of times when we were completely outnumbered." He went on to describe his group of thirty men running for two days ahead of a hundred pursuing insurgents. "Our radio batteries were flat, so we couldn't call for help, and the three contacts we'd already been in had used up most of our ammo." They escaped.

"Would you believe when we first got those cars, no one wanted to use them?" said Dreyer. "I actually had to order the group leaders to take them." The first contact involving the Hippos resulted in eighteen dead insurgents. "And that was with only two cars. After that, everyone wanted them." Koevoet's course was charted.

To the horror of the Hippo's designers, the inventive operators set about customizing their new toys. "Hell, the Hippo had a closed top. Not only did it make it too damned hot inside, but cut way down on visibility and fighting capability. Shooting out the gun ports is fine, but there are definitely times when the people in the back need to stand up and shoot. So we just got some cutting torches and opened her up. No problem, but the factory people back in South Africa went ape shit." Interior water tanks were added, as well as extra radio racks and more armor protection for the man standing behind the gun turret.

"We really didn't know much about arming the cars," explained one of the unit's early members, "or even the best way to use them. There were lots of midnight bull sessions, trying to work out the best tactics. It was all new. There weren't any books on it. No one had ever used APCs in the bush the way we were trying to do. We experimented with all kinds of weapons. Our first gun mounts were all homemade things that didn't work too well. We stuck .50 caliber Brownings in them, .30 caliber Brownings, GPMGs, Russian PKMs and RPDs. Some people even got some captured Russian 14.5-mm guns from the army and tried them out. One group leader actually tried *two* of those 14.5s. Took a big man to swing that turret! Another group leader talked someone in the air force out of a 20-mm gun and mounted that on his car."

"We had one of the 14.5s," said another. "Someone shoved a rag up the barrel to keep leaves and branches out while driving through the bush. He didn't understand the ammunition was high-explosive stuff designed to detonate as soon as it hit something. Man, the first contact, the first round down the barrel hit that rag and exploded. Blew the end of the barrel off and peeled back part of what was left like a banana skin. After the contact was over, we got a hacksaw out of the tool box and just sawed the barrel off behind the split. Still worked fine."

Listening to his operators in the field, Dreyer soon backed away from the Selous Scout idea, deciding that highly mobile and heavily armed hunter-killer teams were the best way of dealing with insurgents in the thick bush of Ovamboland. After much experimentation and discussion, each group was eventually organized into forty Ovambos, four whites and four diesel-engined Casspir APCs. Added to each group was a Blesbok supply vehicle to carry extra fuel, water, ammunition and food.

Living up to his reputation for contrariness, Dreyer began butting heads with the army over defined areas of operation. He wanted—and demanded—unlimited freedom of movement throughout the operational area. Dropping a hot spoor just because it crossed into an army unit's area was unacceptable. As usual, he got his way.

"We've got a good boss," one group leader said proudly, "he lets us go where we want. And if the terrs head back across the border into Angola, we'll chase them as far as they want to go."

Men, tactics, equipment and a maverick in the driver's seat had made Ops K one of the world's most spectacularly successful counterinsurgency units. Nonetheless, all its people — black and white — insisted that they were still policemen. "We're just stopping criminals and preventing crimes."

11

War Stories and Patrols

December 12, 1986.

The white, late-morning sun already had turned the interior of the car into an oven. The other three Casspirs and attendant Blesbok, spread well apart from us in a ragged skirmish line, rumbled slowly through the bush a few kilometers north of the Namibian border. The group leader stood in the hatch behind the machine gun turret, monitoring the radio and keeping track of the other vehicles. The black policemen, oblivious to the ever-present threat of ambush, rode sidesaddle on the coaming, scanning the passing ground for spoor. It was a scene that had been repeated daily year after year across Ovamboland and southern Angola — constantly moving, looking, questioning.

The radio crackled. "Zulu Alpha, Zulu Mike."

Marius Brand raised the handset to his ear and pressed the transmit key. "Koos, Marius. *Gaan.*" Go ahead.

I listened to the one-sided Afrikaans conversation between Brand and Koos Combrinck, the new group leader of Zulu Mike. Brand slipped the handset clip through the epaulet on his shirt and leaned down to order the driver to stop. He straightened and spoke briefly with the young Ovambo warrant officer sitting on the rim of the car. He then turned to me as the Casspir slowly coasted to a halt, engine idling.

"Zulu Mike's trackers have fresh info. Four terrs were in this area last night, heading east."

Otto Shivute stood atop the car and scanned the horizon. He leaned over and touched Brand on the shoulder, the other hand pointing off to the left. Just above the trees half a mile away, the haze of yellow smoke rose from a grenade thrown by Koos to mark his position.

"Maybe we have something," Brand mumbled, massaging the back of his neck. He looked down at the driver and pointed toward the smoke. "Hey! Kom! *Komesho!*"[a] he said irritably in a mixture of Afrikaans and Oshivambo, waving the car forward with the palm of his hand.

The driver, who had worked his way through Brand's legs to stand next to me, wiped the sweat from his face, gulped the air and dived back to his seat. He worked the gearshift lever with a gloved hand, let in the clutch, and we lurched forward, bush and small trees falling under the armored nose of the Casspir. The driver of the Blesbok supply vehicle alongside us disappeared into his cab, pulling the hatch cover over his head. There was a belch of black diesel exhaust, and the Blesbok tucked in behind us, following in our flattened wake.

By the time we found Koos, Zulu Mike's trackers already had the spoor. But the terrain here was hard, making it difficult for even the keenest eyes to detect and follow the insurgents' trail. When the spoor was lost, the trackers spread out side by side to pick it up again, while cars from the other team cut ahead — *voorsny* — to try finding it farther on. When the voorsny cars found it, another smoke grenade or thousand footer flare was fired. The following group recovered its trackers and raced to catch up.

We were plowing through the dense undergrowth when the Casspir hit a dead, termite-eaten tree, shearing it off at the base. The tinder-dry and brittle branches above us exploded in an avalanche of debris. Before I could duck under the overhanging rim of the Casspir, a section of tree limb landed squarely on my head, splitting the scalp and bringing forth a torrent of blood. Sinking to one of the seats, I grabbed my bandana and tried to staunch the flow. Shivute shouted at Brand, who glanced at me, then immediately grabbed the handle of the Browning and swung the gun mount in an arc across the bush around us. When Otto told him what had happened, he relaxed against the armored back plate and they both started laughing. A little annoyed at the level of their humor, I asked what the hell was so funny.

[a] Oshivambo for "forward."

"For a second we thought you'd been shot," said Brand as Shivute handed me a wet rag to wipe the blood away. While the Ovambo medic gently parted my hair to daub the cut with Mercurochrome, the two of them were still choking on suppressed giggles at the idea of someone so clumsy as to be hit on the head with a rotten branch. *Shot.* Well, Brand did have a tendency toward the dramatic. I started to dismiss it as one of the more improbable jokes I'd heard, then realized that his immediate reaction wasn't theatrics. Never mind that I was a noncombatant; somewhere out there were people who would kill me if given the chance. I was white and dressed in the uniform of their deadliest and most hated enemy; clearly, that made me as legitimate a target as any of the men around me. It was a sobering thought as I winced under the ministrations of the medic.

After a three-hour chase, the spoor finally disappeared as the result of heavy anti-tracking on difficult terrain. The four insurgents were more expert than most. They escaped.

At the next kraal, the Ovambos started bargaining for a few chickens until they cast their eyes on a herd of goats. The head of the kraal agreed on a price for three of them. I chipped in my share, and South African rands were passed to an ecstatic Angolan peasant. The goats were quickly trussed and lifted into the back of the Blesbok. Supper.

"We got robbed on the price, but it's a nice break from rat packs," allowed Brand.

"How is he going to use South African money?" I asked, puzzled that the farmer accepted it so readily.

"No, he'll go across the cutline some day to buy a few things he can't get here. Or he'll trade them with another Angolan for something. If we had offered him kwanzas—Angolan money—he'd've laughed in our faces. They all know rands are worth something, but kwanzas? Kwanzas are just a little more valuable than dirt."

He laughed. "Did you hear about the guys who rustled a couple of cows last year? They decided the boys deserved some fresh meat, so they shot two cows they found in the bush. Didn't pay anyone or even bother to find out who they belonged to. That night they had a hell of a nice braai.

"A few days later, the old Ovambo who'd owned them marched

into the Brig's office. His donkey—with the heads of those cows tied on it—was out in the car park. He was quite pissed off. He'd done a little detective work himself, talking to the local pops from neighboring kraals who'd seen what had happened and got the group letters from the cars. He wanted payment for them, and he wanted it in rands. The boss called in the two group leaders, chewed them up one side and down the other, and made them pay the Ovambo twice what those cows were worth. No one's tried that trick again."

An hour before sunset, the teams found a spot for a TB. Cars were parked around the camp, guns facing outward. Bedding and food were unloaded, dried branches dragged in, and cooking fires lit. Tent poles were cut, and ponchos stretched over them and pegged down. Although SWAPO had never been so imprudent as to hit an overnight Koevoet TB in the bush, the trackers still placed their short-barreled R5 assault rifles within easy reach of their sheltered sleeping bags.

The throats of the three goats were cut, then the carcasses hung from trees, where they were skinned and butchered. Haunches and ribs were hacked off and distributed. As water boiled in fire-blackened kettles, coffee bags were dropped in and allowed to steep. The aroma of sizzling meat was savored; unless we stopped at a base, the balance of the week's meals would be whatever came out of cans in the rat packs. As we ripped the tough flesh from the ribs with our teeth, I asked Brand about the long history of animosity between Koevoet and the army.

"I guess it started in the early days of the unit," he explained, licking his fingers. "Because no one was supposed to know we existed, the army got the credit for all our kills in official press releases. Even back then, we were getting a lot more than the defense force. Then, when the army saw that we were getting the successes, they tried to bring us under their command, but the boss wouldn't go for it. You can't do what we do and operate according to a book the way the army does. The army finally copied our tactics with 101 Battalion. They even stole a lot of our best Ovambos by offering higher pay, but they still couldn't get the kills that we do."

"Why not? If they have Casspirs and they're using trackers the same way, what's the difference?"

"No, for one thing, we use basic police techniques of investigation and follow-up. And we're flexible—the boss knows we understand what's happening on the ground and lets us make the tactical decisions. But the army, they work according to set rules; the group leaders don't have the same freedom to act independently without first getting permission from a senior officer. Once you start going through all that bullshit, you lose tactical control. If you've got spoor, you have to make decisions now-now, not half an hour or an hour later. Also, the army guys are assigned up here, rather than being volunteers. And usually they're not here more than a year, so when they're finally getting to know the terrain and getting a little experience, they're sent back home. It takes at least two years in the veld before one of our people has the experience to be a group leader, but the army puts lieutenants in those positions who don't have any at all. And the press releases *still* don't use our unit name when they report contacts. It's just 'the security forces killed so many terrs,' so everyone back home thinks its the army." He shook his head at the unfairness of it.

"But why do you guys get into so many fights with them?" I asked, still not understanding.

"Because we don't like the bastards."

"Right, well, yes . . . ," I coughed politely.

Afterward, with the men sitting around the flickering fire with a last cup of sweet, milky coffee in hand, the inevitable stories were taken out and brushed off. They were told matter-of-factly, without embellishment, as an accepted part of the profession these men had chosen to pursue. I always had to remind myself that these weren't tales repeated third or fourthhand, or plucked from books or magazines. They were what Brand or Otto, Dean or Nella or Jackie or any of a dozen others had experienced themselves, when they either killed first or died. I settled myself on the ground, laid out cameras and cleaning equipment on my shirt, then leaned back against a tree to listen.

"We picked up the spoor of about thirty terrs, but most of the cars got stuck in a 'shona. The trackers were out trying to find the spoor. Only my car was free—and the Blesbok—and I said to the Blesbok driver over the radio, okay, you stay with the trackers, I'll go forward. And as I passed the trackers, I saw something near a kraal ahead. I didn't know if it was a terr or something I just glimpsed from the eye. As I rounded the kraal, I gave some flashing fire to keep the terrs down, then I saw the trackers coming towards the kraal, and I realized it was a terr that I saw. There were no civvies around. They had all run away when the terrs had come through, so I told the driver to go into the kraal, and we were circling around through the kraal, and the terr jumped out of a hut with an AK next to me—and he fired at me. He missed, and I got him with my pistol. Nailed him. Emptied my magazine into him."

"Remember Simon? He was the Ovambo radioman you met with Zulu Mike last year. Incredible tracker and really good guy. We were on a follow-up on foot, and he saw the trip wire for a pom-zed [POM-Z]. He stopped, but one of the other trackers walked straight into it. The top of the pom-zed hit him under the arm and went all the way through his chest. He walked about five steps and died."

"We were trying to get to Elundu on the dirt road before dark. We should have stopped and TB-ed in the bush because it was getting late. There's one place along that road where the terrain along the side is higher than the road, perfect for an ambush, and that's what we hit. They were waiting for us. I was driving, and we took three RPGs. Bang, bang, bang! One went through the engine, the other two behind me. One hit Captain Koch, who was sitting behind me. If it hadn't hit his rifle first, it would have killed him for sure. The engine stopped when the RPG hit it, and I just instinctively pushed in the clutch and we kept rolling until we were past the ambush. I had picked up lots of little pieces of shrapnel in the back of my head, neck and shoulders from the RPG that hit the captain. We were still moving, and I reached up and touched the back of my head and felt my whole scalp move. I looked at my hand and there was a big lump of flesh in it, and I put it back really fast. I thought it was part of my head. It was actually part of the captain's arm. They really hammered us."

"You know Louw, the Afrikaans guy with the scar on his cheek? Well, they had a contact, and this terr surrendered at the end of it. Louw's driver stopped in front of him, and Louw climbed down from behind the guns onto the car's bonnet. As he jumped from the bonnet, the terr reached down and grabbed his

AK and fired while Louw was still in the air. He had his mouth open, and the round went in his mouth and out the side of his cheek. Missed his teeth, jaw, everything, just went through his cheek. The terr didn't get a chance to fire a second round."

"Sakkie—maybe you didn't meet him when you were here, Afrikaans guy—he never saw the terr. They were on a follow-up when a terr jumped up in front of the car. Heatstrim came through the gun mount and caught Sakkie in the chest. Never had a chance."

"I was passing a tree as we were going into the contact, and I caught a glimpse of something behind, and I looked back, and a terr was just standing there with an RPG-7. He was too far back, and I was already busy shooting. I looked at him and realized I must get my guns around before he killed me; I didn't even think about my pistol at that time. I should have pulled my pistol, but I wanted to shoot him with the guns, the five-oh. I realized it's too late and yelled at my driver that there's one right behind us, and he turned. I looked at my LMG; it's empty. Looked at the five-oh; there was only a short piece left, maybe ten-twelve rounds, and I had to keep this gook worried, and I just squeezed off the shots, one by one. I shot off three–four before I could reach him and then gave him everything I had. Blew his head off. It was close . . . exciting."

"One night only a couple days after you left last year, the terrs revved Ohangwena and ran back across the border, heading for Namakunde. Next day on the follow-up just south of Namakunde near the tar road, our cars got stuck in some 'shonas. The other groups were trying to find a way around, so we were out and following the terrs on foot. Me and Nella, we were wading across this 'shona, the water was right up to our chests in some places, and suddenly one of the Ovambos was pointing and saying, 'There, there!' Man, there were terrs in the weeds right in front of us, and we were firing, and they were firing, and the cars were firing behind us, water was kicking up all around us. There were more terrs in the bush on the other side of the 'shona, and they were shooting. Shit, we were getting machine guns, mortars, RPGs, everything thrown at us. Man, it was really something. We kept moving into the 'shonas, out into the bush, and back into the water. We had three more contacts that day. Killed fourteen terrs, altogether. Man, you should have been there. Afterwards, we were saying you really should have been with us. You could've really got some good coverage there."

"I've never had my car shot out, but they've come quite near — hit the tree next to me with an RPG, but never did they shoot my car out. I think there's about three, maybe four, bullet marks on my car that I've been driving for the past two years. That's all. I was lucky, and I believe God looked down on me. There's a lot of times that they lined me up, but I saw them first. And I don't miss at that stage . . . "

The fires slowly died to embers, and conversation faltered. From different places inside the perimeter, there was low murmuring and quiet laughter from the Ovambos. Some winged insect, only slightly smaller than a B-17 bomber judging from the sound, droned determinedly across the camp. A black velvet sky dripping with brilliant stars draped itself from horizon to horizon above the trees. The sudden streak of a shooting star appeared and disappeared so quickly you wondered if it had really been there. The faint, pulsing glow of lightning far, far to the north in Angola was a reminder that the rains still had not arrived.

The rains, you wondered, snuggling into the sleeping bag, *when will they come? And what happens when they do?*

The next day followed the same pattern as the day before: moving through the bush, stopping to question members of the local population, moving on, stopping, and on and on with no good info or even a trace of spoor. Late that afternoon, Brand turned to me. "I think we'll try setting up an ambush tonight near the *yati* [border]. Me, Koos and about ten of the trackers. Want to come?"

The invitation took me by surprise. If the ambush were successful, it would certainly be too dark to take photos. I would be a useless addition to the enterprise. But the invitation had been tendered, and I had come to experience as much of the war here as possible.

"Yeah. Thanks," I said, wondering if I was getting in over my head.

We stopped at the Security Branch base at Ohangwena, the scene of the failed SWAPO attack the previous April. It had come during a full moon only one night after I'd departed eight months earlier. Brand had been involved in the follow-up and was the one giving covering fire to Dean and Nella as they waded across the 'shona against heavy SWAPO resistance. As we made our preparations for the ambush patrol, I listened to his description of the attack and follow-up. What a story that would have made, I thought, disappointed that SWAPO hadn't done it while I had been here. Why couldn't they have tried it just one night earlier? I shook off the picture. You were either there for it or you weren't, and the opportunity was gone. After the reception and subsequent losses they had suffered, it was unlikely SWAPO's planners were ready to try it again. Forget it. But what a story.

I turned my attention to the present as Brand picked a dozen trackers with the most night-work experience. The majority of the two fighting groups began setting up a TB under the trees south of the Security Branch base. Those selected for the ambush attempt loaded extra magazines and packed rucksacks with the barest essentials. Koos, another tall and quiet one with an infectious grin and all the easy grace of a natural athlete, pulled on a camouflage jacket as I began snapping photos of the preparations.

"Don't take my picture with this thing on," Koos said in a moment of seriousness. A few months earlier, Dreyer had changed his men's uniforms from camouflage to a solid olive green. This was to differentiate his people from those serving in the Security Branch police, who continued to wear the same mottled pattern. Dreyer wanted no one mistaking his men.

"We're not supposed to wear them anymore," Koos explained. "If the Brig saw it, he'd kill me." I promised not to photograph him in the old-style bush jacket.

We boarded one of Zulu Mike's Wolf Turbos and drove east for a few miles. We were dropped off three miles from the border as the sun began to slip toward the horizon. Brand gave me a quick briefing.

"Stay behind me and don't talk. If we hit something, get down and stay down until I tell you it's okay. When we get close to the yati, the boys will play terr-terr and drop into some of the kraals to ask about any other Swaps in the area. Some of the PBs around there are pretty pro-SWAPO, but in the dark they won't be able to tell the difference between our people and the gooks. If everything seems quiet, we'll set up about a hundred meters south of the cutline. Okay?"

We spread out and moved silently through the bush, detouring widely around any kraals. As we were crossing a dirt road just after sunset a battered pickup truck, headlights shining, appeared through the trees. The policemen waited in cover until the pickup truck neared us, then two of them stepped out to stop it. The driver slammed on the brakes and came to a sliding stop in a cloud of dust that rolled over us. Clearly surprised by our presence, he scanned the bush on both sides as dark, silent figures emerged and surrounded the car. One special constable, assault rifle at the ready with another covering him, approached the door and opened it. He crooked a finger at the driver, who slowly stepped into the road. The identification he handed over showed that he was the domini, or minister, at a nearby church. As Brand questioned him, the special constables carefully searched the vehicle but found nothing to arouse their suspicion. The documents were returned with a warning about driving after curfew and an order to return to wherever he had come from. "I'm sorry, domini," Brand told him when he began to protest, "but it is after curfew and this road is closed."

We watched as he angrily slammed his door, turned the pickup truck around and sped back into the gathering dark. By the time he disappeared, we were moving again. We were 100 meters beyond the road when we heard the bakkie returning, horn blaring, as the Ovambo preacher passed the spot where he'd been stopped and continued down the road toward his original destination.

"So much for surprise around here," Brand hissed.

Soon after last light had faded, a brilliant half-moon rose to throw enough light to keep us in the cover of shadowed bush. We came to a trail snaking through the bush. The trackers at each flank covered the approaches, while the rest of us slipped quietly across in twos and threes, appearing for a brief second in the soft light before disappearing eerily back into darkened cover.

Half a mile from the border, we found ourselves winding between closely spaced kraals. Fires flickered inside the enclosures, casting orange glows against the roofs of thatched huts we could see above the crude log palisades. Occasionally, we could hear laughter and conversation.

We froze in the moonlight and crouched as a woman came out of a kraal ahead of us. We watched as she hoisted her dress and squatted to urinate. When she disappeared back through the kraal wall, we slowly rose and began moving again.

We were passing another kraal when a dog began barking. Again, we stopped and sank to our haunches. A barely visible figure appeared at the entrance to the kraal. The figure stood there for perhaps half a minute while we held our breaths. There was a loud belch, followed by a slurred command to the dog. It quieted for a moment, then started barking again as we rose and took the first step. We halted, cursing silently. The figure reappeared. There was a sharp yelp, and both dog and master disappeared. We stood and distanced ourselves from that one as quickly and quietly as possible.

Not far from the border Marius and I settled in the moon shadow of a makelani palm. The trackers dissolved away into the night to play terr-terr, posing as SWAPO insurgents. We waited without talking. As the moon rose higher and higher, we shifted to stay in the shadow. An hour later, two of the trackers silently materialized. One whispered close to Brand's ear, his teeth flashing in a shared joke.

Marius smiled, leaned close to me and whispered: "He asked a woman at that kraal over there if it was safe to cross the yati back into Angola. She told him there were no security force people around and that if he walked down that trail, it would take him to the border. She told him many of the freedom fighters used it."

When the rest of the trackers returned from their reconnaissance, we moved down the path the woman had indicated to our pseudo-SWAPO. Brand picked a spot where high ground on either side commanded the approaches from both the north and south. Our group split to the east and west, each half moving 30 to 40 meters up the opposing slopes to where the first thin cover began. The Ovambo policeman next to me set up his pack mortar, carefully laying out half a dozen illumination rounds. We settled in and waited. I lay on my stomach and faced down the slope, propping my chin on crossed hands and wondering what the hell I was going to do if anything happened. *Stay the hell down and hope an unlucky round doesn't catch you.* My head lifted as something large and scaly climbed up one elbow and crept slowly across both arms. It dropped off the other side and continued on its way into the darkness.

Just before midnight, two old men staggered by, black silhouettes in the silver moonlight and drunk as coots. They passed under the guns, unaware. I ignored the urge for a cigarette and concentrated on trying to pick out the policemen scattered under nearby bushes. There was nothing I could see to betray their presence. The occasional pulsing glow of lightning on the northern horizon captured my attention for a while. Towering clouds would suddenly appear, lit from inside as the lightning flickered on, then off again, the cloud disappearing once more into the night, too far away to hear even the faintest rumble of thunder. As if awakened by the distant glimmers, something chirped sleepily in the calm night, then fell silent again. I stifled a yawn and rested the side of my head in the crook of my arm.

I opened my eyes to the first pale light of early dawn. I'd been sound asleep. Some war correspondent, I thought, rubbing my eyes and stretching casually in the hope no one had noticed. Brand was on the portable radio, telling Otto that nothing had happened and that we were ready to be picked up.

"Have a nice sleep?" he asked pointedly, turning to pack the radio.

Looking around me, I saw that the ambush team members already were standing and stretching stiff backs and arms. With morning, the ambush site was no longer tenable. Too many of the local population used it. Koos waved me across to his side, and we walked to the yati, a wide swath through the bush that separated Angola from Namibia. He pointed toward a muddy pool of scum-covered water reeking of cow urine and asked if I wanted to wash. I took a whiff and politely declined. Koos carefully scanned the tree line on the other side of the yati and grinned at me. "Christ, my back teeth are floating." Yeah, me, too," I allowed. And like a couple of kids on a dare, we scuttled across the border to relieve ourselves in Angola.

Brand liked working on foot, I was beginning to discover. "We're going to try a silent follow-up on the other side of the yati. Ten, maybe fifteen klicks is all. You want to come with us?" Which was sort of like adding: If you think you can handle it. Which didn't give me any choice at all. I also understood that the invitation was a mark of confidence; these black policemen had conferred a special trust just by allowing me to accompany them. If at any time they had told Marius or Koos that they didn't want me there, I would have been out. I already knew of at least one white policeman who had been transferred out of Koevoet at the insistence of the Ovambos.

"Where's so-and-so?" I had asked when I'd returned.

"Gone," was the brief answer.

"How come? He hadn't been here that long? Did he get hurt?"

"The blacks didn't want to work with him any more."

"Why?"

"We went into a contact, and a terr jumped out of the bush next to his car and opened up on him. He ducked down inside the car and froze. After it was all over, my senior black came to me to say he and the boys had talked it over, and they didn't want to go on another deployment with him. He told me they couldn't trust him after what happened."

"What should he have done if he couldn't get his guns around?"

"Used his R5 or pistol. Whatever. But he shouldn't have frozen."

We crossed the border and stopped in an area SWAPO insurgents often used on their way from the Angolan army base at Nama-kunde into Namibia. The idea was to move northeast; according to Brand, with a little luck we might intercept some of them before they reached the border. Unlike the night ambush attempt, where too many people were a liability, this time there were over thirty of us. Getting everything together, we had just started moving when we were called to a stop by some of the Ovambos. Shivute was doing the talking and pointing at me. Brand listened and turned to me.

"Otto's saying the boys are asking where your weapon is," he said with a deadpan expression. I asked him what the hell they were talking about. "They say you should have a weapon," Marius translated from Otto's Afrikaans. "They say if a terr jumps up in front of you maybe they won't see him in time, that he's going to shoot you while you're taking pictures of him. What they're saying is that if you're going to come along, they want you to carry a weapon."

I looked at the trackers. Behind their grins they were deadly serious. "Well, uh," I temporized, playing for time and shifting excuses through my mind. But the reality kept coming back. This wasn't some little boy's game where you fell down and got your clothes dirty after a playmate pointed his finger and said, "Kapow! I gotcha, yer dead!" When you were dead here, it was for keeps: no arguing with the other kids on the block over whether they got you or not.

I knew that many journalists in Vietnam had found themselves with weapons in their hands as part of the basic survival game. Some had actively participated in combat. When the shooting started, no one was going to ask if you were a noncombatant before taking a bead on you and squeezing the trigger. In spite of that, could I still justify going armed? I had known the risks before arriving and accepted them in my role as an observer. Where was the line drawn between journalist and participant?

"But why didn't they want me to carry one last night?" I asked, still holding out.

Marius spoke to them. Their faces broke into grins again.

"They say at night all blacks look the same," Brand answered. "They didn't want you to shoot one of them by mistake." Otto took an R5 from one of the Casspirs. He snapped a full magazine into it, drew back and released the charging bolt to chamber a round, clicked it to safety and brought it over to me. With another look at the determined faces, I accepted the short-barreled assault rifle and slipped the sling over my shoulder with a lot more casualness than I felt. Koos dropped an extra magazine into the deep pocket on the side of my trouser leg and patted my shoulder.

"You never know," he smiled.

As we began moving again, Brand glanced at me walking at his side. "Stay away from me and Koos. If we hit a contact, the three of us are going to be priority targets for the gooks, and two of us together are more likely to be seen. They're told to try to kill any whites they see first. See you later," and he strode away toward the left flank.

Thanks a lot, I thought. *Terrific.*

During the next two hours, we moved hard and fast through dense bush, slowing only when we came upon the occasional kraal. As we'd approach it across open fields of freshly sprouting mohango, the lack of cover was intensely uncomfortable. The feeling of naked vulnerability was eased when I looked to either side. Even to me, the skirmish line emerging from the bush to advance silently had a sinister, almost spooky aura about it. I could imagine what the Angolan peasants in their simple kraal felt at the unexpected sight.

Eyes flicked back and forth across the far undergrowth, everyone tensed and ready for the first shot of an ambush. We'd stop briefly in the primitive enclosure as the farmer and his family were separated and questioned. There would be a quick conference and then we'd immediately begin moving, regaining the welcome security of the bush on the other side.

We'd left one kraal ten minutes behind when I saw one of the trackers stop and wave two others toward him. They motioned me down, and I squatted on my haunches, grateful for the break. They alternately examined something on the ground and stared into the bush ahead. Tracks. One trotted off to find Brand, who soon weaved his way from the left to see what they had found. He squatted down next to the fresh, distinct spoor.

"FAPLA," he agreed with the Ovambos. "See the tread pattern of the boot?" he said to me. "SWAPO cuts them off the soles of their boots. This guy was probably heading south to visit the mission hospital just on the other side of the cutline. We arrested three of them there a few months ago. Their own medical care is so bad some of them sneak down to our side." His eyes traced across the terrain ahead. "We'll let him go. As fast as he's moving, he's already long gone. Probably saw us." Brand stood and laid the side of the rifle across his shoulder. "If there are any terrs between us and Namakunde, this guy has warned them for sure," he said disgustedly and stalked away. I rose to my feet at a sign from the

Ovambos. As we continued cautiously on our way, I noticed that the black policemen had casually repositioned themselves to my front and sides, keeping me covered in case we stumbled into an ambush. If the escaping FAPLA soldier had seen any SWAPO and warned them . . . .

For the entire two hours, I juggled the automatic weapon from shoulder to shoulder, across the back of my neck, slung under one arm and then the other, wondering just what would have to happen before I would use it. Only in self-defense? Of course that was the only justifiable scenario. Sure it was. They couldn't expect me to use it for any other purpose. They had to understand that the most exciting photos would be taken in the middle of a contact, when everything had gone for a ball of confusion. That's why I was here, looking for that one-in-a-million snap. I didn't have time to be shooting guns. That was their job, not mine. But what if I saw an insurgent taking aim at one of the Ovambo policemen around me? Was I to drop the gun and go for the camera and photo that might make me famous? Could I live with letting someone die — someone who trusted me — when I possibly could have prevented it? For the sake of a picture?

God knew, I wasn't there to kill anyone. Whatever adolescent fantasies I might have held about war, they had never included taking a life. My job was to observe, to take photos and notes, to report; yet here I was, carrying a loaded assault rifle. Once you had it, you couldn't be a shooter *and* a journalist-photographer, though the automatic rifle joined the three cameras as if to say: Don't worry, I can choose when the time comes, no problem, right? I tried to use the excuse that the Ovambos had forced me to carry it by not giving me the option of going unarmed (I would never get over their practical, down-to-earth paternalism toward me). But I did have the choice, and it had been mine alone: go armed with them, prepared to use the firepower in my hands as they had the right to expect, or stay with the cars until they returned. And without thinking of the consequences, I had chosen to go with them.

I struggled for two hours with doubts and questions. My acceptance of that weapon had raised a double-edged set of moral and ethical dilemmas that I never was able to resolve totally. The patrol was without incident. In the end, I knew there was only one answer. But I would never really know for sure.

("Hey, man, you ever carry a weapon on one of these trips?" "Are you kidding? That's the *last* thing I'd ever do.")

12

To Be Cruel in the Struggle Is to Do Good for the Future

S ERGEANT Jerry Mbwale was twenty-four years old, a bright, good-looking six-footer with six years in Koevoet. He couldn't really remember the number of contacts he'd been in, just laughing and shaking his head. "A lot, very many," he said.

Jerry was typical of the dedicated and aggressive young Ovambos who made up the bulk of Koevoet's NCOs. A member of Boesman's Zulu November when it was ambushed by the forty-man SWAPO detachment, Jerry had been seriously wounded when an RPG hit the Casspir he was riding in. Shrapnel from the Soviet-made rocket blinded him in one eye and left his chest and shoulders covered with a mass of raised scar tissue. As a result of his wounds, Jerry was taken off operations and made a special investigator.

Although most of his duties now entailed plain-clothes office work, he was not above dressing in captured camouflage, shouldering an AK or RPG, and with one or two of his operatives, slipping into the bush to visit remote pro-SWAPO kraals and beer-drinking Cuca shops. Posing as SWAPO freedom fighters, the information they picked up was often invaluable to Koevoet's counterinsurgency efforts.

When not working, Jerry studied hard to pass his exams so that he might eventually be eligible for a commission. It was difficult not to imagine him as one of Koevoet's first black officers.

Although his mother tongue was Oshivambo, his Afrikaans was equally fluent and his English more than passable. Over a cup of coffee one morning, he told me a little about himself.

"You know, my father, he doesn't have any [educational] qualification and did not understand why I should go to school. He just sent me to watch the cattle when I was a boy. At that time, I was very stupid and very young and didn't know anything. There was no difference between school and life. I told my father I wanted to be a policeman, but he said it was more important to have cattle than to be a policeman.

"Me, myself, I discussed things with political people who said we must go outside [to Angola] for better education so that we can bring freedom to Namibia, and that we must take the white people out and bring another white people in we can work with. But I couldn't understand why we should bring another white people in. I saw that SWAPO only wanted to take schoolchildren outside to become soldiers, not for education, but I didn't want to go. I discussed with myself that it was better to go to school here and become a policeman than to go outside.

"In 1979 I had to leave school because SWAPO took my uncle outside, and he was the one helping me with school and money. I did not understand the politics of SWAPO, but I thought this was very bad. They came during the night and just took him away. So, in 1980, I didn't tell my father I was leaving to become a policeman, because I knew he just wanted me to watch the cattle. But when I came to the police I did not know anything. But I could see that SWAPO was much worse than the South Africans. I wanted to fight against SWAPO. I thought to free my uncle from SWAPO in Angola, but I was very stupid because, perhaps, really he was already killed.

"You know, the black people in Namibia can go where they want, even they can live where they want. They can have good businesses, too, if they work hard. There are many rich black people in Namibia. I think, really, education is not so good, but it comes better, but SWAPO want to take the schoolchildren outside to make them soldiers. SWAPO, they are telling us this is freedom.

"I, myself, I have nice clothes and a car and a good house, and I am working for more education because for a policeman this is very important. I think, really, anyone can do this in Namibia. You know, these SWAPO who work in the bush are just stupid people who make a lot of trouble. They are telling us it is for freedom, but I, myself, I do not believe it."

The following document was taken from a SWAPO insurgent by the name of Jostu Tutaleni, the intelligence secretary of the Central Region. He was killed by Koevoet on September 20, 1985.

Copy No 02

RHQ [Regional Hq]

NF [Northern Front]

17/03/85

TO ALL DET COMMISAR

Dear Comrades,

Our liberation struggle is now approaching . . . another stage of criticality which of course created by the powerfull forces of occupation with the sole purpose of the independence of our country Namibia.

The RHQs has critically tried to analyse the situation in Namibia and in our operational sector in particular and drawing examples from our many setbacks and the work of our political department in regard with the political mobilization of the masses and political work among our Combatants were reassessed. Viewing the facts of the past we concluded that drastic measures should be taken to regain the support of the masses. The RHQ put emphasis on our organization standing through these difficult times. The following guides should be followed during the Political Mobilization among the masses and own troops.

—Try to make the masses understand the critical situation for PLAN and they must stay in high morale for the future.

—The use of force is allowed on those who do not want to support the organization.

—Enemy propaganda should be countered as soon as heard or dropped in an area of our jurisdiction because we cannot alow a further drop in morale.

—Meetings should be conducted to individual persons or collectively whenever applicable but always remain vigilant of the large number of puppets and agents of our regime in our midst.

—Murder should be limited only to suspected enemy agents and supporters.

—Large numbers of children if possible a whole village or school must be captured to rebuild our organization.

—A revolutionary has always a goal to achieve. To be cruel in the struggle is to do good for the future.

—We must expose the atrocities committed by our own people, but side them to the enemy. Therefore atrocities should not be committed in front of masses.

—The firing squad will be re-implemented for cases of desertion among own troops. Only detachment cmdrs are authorized to judge and execute after recommendation by det cmsrs. Personal belongings and statements must be sent with monthly report. This aforementioned is the task that is on the shoulders of all det commisars and their substitutors to be carried out through the struggle.

—The revolutionary movements which is separated from the people will not in any way win Victory, or it victory cannot last long.

EVERYTHING FOR THE STRUGGLE, ALL FOR FINAL VICTORY

···   ···

MAPAYA YA MAPAYA   JOE ANCALA
RC [Regional Commander]   RPO [Regional Political
                                    Commissar]

Date: ....   Date: ....
CC   [Detachment Political
                                    Commissar]

Copy	no	01-Det	"D" DPC
"	"	02- "	"F" DPC
"	"	03- "	"E" DPC
"	"	04- "	"B" DPC
"	"	05- "	"C"

13

"I Am Going to My Daling Today"

January 2, 1987

Dear Sugar,

Have been here just over a month now, with most of that time spent in the veld. It's been exhausting, dirty, and frustrating, with everyone assuring me that it's still the quiet time, that we're still at least a couple of weeks away from the beginning of the annual summer infiltration. "It's always like this right now," they keep saying. "Don't worry, the terrs will come. Genuine," they add, as frustrated as I over the inaction. "The rains are still late; the terrs will come with the rains." So it's been lots of days rumbling across the landscape, watching the Ovambo special constables questioning the locals at their primitive kraals in the middle of nowhere, chasing and losing the occasional spoor, but all in all, a fairly undramatic time. Until three days after Christmas.

For two days I'd waited at Eenhana, a company-sized fire-support base, just south of the Angolan border, which Koevoet shared with the army and a small air force helicopter detachment. Teams used it for rebunkering, occasionally overnighting there. More important, it was their tactical radio link with the helicopters that served as airborne spotters and gun platforms. They could also provide immediate casualty evacuation in the event of injuries. My plans were to spend the week in the shade of a camouflage net, catching up on notes and hanging loose should a team scramble the choppers, the pilots saying they could set me down alongside or even right on top of one of the cars; "No problem," with the typical braggadocio of military pilots the world over.

So I buckled down to work, pounding the keys of the portable typewriter that had seen me through five other African countries (and been impounded in two). My dedication was short-lived. I found myself wandering more and more frequently to the ops room to ask Van, the radioman, if any group was following spoor. But each time he would raise his eyes, shake his close-cropped head and return to reading a well-worn paperback war novel. The lurid cover depicted a square-jawed, muscular hero firing an AK-47 one-handed, while the other arm encircled the waist of a statuesque blond clutching a ripped safari jacket over luscious, melon-sized breasts. Just like in real life.

By noon I'd closed the case on the typewriter and settled inside the air-conditioned ops room, thumbing through tattered back issues of *Huisgenoot,* a popular South African magazine. The only calls Van received were routine position reports. I'd watch him move the map pins that marked each group's updated location, then return to seeing how many familiar Afrikaans words I could pick from the journal—in between shooting surreptitious looks at the blond on the cover of Van's book.

"How much Afrikaans have you picked up?" Van asked, laying down the book and stretching.

I tossed the magazine aside in frustration; it might as well have been printed in Greek for all my understanding of it. And there wasn't a thing in it that compared with Van's blond. "In the bush I guess I can already understand about a third of what's being said," I allowed, shaking the last cigarette out of a crumpled pack and lighting up.

"Genuine?" he asked, visibly impressed.

"Sure," I said, tilting back my head and blowing a smoke ring toward the ceiling. "It's pretty easy when about every third word is 'fuck.'"

"Oh. Yeah," he admitted, blushing furiously.

"By the way," I asked casually, "mind if I have a look at your book?"

After two days of no calls and feeling guilty about not sharing the heat, dust and tedium of the bush (if I was going to do this story, understand what was happening, I had to be out there with the rest of them, not sitting safely in an air-conditioned radio room), I decided to join the next group to come in for rebunkering.

Among the fighting groups that rolled through the gates late on Saturday afternoon was Boats Botha and his team Zulu Foxtrot. Over a beer in the air force compound that night, I singled him out. Still a little unsure of myself and not knowing how individual members of the unit felt about an outsider taking up extra space in their already crowded cars, I talked around it until finally deciding that he was approachable. "Is it okay if I go out with you guys tomorrow, Boats?" I asked.

"Sure, Jim, yes, sure, no problem," he shrugged.

Small, married and thirtyish, Boats was one of the longest-serving members of the security forces in the operational area. Eleven years in the Eastern Caprivi, where he ran police boat patrols along the Zambezi River, preceded his three years with Koevoet. Behind an easy-going, almost placid personality, Boats Botha was an intense and extremely capable counterinsurgency professional. He was, in the parlance of the unit, "a good operator." But even good operators tended to make mistakes now and then, it seemed.

"There used to be a lot more ambushes along the Chandelier Road east of here," Boats reminisced a little sadly, as though disappointed they had tapered off. "We were here at Eenhana one morning, two, maybe three years ago, I guess. A couple of groups had already left. It was raining, so we weren't in a hurry to go. I was in the toilet when I heard firing. I thought it was only the army. You know, just practicing near the base or something, when one of my people ran in and said the groups that already left had hit an ambush not so far down the road. The choppers were already being scrambled. We jumped in the cars and got going. We were a couple of klicks down the road when one of my boys saw spoor going off the side, and I yelled at my driver to turn. When we turned off the road, the cars behind us didn't see us, so we were by ourselves. We were trying to follow the spoor, but the rain was washing it away fast so we knew they were bloody close. We had gone just a few hundred meters south of the road when I saw a terr standing behind a tree with an RPG. He was aiming at us, but he was already to our side, and I didn't know if I could reach him with the guns. I swung the guns as far as they could go and fired and saw him go down. We drove up to him, and I jumped out without my R5. He was still alive, and as the medic was working on him, I was trying to get info—you know, how many terrs, which way they had gone, what they were carrying.

"Suddenly, on my car's radio I heard Dave Atkinson, the chopper pilot, yelling, 'Boats! Boats! Behind you! Look behind you!' I looked around, and man, there was a terr not more than thirty meters away coming down on me with a Dragunov sniper rifle. There was nothing I could do. No weapon, no time to get behind something—I was a dead man. That terr had me. Major Dave just put that chopper on its side, and the flight engineer floored him with his 20-mm on the first burst.

"Guess I was lucky," he sighed, running his fingers through his short, sandy hair. "I still have that Dragunov. Nice scope on it. And accurate. But we don't get many ambushes along there any more," he added.

Of Botha's car commanders, Flip Fouche was wiry and red-headed with a quick, aggressive temper to match his hair, while Marius Gous was big, quiet, dark-haired and tending to weight. Both Flip and Gous had a few years behind them in Koevoet. Herman was the new guy in Zulu Foxtrot. Well built and athletic, he was, like Flip, a graduate of the police special task force school.[a] Unlike Flip, however, he had yet to experience his first contact as we pulled out of Eenhana the next morning and headed east.

By midmorning, we received a radio call from the group leader of Zulu Charlie; his men were following the tracks of five insurgents who appeared to be moving north. We rendezvoused with them half an hour later, and Zulu Foxtrot took the spoor while Zulu Charlie moved ahead in overall command of the follow-up. (Protocol dictated that the leader of the group that discovered spoor had tactical control of the chase, regardless of his rank. If a group leader with the rank of sergeant requested assistance from another with the rank of warrant officer, the warrant officer responded to the sergeant's directions.)

Not fifteen minutes had gone by when Zulu Charlie's trackers

---

[a] Equivalent to SWAT in the United States.

scrambled the helicopters; they had fresh spoor that was no more than ten minutes old. A third fighting group joined us in the suddenly fast-moving chase that led us and the orbiting gunships across the border and increasingly deeper into Angola. After two hours of steady pursuit, the spoor quickly petered out on hard ground, and the groups fanned out to try finding it again.

With the sun almost directly overhead, the helicopters landed to refuel from the barrels of jet fuel carried in the supply vehicles. The cars pulled under scattered trees, while the trackers set up a defensive perimeter to provide security for the vulnerable choppers. Boats was talking over the radio when the frequency he was using was overwhelmed with a curious static. Puzzled, he waited a moment and tried again. Within seconds, his conversation with Zulu Charlie's group leader was blanked out once more by the same static. He dropped inside and switched to another frequency. Again, it was interrupted. "Maybe someone's trying to jam you," I suggested.

Boats continued going through different frequencies. In each case, there was an overriding signal. "Shit!" he suddenly exclaimed. "That's not jamming, that's another radio set! There are terrs right here with a radio!" He shouted his discovery to the pilots, who immediately suspended the refueling and lifted off, the long barrels of the 20-mm guns sweeping the bush to the left of the choppers' flight paths. As soon as they were clear, we set off again, searching rapidly through the nearby bush in ever-widening circles as weapons were cocked and heads swiveled back and forth, looking for running insurgents.

We stopped briefly alongside the decaying, pink shells of once-graceful Portuguese villas at Chiede while the trackers swept through the crumbling ruins. A platoon of gray-green lizards darted ahead of us into the safety of shadowed rubble, annoyed at the unexpected intrusion. Long-untended bougainvillea straggled over the bullet-pocked stucco. I stared at sun-blistered walls daubed with the fading slogans of three black liberation movements and tried to imagine what these homes must once have been. Where were the people who had lived here in the days before independence? On nostalgic evenings somewhere in the Algarve, were photo albums still occasionally opened to memories of a life long since gone? Did a mother in Lisbon or Estoril point to a curling, faded picture and say to her daughter, *And that was me when I was your age in Angola. It was such a beautiful place; I wonder what it's like now . . . .*

The trackers piling back into the car snapped me out of my reverie. One of the groups working voorsny had picked up the spoor again, and we raced on, leaving the villas at Chiede to the sun and silence and faraway memories. As the sound of our engines faded, the lizards slowly emerged from hiding places to reclaim what was theirs now.

The insurgents continued fleeing north until their anti-tracking techniques saved them from the chaotic manhunt going on around them. They escaped, disappearing into the bush. The groups turned south and headed toward the border. Shortly before reaching the cutline, Boats stopped to question an old man who was driving a pair of heavily laden donkeys northward. As the Ovambo policemen asked him about any insurgents he might have seen, I snapped a photo of his animals, each of which was carrying two large sacks of mealie meal. The sacks were clearly stamped Produce of South West Africa. I pointed them out to Boats, who smiled at my surprise.

"No, a lot of them cross the border to buy things. Haven't you noticed there aren't any Cuca shops on the Angolan side? They'd have to go a long way north to buy anything, and even then there's not much available according to guys like this one. It's a lot easier for them to get what they need in South West. They're supposed to cross at Oshikango and show their papers, but most of them just cross the cutline wherever they feel like it. The only reason we even bother to stop and talk with them is that we usually get a lot of good info. Not many are what you'd call pro-SWAPO. The terrs treat them like shit because they can get away with it. And if they complain to the FAPLA, well, SWAPO uses FAPLA bases all the time, so they're not going to do anything about it. The civvies up here have it a lot worse than the ones on the other side. You don't find too many that are pro-SWAPO, I can promise you.

"No," he said, watching as the old fellow laid a switch on the rumps of his donkeys and continued unmolested into the bush, "we'll stop and talk to them about the Swaps, but we don't bother them about crossing the cutline. They've got to make a living some way."

That night outside the Security Branch base at Ohangwena, Old Tom, Zulu Foxtrot's senior Ovambo warrant officer, sat cross-legged side by side with Boats next to the campfire and analyzed what had gone wrong with the day's follow-up, drawing diagrams in the sand with his finger. As one of the founding members of Koevoet, Tom had seen everything there was to see in this war. Boats listened attentively, nodding and asking questions as Tom made his points. Tom finally brushed his hands off against his legs, stood and walked off to check on the men.

"What was all that about?" I asked.

"No, Tom reckons we lost them because Neil — Zulu Charlie's group leader — was just too uncoordinated. The hell with tradition — Tom thinks we should have taken over. He's sure we went right by them, probably within a few feet. He said that at one point we were only five minutes behind, that we were just too close for them to have gotten away. I think he's right. That old man knows what he's talking about. Did you hear what he did last week?"

I shook my head.

"We were on a follow-up. The bush was really thick, so we were moving slow. Tom was in the front. Man, he looked up, and there were two terrs. One of them had an RPG on his shoulder, lining up on one of the cars. Tom had left his R5 in the car — all he had was a stick in his hand — and there wasn't time to pull his pistol. The other terr was just moving some bush out of the way to give his pal a clear shot. Tom raised his stick over his head, screamed and charged them. Yeah. Took them by surprise just long enough for the trackers behind Tom to kill them before they could shoot. Genuine."

Early next morning, Boats switched areas, and before the dew had dried, Zulu Foxtrot had good information: five SWAPO, armed and uniformed, had stopped the night before at a small Cuca shop in a nearby village. None of the locals questioned by the Ovambo constables knew which way the five had gone, only that they had been drinking there until midnight. Although the information was solid, the ground was hard and blanketed with the sharp prints of cattle hooves. Flip suspected the five insurgents had friends or relatives in the area who had intentionally obliterated the evidence by driving their herds along the path they had taken. Even if the constables found spoor, it would be almost impossible to separate and identify from the fresh civilian and cattle tracks crisscrossing the area.

We stopped near the collection of traditional huts and tin shanties of the nondescript village. Feverish from the onset of my first malaria attack, and bored at the prospect of another long and inconclusive day, I stood inside the Wolf and leaned forward, crossing my forearms on top of the open well and resting my chin on them. Aside from someone's admission that SWAPO had been here a few hours earlier, there was nothing to suggest this place was any different from a dozen other villages scattered along the length of the Oom Willie Road. Wondering if I had been too optimistic about pursuing what so far was a non-story, I quietly took in the scene. A few elderly men sat in the sun, puffing pipes filled with homegrown tobacco. Women passed to and fro with bundles of firewood or buckets of water balanced on their heads. Half-naked children played in the dirt. All seemed oblivious to our presence.

Boats and the trackers were out of the cars, casting about for spoor. In spite of a splitting headache and stiff joints, I climbed out to join them. The one Ovambo policeman still in the Wolf leaned over the side to pass a spare R5 down to me. I started to reach for it, then shook my head. Although there seemed little chance the insurgents were still in the area, I switched on my cameras, did a battery check and wiped a cleaning tissue over the lenses. In theory, at least, a contact could explode at any moment.

Of the other three car commanders, Herman and Gous were moving their cars slowly away from us toward the southeast, keeping their trackers covered. Flip, with a keener eye for identifying spoor than most of the whites, had dismounted to join them on the ground. Boats, the two trackers who had stayed with us, and I reboarded the Wolf to move up with the others. The other three cars were just to the east of a patch of low, scattered mopani bush about the size of a football field, surrounded by freshly tilled farmland. The morning air was still cool; the blue sky streaked with high, wispy mares' tails; the only sound the low rumble of idling diesel engines.

Daniel Taiko, one of Zulu Foxtrot's most experienced trackers,

"Running the cutline," the cleared strip separating Namibia from Angola, which lies to the right. These men constantly scan the ground for the spoor of infiltrating insurgents.

Lesch (group leader of Zulu Juliet) and Koevoet constables relax after a day of search-and-destroy operations. Note AK-47 hits on armored glass.

The 40-mm armored glass of this Wolf Turbo was easily penetrated by the RPG that killed Betoger, who was standing behind the twin .30-caliber Brownings.

Two Wolf Turbos and a Casspir pause on the southern edge of the cutline between Namibia and Angola to wait for the rest of their groups before continuing north.

The driver and gunner of Zulu Foxtrot's Strandwolf supply vehicle halt behind the lead Wolf Turbo in extremely dense bush. In areas such as this, where visibility was often down to 3 or 4 meters, ambush was a constant and very real threat.

Special warrant officer Otto Shivute, a six-year combat veteran with Koevoet, rests after running on the spoor of fleeing SWAPO insurgents.

Toit examines Phillip's wounds while Frikkie prepares a painkilling injection after the contact in Angola.

Ryno, Zulu Quebec's ops medic, in a private moment after trying to save Porky's life.

The ancient warrior, Piet Cronje, scans the harsh horizon of the Kaokoveld. His car carries a South African manufactured 20-mm cannon. The 60-mm mortar on a 360° swivel was a personal modification.

Toit, carrying a portable radio and an assault rifle, moves with trackers on the spoor of five insurgents.

Ovambo trackers have just kicked sand over the body of a SWAPO insurgent to show their contempt.

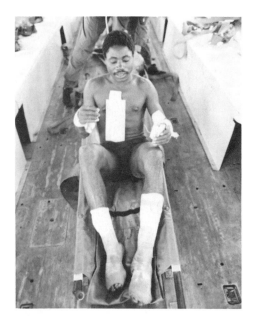

Caprivian member of SWATF, wounded by an exploding POM-Z antipersonnel mine, was flown to Eenhana and loaded on a C-47 for the flight to the primary trauma center at Ondangwa Air Force Base.

Two Alouette III gunships, 20-mm guns projecting from lefthand doors, lift off after being refueled from Blesbok supply vehicle deep inside Angola.

A badly wounded Koevoet constable is rushed to a waiting Alouette III helicopter.

Rapidly moving trackers use sticks to point out the individual footprints of fleeing SWAPO insurgents. The scarf, which is red, is considered a good luck charm since the color has certain magical qualities for some Ovambos.

Christo of Group Zulu Alpha cleans debris from the ammunition belt of his .50-caliber Browning.

From left to right: Flip Fouche, Daniel Taiko and Boats Botha with captured AKMs after the contact near Ondobe. Taiko was later killed in the April 1989 fighting during which fifteen-hundred heavily armed insurgents crossed the border in violation of truce agreements leading up to elections.

Riaan, hit through both arms, is supported by one of his men, who shields his face against sand blown from a descending helicopter while the ops medic yells that he is the next to be casevacked.

Wolf Turbo of Group Zulu Mike crosses the 'shona east of Oshikango in pursuit of SWAPO insurgents.

"Contact!" Ovambo trackers and Constable Jim duRand firing at SWAPO insurgents from a Casspir. White spots are debris from firing and grass kicked up by the Casspir's wheels.

Marius Brand, Ovambo trackers and Koos prepare to set out for a night ambush attempt as the sinking sun casts long shadows.

This young Ovambo special constable carries a belt of .50-caliber ammunition from the Koevoet stores to his Casspir.

Koevoet special constables disembark from a Casspir to follow spoor of SWAPO insurgents. Each man carries an Armscor 5.56-mm R5 assault rifle with 50-round magazine. For additional firepower, a captured RPG-7 accompanies them.

Tony of Group Zulu Hotel holds a TMA-III antitank "cheese mine" recovered from a cache pointed out by captured insurgents. The SADF sapper on the left and the Koevoet special warrant officer on the right hold 200- and 400-gm blocks of Russian TNT.

Sergeant Stephanus du Toit lights the fuse leading to a lump of plastic explosive atop a pile of captured "heatstrim" (anti-armor rifle grenades) after a contact in Angola.

SWAPO prisoner Petrus Hatutale is stripped and searched minutes after being captured by Group Zulu Hotel. Martin Hangula, arms tied behind his back, stands trembling and sweating at right. The two freedom fighters were sent into Namibia to murder a local elder suspected of passing information to the security forces.

Officers and men of Zulu Quebec and Zulu Uniform bow their heads in prayer before setting off from their TB outside the SADF base at Eenhana.

Just seconds before the author was hit, Casspirs of Zulu Quebec and Zulu Uniform race into the contact.

This Koevoet member, muscles tensed and eyes scanning the terrain, is caught by the camera just minutes before the first shots of a contact.

As Boats' Wolf Turbo races into the contact near Ondobe, these two constables, assault rifles ready, scan the surrounding area for insurgents.

Interior of a Casspir APC showing Armscor R5 assault rifles plus two captured Russian 7.62-mm PKM GPMGs and two 7.62-mm FN GPMGs, which are positioned to be fired through the spring-loaded gunports.

Author Jim Hooper moves with Zulu Quebec's trackers as they follow the spoor left by SWAPO insurgents.

had separated himself from the others when he spotted spoor that aroused his suspicion. He acted on a hunch and followed what at first appeared to be civilian tracks. A sixth sense that had come from years of combat told him that there was something different about these. The tracks led him into the mopani cover. Glancing up from the spoor, he saw a crouched, camouflage-clad figure whose attention was focused on the approaching cars and the cluster of men moving ahead of them. Unaware of Taiko's presence, the man was slowly backing deeper into the low bush. On the end of the insurgent's Soviet AKM assault rifle was a heat-strim anti-armor rifle grenade. Launched with a blank ballistic charge, the grenade had a range of 400 meters and was designed to burn through up to six inches of steel before spraying the inside of whatever it struck with white-hot shrapnel. The quarter-inch skin of the Wolf Turbos offered as little protection from the shaped charge as a sheet of tissue paper. As the figure ducked into thickening cover, Taiko brought his R5 up to his shoulder and opened fire.

We were 100 meters away when I heard the shots. I looked up at the sound and saw a red tracer spinning crazily through the air. As if confirmation were needed, red smoke spewed from the grenade Taiko had thrown to mark his contact position. I looked at Boats confusedly. What the hell . . . ?

Boats and the radio both yelled "CONTACT!" and I stumbled backward as the Wolf bellowed and lurched forward. I pulled myself up again and fumbled for the tape recorder. I wedged it next to Boats and stood in the open well behind him, Y-legged across the seats. Behind me, the two trackers were leaning out on either side, R5s chambered and ready, looking for targets.

We cut across the northern edge of the bush, then swung hard left to go down the western side. I dragged two cameras out, trying to keep my balance as the stiffly sprung 16-ton car took the choppy ground with jarring, knee-buckling shudders. A hundred feet to the left, I saw an armed figure in dark camouflage running through the low, scattered bush. One of ours? What would he be doing there? Then I saw geysers of sand erupting around him. I jerked the camera up and panned with my longest lens, trying to keep him in the viewfinder as we moved in opposite directions.

A fifteen-foot anthill was coming up on our left, and as we started to come abreast of it Boats saw another green-clad insurgent kneeling in thick bush at its base and firing at us. Boats swung the machine gun mount, but we'd gone too far to traverse the guns enough to hit him, and Boats was yelling "KOLOMOSHO! KOLOMOSHO!KOLOMOSHO!" (LEFT!LEFT!LEFT!) and the driver took us sharply around the anthill in a wrenching U-turn, heading north. Boats and the two Ovambo special constables were firing steadily. Bits of the anthill were exploding into dust and crumbling twenty feet away, the bottom of the fifteen-foot column punctuated by the bright orange spots of burning tracers from Boats's guns. Branches jerked violently and snapped off as the streams of bullets scythed through the hiding place.

At that moment, a bullet ricocheted off the opposite side of the car and whined quickly away (though I heard it only later when I replayed the tape). Unknown to us, another insurgent was hidden not more than seventy-five feet away, firing at us on full automatic. The overwhelming roar of machine guns and R5s completely masked the sound of the Soviet assault rifle. That he managed to miss as we passed broadside to him, and continued to miss as we pulled away, giving him almost a zero deflection shot, was no tribute to his Cuban instructors in Angola.

Ahead, Gous was also racing north in pursuit and firing on the one I'd seen running. This was the same insurgent Taiko had first seen and fired at. The heatstrim was still on the end of his rifle. Closing rapidly from behind, Marius couldn't hit him from the bouncing vehicle. The insurgent looked over his shoulder, then started to swing around to bring the heatstrim to bear on the Wolf. He was too slow; the car hit him, knocking the body forward and rolling over it with barely a bump.

Neliwa, the Ovambo manning the guns on Herman's car, now saw the insurgent who was firing on us as we pulled away from the anthill. I looked quickly over my shoulder and saw their car racing in at right angles to the path we had taken through the bush. The twin .30 caliber machine guns were firing, the close concentration of bullets raising a thick cloud of dust just ahead of the Wolf. I twisted around and clicked off one frame with the camera, not realizing that Neliwa had just killed the SWAPO insurgent who was firing at Boats and me.

Immediately to the east, Flip and the rest of the trackers were down, hugging the ground and hoping they were out of the line of fire. They were out of the fight. Boats knew they were there and was handling the contact with his .30 caliber Browning, leaving the .50 caliber alone. There was too great a chance of accidentally wounding or killing one of his own men with a ricocheting bullet from the heavier gun.

Then Boats was yelling "KOLOMOSHO!KOLOMOSHO! KOLOMOSHO!" again, and we heeled over in another U-turn, roaring south once more. Boats was firing sustained bursts with the .30 caliber Browning, raking the bush around the anthill. I was braced against the side of the car, pointing the wide angle where he was aiming, frame after frame clicking through the camera, when I was slammed forward as the Wolf hit a hidden tree stump, snapping the right front suspension with a loud crack. Then Boats was yelling "STOP! STOP!" and for a moment there was silence before the air was split with the whistles and shouts of adrenaline-stoked excitement.

I jumped out of the Wolf and ran after two of the black constables who were advancing into the mopani bush, R5s at the ready. Following ten feet behind them with a camera at my eye, I pushed through the leafy branches. As they stopped and leaned down, I felt something wet on my elbow. Glancing down, I saw a smear of blood. At first, I thought that it was mine, that I'd cut myself on something. Then I saw that the leaves around me were sprayed with it. Beneath my feet, a trail of fresh blood led toward the two policemen. When one of the constables looked up and waved me forward, I quickly backed out and took another route.

The insurgent at the foot of the anthill lay curled in a fetal position, still alive, but unconscious and dying. This was no Hollywood death scene. A fist-sized hole gaped on the side of his head; splintered white bone protruded from the left arm, and one leg below the knee lay at right angles, shot almost completely off. His other arm moved slowly, and involuntary mewing sounds came from his throat as the trackers dragged him clear of his hiding place, cut off the webbing and looked through his Libyan uniform for papers. A small notepad pulled from a hip pocket carried two fresh bullet holes. I photographed the scene and turned to look at the others. As I walked away, two closely spaced shots broke through the excited voices.

The insurgent Gous's driver had killed lay 100 feet to the north. The heatstrim on the end of the assault rifle was flattened from the 16-ton car that had rolled over it. My eyes traveled from the weapon to the insurgent's body; the same tire had gone over his head. I raised a camera, then lowered it, recording the scene only in my mind. (Mind, mind, which was what bubbled from his mouth.) I turned away before I gagged.

I walked to the southeastern corner, completing the triangle. The third insurgent was sprawled face down, and two Ovambo policemen were stripping the body of leather webbing and equipment. He had been the one firing at us as we rounded the anthill. As I was photographing the scene, Boats walked up behind me. Neliwa rolled the body over and spoke to Boats in Afrikaans. He pointed at the body, then stood and scribed imaginary lines through the air from where the body lay toward where we had made our first U-turn around the anthill. Boats shook his head and turned to me.

"Did you see any tracers?" Aside from one at the beginning of the contact, I couldn't remember any. "Neliwa said he didn't know there was a third terr till he saw tracers going by us coming from this one," he nodded at the body.

The Soviet assault rifle lay alongside. An empty magazine nearby emphasized the profusion of grayish-brown casings scattered over the ground. Taking my eyes from the scene at our feet, I looked over my shoulder at our tracks to note how close we had passed, then looked back at Neliwa. It all started to come together. The insurgent we were standing over had been right here, firing as we went by him. *How could he have missed?*

If Neliwa had not killed him at that moment, might the next round . . . or the one after that . . . ? I asked if I could fire off what was left in the weapon. Boats nodded, and we walked to another anthill. I flicked the selector to automatic and in a series of short bursts emptied the weapon's load of ball and tracer ammunition into the pillar of dirt.

Handing it back, I looked at the empty cartridge cases littering the ground, wondering if . . . and *if* . . . then which one? Walking to the car, I ran my finger over the bright scar a few feet from where we'd stood exposed during the contact. Where had the others gone? How close? Pointless to contemplate; impossible not to.

Yet through it all, there was a feeling of exultation. It was as real as any fantasy: too immediate to ignore, too intense to believe, too *now* with nothing ever before nor ever after—only a deep-welling and primitive immediacy of sensation. And as I listened to the tape afterwards, hearing the firing, the shouted commands from Boats and the two Ovambo policemen, the clatter of empty cartridges and links dropping on the steel plate under the machine gun, the whine of a ricocheting bullet aimed at us, I was stunned at the sound of someone's laughter.

The bodies of the three insurgents were stripped of equipment and searched for papers. A tattered pamphlet with a photo of SWAPO President Sam Nujoma on the cover was tossed on the ground. I picked it up and thumbed through the pages, surprised to find it printed in English. An article by Nujoma attacked the "murder squads" of Koevoet, 101 Battalion, and the Portuguese-speaking 32 Battalion and eulogized "the many comrades who have sacrificed." There were long, creative tallies of racist bases destroyed, South African soldiers killed and aircraft shot down. Whether wishful thinking or morale boosting for the benefit of simple peasant guerrillas like the three who lay here in the dust, none of it was true. The article finished by promising that this was "the year of final victory over the racist South African regime in Namibia."

Boats took the pamphlet from me and read sections to the Ovambo policemen, translating into Afrikaans as he went along. Those who listened hooted in derision and laughed aloud. "Sam's been promising for years that a military victory was right around the corner," Boats explained. He pointed at one of the bodies. "And he keeps convincing youngsters like these that he's right."

Boats laid the pamphlet aside and sorted through the rest of the papers taken from the body next to the anthill. A sheet of paper was unfolded to reveal a crudely drawn picture of an army base that the policemen recognized as the one at Okankolo. Stick men holding guns represented soldiers. Childishly sketched trucks might have been Casspirs entering and leaving the base.

These three had obviously been returning from a reconnaissance mission. Their ages and the fact that the leader had stopped where there was no chance of escape testified to their lack of experience and training.

I saw Boats thumbing through the damaged notepad. He stopped on one page and read it slowly. He shook his head and handed the opened note pad to me. I took it and began to read.

> it is good to have this opportun-
> ity to ratty to you
> because of love to you daling.
> Please tell me if you love me
> baby. But to me I love you and
> I love. Please daling dont forget
> my lovest to you daling.
>   I dont have meny to ratty
> to you Good bey daling.

I glanced up at Boats and turned the page.

> I love you daling
> I love you forever.
> Kiss me baby.
> I am very happy of you.
> I will not forget you baby.
> six is good to me and you.
> I am going to my daling to day
> I will cam to slipp to you.
> Yes or not daling?
> I will not forget my love to you daling.
> From Nakale Ya Nakale

I closed the stained pages and walked over to where Boats was standing next to his broken Wolf Turbo. I passed it back to him. He took it and raised an eyebrow.

"Poor bastard."

"Yeah."

"Didn't know what he was getting into."

"No. He didn't."

"Should've stayed home and married his girlfriend."

"Yeah. If they'd have let him."

The three bodies were tied with strips of bark to the bumper and spare tire of one of the cars. We drove back to the Oom Willie Road and stopped at the village of Ondobe to wait for a Casspir coming up from Oshakati. The investigative center had radioed to say they wanted to collect the bodies for possible identification by recently captured insurgents.

While we waited, Herman went into the Cuca shop and brought back a dozen beers for his first contact. Willem, one of Boats's senior Ovambo warrant officers, climbed into the car to join us. The Soviet-made compass he had taken from one of the dead insurgents was a rare find. Gous tried to bargain for it, but Willem only smiled and slipped the thin strap around his neck. Gous winked at me and rubbed his thumb and forefinger together: he'd eventually get the compass, but it was going to cost him. The other Ovambo special warrant officers climbed in to join us, and the beers went from mouth to mouth as the contact was relived.

Flip became the butt of jokes for being flat on the ground during the contact. All he could do was stay down and hope a stray bullet didn't catch him or anyone around him. His tight lips finally relaxed under the ribbing from the others. No one needed to point out that if Taiko had not seen the first insurgent, Flip and his men might have walked directly into the ambush. Instead of sitting here in the shade and sipping beers, some of them might at this moment be on casevac choppers racing for the primary trauma center at Ondangwa. Beers tilted gratefully towards Taiko.

One of the Ovambos lifted his chin toward me as he spoke to Boats. I looked at him and raised my eyebrows questioningly. "He said the boys are talking about the foreign *shirumbu*[b] who was standing up taking pictures," Boats translated. "They think you should stay down inside and take your pictures. So do I."

"I can't get the snaps if I can't see what's happening," I protested, surprised but childishly pleased they had noticed and remarked on it. "Besides, you're even more exposed up there behind those guns," I pointed out.

"Yeah, and that's why we take more injuries, man for man, than the Ovambos. But I'm up there because it's my job, and I

---

[b] Oshivambo for "white man."

know what I'm doing. That's what I get paid for. You're a big boy, so I'm not going to tell you what to do, but you get killed and I'm going to have a lot of paperwork to fill in." I smiled at him and said something stupid about everything being a calculated risk. Boats shrugged and let it pass.

Everyone agreed that the contact had been totally unexpected. The insurgents should have been gone long before we arrived. Had they been moving through a heavily patrolled area during broad daylight to show their contempt for the security forces? If so, it was a fatal decision on the part of an inexperienced reconnaissance team leader. It might have been a youthfully brave gesture to impress the locals—had they succeeded—but their mission was to bring back information. They had failed on both counts. Or had they made their overnight camp right where we found them and fatally overslept, waking to the sound of Zulu Foxtrot's Wolf Turbos? Christ, I thought, imagining the dread they must have felt when they first heard the cars. And what must have gone through their minds when they saw the entire group moving slowly toward them, knowing then there was no escape? No one would ever know.

I made my way through the tangle of black and white legs inside the car and climbed down to the ground. The Wolf Turbo with the three bodies tied to the outside was parked under a large tree next to the road. Ovambo civilians passed with hardly a glance at the grisly scene. Two women sat under the tree drinking Cokes, while not fifteen feet from them a steady drip of blood spattered the ground. The body of the insurgent who had been firing at Boats and me was draped over the spare tire high on the side of the car. I looked up at his young, handsome face. *If he had killed either of us,* I thought, *what difference would it have made? And what had his death done for the liberation of Namibia? Nothing. It was all such a waste. You poor, poor kid. Why did they have to send you down here?*

At some point while we were parked there, a passing Ovambo clergyman snapped a photo of the scene, showing the two bodies lashed to the front bumper and the third over the spare tire. It was sent to South Africa where it would be angrily splashed across a number of newspapers. Scathing editorials would attack Koevoet for its lack of respect for the dead, for its callousness in exhibiting the bodies. None would mention the atrocities committed by SWAPO against unarmed Ovambos who refused to support the liberation movement.

When the car from Zulu Three arrived, the bodies were transferred and the Casspir left for the trip back to Oshakati. Word came over the radio from headquarters that the three insurgents had brought the total of SWAPO killed or captured by Koevoet to 399 for the year. A cheer went up among the policemen. They shook hands and slapped each other on the backs as we rolled down the road.

Somewhere behind us the insignificant patch of low mopani bush was silent now save for the sound of bloated flies around thickening pools, while columns of ants marched to and from unexpected feasts on things more solid. Crimson spray splashed over bright green leaves had turned black under the heat of the sun. The faces of those it had all belonged to already were fading from memories. The only reminders would be their Kalashnikovs, spoils of war, which had been thrown carelessly on the floor of one of the cars. On the third day of Christmas.

I will not forget my love to you daling.
From Nakale Ya Nakale

14

Feeling Sorry for
the Poor Bastards

W E worked slowly eastward the rest of the day. As the adrenaline wore off, the sweats and fever and dull ache of the malaria returned. Herman handed me a handful of antimalarial tablets to swallow, promising the shock of them would make me feel worse for a while, but would knock the malaria back.

He was right. Before long, I felt much worse. We pulled into Eenhana base late that afternoon, and I decided to stay there the next day. I did, and then I didn't.

December 30, 1986

Boats and his group had been gone for an hour. I was sitting in the shaded air force compound trying to catch up on my notes again and not feeling at all well. Roelf Maritz, the Koevoet operations officer for the week, walked over from the radio room. He poured a cup of coffee and joined me at the expanded metal table. Smirking at my haggard appearance, he made a show of holding up an antimalarial tablet and washing it down with a swallow of milky coffee. True to form, I'd been following the example of my mentors by foregoing the bitter pills; screws up your tan, they'd told me.

"Looks like we might have a little activity already," Maritz said brightly, stirring his coffee. "Zulu Hotel's got good info on two terrs just up the road."

The Alouette pilots and flight engineers had dragged themselves from under their mosquito nets in the doorless, sand-bagged sleeping quarters. Hair tousled and dressed in loose-fitting flight suits, they sat or stood around the table under the plastic and nylon camouflage net, working on cups of milky tea or instant coffee.

"Zulu Hotel just called," Maritz told them, speaking English for my benefit. "They've picked up spoor not too far from here." He jabbed his cup toward the east, coffee slopping over the rim. He placed the cup on the table and wiped his hands. "Jasper said the PBs put them on to two terrs. He reckons they're about thirty minutes behind them and moving this way."

A few minutes later, Zulu Hotel called again to say they were less than three miles from Eenhana and following two insurgents dressed in civilian clothes. The chopper pilots moved quickly into their ops room to slip on shoulder holsters and plot the reported grid references. The flight engineers were already trotting out to make their preflight checks on the Alouette III helicopters. I laid the notepad aside and slipped my arms through the open sides of my camera vest, which was draped over the back of the chair.

Major Grant Brooks, the air force officer commanding the unit, came out of the radio room and settled into another chair at the table. Slender, bald and the fastest talking man I had ever met, he had put his neck on the line by officially-unofficially authorizing me to ride in the helicopters; "As long as the pilots don't mind you going along," he'd added. "It'll be up to them." I thanked him, knowing that not only was he doing it on his own responsibility—if something went wrong he'd be the one taking the heat—but that he was allowing me to see tactics and equipment that were considered somewhat sensitive.

"Well," he said when I expressed my gratitude, "sometimes you just have to take the chance." I suspected that had a formal request been passed up the chain of command, I'd have stayed firmly on the ground. "Just don't do anything silly," Brooks said, waggling a finger at me with mock severity. I crossed my heart and promised that I would do my very best not to embarrass either of us.

The pilots returned and took up their positions around the table again. The topic of conversation was unvarying. Like every pilot I'd ever met, their favorite subject was flying. As a pilot myself, we immediately had a common language and stories to swap. Although all of them were proficient in both Afrikaans and English, English seemed the language of choice. It was something of a relief not to have to struggle to understand Afrikaans or wait for a translation of what was being said.

Thirty minutes later, the call came to scramble, and I ran with the crews along the path that led over the berm, across a short bridge spanning a drainage ditch, and onto the hot tarmac where the choppers were spotted. A camouflage-painted C-47 transport, engines running, held its position inside the sandbagged revetment, waiting for our departure. The pilot showed me where to sit, and I settled on the aluminum deck next to him while he strapped himself into his seat and started the engine. As soon as the instruments were in the green, the Allouettes taxied on to the runway, and after a short takeoff roll, lifted into the hot, thin air. The flight engineer grasped the handlebar and chain attached to the breech block of the 20-mm gun and drew it backward against the heavy spring. He carefully eased it forward to chamber a yellow-nosed, high-explosive shell.

Climbing steadily, we were still within sight of the runway behind us when the pilot tapped my shoulder and pointed ahead and to the left, where a brilliant white cloud was billowing out of the gray-green terrain. It was from a white phosphorus grenade thrown by the Koevoet group that had scrambled the helicopters. We homed in on the smoke that was curling out of the bush and quickly dissipating. Over the spare set of earphones I slipped on, I heard the C-47 pilot advise that he had us in sight and was starting his own takeoff roll.

Jasper, Zulu Hotel's group leader, radioed the pilots that they were chasing two suspects in civilian clothes. Members of the local population had told them about the two men who had been hiding in the area for some weeks, intimidating the Ovambos in their scattered kraals. The locals had finally had enough when the two bayoneted an old man to death after accusing him of passing information about SWAPO movements to the security forces.

The helicopters passed over the Casspirs and set up wide orbits ahead of the trackers. Below us, I could see a dozen Ovambo policemen trotting through the bush. Flanking them were two

Casspirs. The other two cars were pulling ahead to look for the spoor farther forward. From above, the bush seemed surprisingly scattered. The impression from the air was deceptive; I knew that on the ground the visibility wasn't more than 30 or 40 meters.

Within minutes, we spotted two civilians a mile ahead of Zulu Hotel's trackers. They were ignored as the helicopter crews scanned the bush for running insurgents. On the next orbit, the two were much farther along the trail than a walking pace could have taken them; they had obviously been running when out of sight of the helicopters. The pilot tightened up his bank and passed over the pair at 200 feet. Neither looked up. I heard the click and hiss in my earphones as the pilot jabbed his finger on the microphone button, opening the channel.

"Hey, what would you do if a chopper was flying low around you, eh? Don't you think you'd probably look up at it? I think we might have a couple of terrs here."

I saw the flight engineer nod. Fingers poised on the heavy trigger, he swung the muzzle of the cannon and began tracking the two walkers. A brief squeeze would obliterate the two in the event we started receiving fire. We banked and flew over them again, circling not more than 100 feet above the ground. Although they appeared to be unarmed, there was still no lifting of heads to suggest they were aware of our presence. The pilot radiod Jasper to tell him he had the two civilians in sight. Jasper asked what they were wearing. The red shirt of one stood out brightly.

"Kill 'em!"

Negative, the pilots answered, we're not taking fire, and we don't see weapons.

"Kill 'em! They're the ones!" Jasper repeated. "The PBs told us one of them had a red shirt!"

Again the pilots refused and continued to circle tightly over the two, who were still walking and carefully ignoring the helicopters. I could see the trackers and Casspirs closing the distance. Minutes later, red smoke marked a spot below us. Contact! The trackers had caught up with them.

As we flew over, I saw two bodies face down next to a Casspir. The red shirt of one was clearly visible. Three or four trackers were standing next to them, weapons pointed down. Suddenly, dust rose around the horizontal figures under the guns. Then we had flown past the scene and I lost sight of them. Had I just witnessed an execution?

"They got 'em!" I heard in the earphones. I looked at the pilot. He was holding up two fingers. "Two, they said. Got 'em both."

I motioned that I wanted to join the cars. He nodded, came around in a wide orbit and set the chopper down next to a kraal a few hundred meters from the contact point. I jumped out and ran low under the whirling blades, glancing back to see the chopper lifting off in a thick swirl of red dust. A Casspir nosed its way out of the bush surrounding the kraal. Tony, one of Jasper's car commanders, stood up behind his gun mount and waved me forward. I ran to the open rear doors.

"Come on," Tony yelled over the sound of cars and choppers, "they've already admitted they're Swaps. They're going to show us where they've hidden their AKs!"

What did he say? Did they get the information before they killed them?

"They said they were carrying a pistol and a grenade, but threw them away when they knew we were behind them. Come on. Let's go!"

Climbing into Tony's car, I was surprised to see a prisoner. He was stripped to his shorts, with wrists tied tightly behind him with strips of bark. Sweating heavily, his chest still heaved from the chase. He looked terribly frightened.

They must have killed the other one to make this one talk, I thought, appalled at what I had seen.

We bumped and crashed through the dense bush for half a mile or so to the Oom Willie laterite road, where we stopped and disembarked to wait for the other cars. The faces of the trackers were sullen as the bound man was shoved out the door. He sprawled face down in the sand and was immediately jerked roughly to his feet and knocked down again by the Ovambo policemen. They spat and screamed abuse at him, hatred etched across their faces. Many had family and friends who had been wounded or killed by SWAPO.

The other three Casspirs and the Blesbok rumbled out of the bush and stopped on the side of road. My growing anger gave way to relief when the second prisoner, as alive and frightened as the first, was dragged roughly from the car and shoved toward his comrade. The Ovambo special constables ripped the shirt from him before knocking him down to yank his trousers off.

A senior NCO, who had once had both shoulders broken when the car he was in struck a SWAPO-laid land mine, threw the first prisoner face down on to the ground. He motioned for me to take a photograph. As I hesitated and then started to raise a camera, he jammed the muzzle of his rifle behind the prisoner's head. The safety catch came down with an audible click.

Oh, shit, I thought, lowering the camera, *I really don't want to see this.*

Tony bulled his way through the circle of trackers, shaking his head angrily. The NCO grinned evilly and drew the bolt back on the R5 to show an empty chamber. I took his photo.

The prisoners, barefoot and dressed only in their underwear, led the group to a spot in the middle of the bush 10 miles away. Yes, yes, they kept saying, we will show you our AKs. Their hands, which had been retied in front, were raised again and again to ward off threatened blows. The first few times that they pointed to a spot and began digging on their knees, nothing appeared. Each failure earned them kicks and punches from the Ovambo policemen. Thin, springy branches were stripped from trees and whipped across their bare backs, raising narrow welts.

When the caches were eventually located, two AK-47s, ammunition, POM-Z anti-personnel mines and moldy sets of Libyan uniforms with Cuban belt buckles were uncovered. When the last of the caches had been found, the two stood trembling and sweating as they awaited the torture and execution they had been told to expect at the hands of Koevoet. To their obvious surprise, they were manhandled back into the cars, and we returned to Eenhana. I was dropped off, and Zulu Hotel headed to Oshakati with Maritz and the prisoners. Intelligence officers were waiting to interrogate the two about the coming infiltration.

An hour later another team called for cover. I joined Maritz's replacement, Captain Klaus Koch, the one I'd heard about with the RPG-damaged arm. He'd recently returned from Pretoria and the latest in a series of operations to rebuild his arm. The stiff brace he wore from hand to the middle of his forearm didn't conceal the mass of shiny scar tissue and skin grafts. Koch took the seat next to the pilot, and I knelt on the floor, noting that this chopper carried a machine gun, rather than the much heavier 20-mm cannon with high-explosive shells. Fifteen minutes after takeoff we picked out four Casspirs and a Blesbok supply vehicle. They were spread out like the fingers of a hand and moving through the bush, trackers between and ahead of the cars. Everyone had his bush hat reversed to show a fluorescent red or yellow patch designed to immediately identify the wearers as friendly forces to the helicopters.

We had made two passes over them when I saw Koch pointing down and to our left. I lay quickly on the floor of the chopper and stuck my head and camera out the open door. Just ahead and below us an insurgent was dodging desperately through the bush and soft sand, a rucksack and RPG slung over his back. The flight engineer aimed through the reflector sight and squeezed off a burst, cursing when the weapon jammed after only a few rounds. As he worked to clear the stoppage, I glanced quickly back and saw a Casspir 50 meters behind the running figure, closing rapidly. It was impossible to hear anything over the screaming whine of the helicopter, but I could see that the Ovambo policeman in the car commander's position was firing, thin smoke erupting from the muzzles of the machine guns. I brought the camera to my eye, but was too late — we'd flown past the scene. I drew myself back to crouch next to the flight engineer, leaning over his shoulder to try to follow the unfolding drama as the pilot banked to the left, holding the turn. When we were on the far side of the orbit, I looked toward the contact point half a mile away and saw a cloud of dust and leaves hanging in the air.

I heard the click in my earphones. "They said a mine he was carrying exploded!" said the pilot. "That terr's just been spread over the landscape in lots of little pieces!"

We diverted to another group a few miles away. They were chasing a second insurgent who had split away from the one who'd been atomized by his own explosives. When it appeared the spoor was just minutes old, the chopper set me down and I climbed into one of Zulu Charlie's Casspirs. Neil, the group leader, took my place on the floor of the Alouette, hoping to spot the insurgent from the air. As it was, this one not only knew his anti-tracking, but could also run. He was eventually afforded grudging admiration by the trackers and car commanders, all of whom were exhausted after chasing him most of the day. We returned at sunset to Eenhana.

The next morning was the end of the week's deployment, and I hopped a ride with another group back to Oshakati. Dropping everything on my bed, I grabbed a towel and soap and headed for the showers. Just the thought of standing under the stream of hot water was enough to make me sigh with sensual anticipation. Lieutenant Chris Pieterse, one of the ops officers, intercepted me.

"Zulu Hotel's taking those two terrs back up, far, far, to lift a few caches they admitted knowing about. Couple days' trip at most. You should be back tomorrow. Interested?"

Hellfire and damnation, I thought, turning in my tracks and heading back to my room, *no New Year's celebrations for you tonight.* I grabbed a fresh stock of film and ran out the door with everything I'd just come in with, including a week's worth of dirt and dried sweat. The two SWAPO insurgents, shirts tied over their eyes to prevent their seeing the interior layout of the compound, were led in leg irons from their cells and shoved into a Casspir. Swollen and puffy faces indicated rough treatment at the hands of their Ovambo interrogators.

There was a quick stop at the Oshakati gate to pick up four freshly scrubbed and starched army sappers who were waiting for us. They loaded boxes containing mine-detecting equipment into the cars, and off we went, retracing the trip I'd just made from Eenhana, then across the border and deep into the Angolan bush.

Directed by the two prisoners, each in a separate Casspir, we leap frogged through the thick undergrowth, stopping at irregular intervals to climb out and follow the two, who wandered about trying to remember where the caches had been hidden. The sappers unboxed their mine detectors, assembled them with loving care and began sweeping the areas indicated by the pair. As we moved from one remote spot to another, a pile of East bloc munitions slowly grew in the back of the Blesbok. Digging into the soft sand exposed dozens of mortar rounds, blocks of TNT, rocket-propelled grenades and antitank "cheese" mines—large, rounds blocks of solid TNT. When the prisoners claimed to have forgotten the exact locations of their caches, memories were sharpened with cuffs and shouts. One buried supply of ammunition had already been lifted by SWAPO; steel bands that had gone around the wooden boxes lay rusting on the shadow-dappled ground.

Jasper, Zulu Hotel's group leader, was a loner even by Koevoet standards. An olive-complexioned, good-looking twenty-four-year-old, he seemed utterly devoid of warmth. When we'd stop at a spot in the bush pointed out by the prisoners, Jasper would stand or hunker down to one side, seemingly detached, but watching carefully as the men searched for the hidden cache. His rare smiles never reached his eyes.

Tony, part Portuguese, with black, curly hair and an easy manner, balanced Jasper's iciness. His easy command of English would later allow me to interview the prisoners after a day of digging up buried munitions.

When we stopped to begin setting up a TB, I noticed the four army sappers in a tight, prim group, casting disapproving eyes on the many cooking fires being started. They looked painfully innocent in comparison to the blacks and whites of Zulu Hotel. Each shout and burst of laughter among the policemen as they unloaded boxes of equipment, cut tent poles and rattled coffee cups brought severe frowns that said clearly, "This is *not* the way we do it in the defense force."

I was stretching my poncho between two saplings when the lieutenant detached himself from his men. "Hello. You're an American journalist?" he asked doubtfully, surveying my grubby bush clothes and dirt-streaked face and arms. No journalist *he'd* ever heard of looked like I did.

"Yeah," I nodded, holding out a filthy hand and introducing myself.

He shook it, wiped his hand unconsciously on his trousers and looked incredulously around the noisy, bustling camp. "How long have you been with Koevoet?"

"Only about a month."

He nodded and pressed his lips together. "Uh, do they always operate like this?"

"I guess so. I don't know, really. What do you mean?"

"Ah . . . well, is a TB usually this noisy?"

"Oh, sure. Sometimes even louder."

"And the, uh, the fires?" he chuckled nonchalantly. "They usually build fires? Just like these?"

"Yeah, sure. Why?"

He didn't answer, just nodded some more, the up and down eventually shifting to back and forth as his eyes took in the scene again. He opened his mouth to say something, then closed it. He cleared his throat and started again. "When do they put out pickets?"

"Put out what?"

"Pickets," he repeated weakly. "Guards."

"Oh, I don't think they bother too much with that," I said, trying to be helpful. "But you don't have to worry," I added reassuringly. "The Swaps can't hit shit anyway."

He stared at me for a long moment. "Bloody hell," he finally breathed, then "Excuse me," and marched grim-faced back to his men, steering a wide course around Tony, who was furiously pegging down the sides of his poncho and swearing obscenely about missing Koevoet's New Year's party.

When I next looked, the four sappers were laying out fields of fire and positioning their weapons from behind equipment boxes. The lieutenant held a notepad and ticked off items as he told his men who would be following whom as pickets through the night. Later, I noticed them clustered tightly together within their redoubt, dipping spoons into cold ration-pack tins as disbelieving eyes followed the outrageous scenes around them.

That night, sitting around a camp-fire where the two insurgents were manacled together, I asked Jasper if I could put some questions to them. Given the situation, I knew I'd have to weigh the fact that the two were still convinced that they were going to be shot and would likely say what they thought their captors wanted to hear. Jasper nodded his consent, and I began by asking them about their years with SWAPO.

Petrus Hatutale, twenty-seven years old, had crossed into Angola in 1978, having heard that joining the liberation movement would give him educational opportunities that were unavailable to blacks in Namibia. On crossing the border, he was taken immediately to Lubango Camp in central Angola, he said. There, the young men who had left Namibia for promised education were given courses in weapons training and political indoctrination. The Cuban instructors told his group that Namibia must first be freed from the racist regime of South Africa at all costs. All men would then be equal. When Namibia was free, they would have all the education they wanted. Until then, however, they would have to fight. To refuse the honor of participating in the armed struggle was to be branded an enemy of the revolution.

For all the talk of equality, Hatutale admitted, the Cuban and Soviet instructors lived in comfortable homes surrounding the camp and had plenty of food. They and the SWAPO cadres also enjoyed *droit de seigneur* with the female "comrades" who had escaped across the border from South African oppression. The Namibians undergoing training slept in dugouts on beds made of branches covered with grass and often went hungry, he said.

Hatutale had made five infiltrations into Namibia since joining SWAPO. On two other attempted infiltrations, he had been wounded in contacts with black forces before his group had crossed the Angolan border. He wasn't sure which enemy units they were, but he thought UNITA or 32 Battalion. He pointed proudly to a scar on his shoulder and lifted his head to show another under his jaw. After his second wound, he thought of quitting, but anyone who refused to fight was taken back to Lubango and never heard of again.

He had eventually been promoted to logistics commander of Echo Detachment, but after a few months was demoted back to the ranks. Why had he been demoted? Tony asked. "I could not remember where I had buried a big weapons cache," he said sadly. "The detachment commander was very angry."

In 1983 he had been part of a six-man unit sent into Ovamboland to ambush only "soft targets," civilian cars and pickup trucks owned by Ovambos. En route to the designated area of operations, the unit's spoor was discovered by a Koevoet team. Near Okatope, Hatutale lost four of his comrades in the ensuing contact.

"I was not told why to kill civilians, just to kill them, because it would help to bring freedom to Namibia."

On his last trip across the border, he had been in command

of a four-man assassination squad. The orders from Shekudike, the commander of Echo Detachment, were to kill an old man named Eliaser Wangushu, who lived near Eenhana and was suspected of passing information to the security forces over a hidden radio. Hatutale had been chosen to lead the squad because he had grown up near Eenhana and knew the old man. Wangushu's nickname, he remembered from his childhood, was Fandi.

"We went to his kraal one night," Hatutale told us, "and questioned him about the radio and helping the security forces. He said he had never done such a thing."

"Did they find a radio?"

"No."

What happened then?

"I told Denga kaGerman—he called himself that because he was trained in East Germany—and one other to take Fandi away from the kraal and kill him while I spoke with the old man's wife. I told Denga kaGerman to stab him with the bayonet of his SKS rifle so there would be no noise."

Tony finished interpreting the answer and added: "There's no way I can prove it, but the odds are that he did it himself. He'd have gotten a big pat on the shoulder from his detachment commander for handling it personally. Killing a suspected informer—especially one he had known before joining SWAPO—would have shown his commitment to the liberation struggle. But you can be sure he's not going to admit it now."

"Ask him what Fandi's wife said when her husband was taken away to be killed," I said.

"She said he didn't have a radio, but that he was not a big supporter of SWAPO, so she understood why we must kill him. When Denga kaGerman took him away, she gave us food."

How did he feel about ordering the death of an old man he had known since he was a boy? Hatutale shrugged; it was forbidden to question orders.

The other prisoner, Martin Hangula, accepted a cigarette with his right hand, touching the forearm with his left fingers as good Ovambo manners required. He could speak fluent Afrikaans from having worked on the railroads in Namibia.

Yes, he also had been recruited by SWAPO ten years earlier with promises of education and money, but the only education he had received was at Lubango Camp, where he learned to use Soviet light-infantry weapons. He was not happy there, but he was not allowed to leave. What did the political commissars tell him about why he was fighting? I asked.

"To make Namibia free so that everyone will have good education and a nice house and a car."

I asked him through Tony if he had ever taken young Namibians into Angola. He shook his head. He had never been ordered to do it, but others he knew in PLAN had carried out abductions. What did they do if the ones they were taking to Angola didn't want to go? I asked. I waited while Tony questioned him. When the answer came back, Tony turned to me.

"He says that whoever makes the most noise about refusing to go—whoever's the most difficult one—is beaten up. He says that usually convinces the others. Sometimes, he says, it is necessary to kill the one who refuses the loudest because the others won't go if that one is allowed to stay. Usually it's not necessary, he says, and sometimes they go without anyone making any problems at all."

This was only his third infiltration into Namibia. He had contracted tuberculosis at Lubango and couldn't run very far, so most of his time in SWAPO had been spent far to the north in Angola, guarding roads against UNITA.

"For someone with tuberculosis you were running pretty fast when we caught you," said Tony.

"I was very nervous," Hangula said seriously. When the laughter from the men subsided, Tony directed more of my questions to him.

Did his political instructors explain the system of scientific socialism that SWAPO President Sam Nujoma planned to impose on Namibia? Martin Hangula had never heard of it. Did he know that SWAPO claimed to have discovered and arrested one hundred South African spies in its senior ranks, or that Andreas Shipanga, once SWAPO's minister of information, was now a senior member in the Namibian Government, or that SWAPO vice president Misheke Muyongo had returned to Namibia last year?

Not only had he never heard the names, he said, but "As simple soldiers, we would never be told such things."

Had he ever thought about leaving SWAPO?

"Yes, but we were told that even if we surrender, the security forces will torture us to death and that if we try to return secretly to our kraals to live quietly, SWAPO will surely find us and kill us."

Tony looked at me. "You almost have to feel sorry for the poor bastards. They can't tell SWAPO they want to stop fighting, because they'll be shot by their own people. They're afraid to give themselves up to us, because they believe we'll kill them. Some of the Swaps have actually committed suicide when they thought they might be captured and tortured to death. A lot of the ones we capture are just like these two, forced to go on fighting until we kill them or, if they're lucky, arrest them. You really almost have to feel sorry for them."

Yeah, I guess you do have to feel sorry for them, I thought, as I crawled into my sleeping bag on that New Year's Eve in 1986, and dropped off to sleep long before 1987 arrived. *You really do.*

Out of sight far to the north, towering thunderstorms battered Angola, the heavy downpours soaking parched earth and filling dry streambeds. Lightning pulsed and shimmered on the horizon, edging slowly southward as we slept.

15

The Most Ruthless
Killing Machine

O N our return to Oshakati, a quick peek at the situation
board in the ops room showed everything blessedly quiet.
From the pained expressions and faltering steps of the men who'd
seen in the New Year, however, it was obvious they'd hit some
serious ambushes and taken heavy casualties in the canteen.

Half an hour under a steaming shower finally left me feeling
reasonably clean and human again. I kicked the dirt- and sweat-
stiffened bush clothes into a corner, pulled on fresh jeans and a
T-shirt, slipped my feet into a pair of flip-flops and wandered
down the street to Bernie Ley's house. I accepted a beer and
dropped thankfully into a soft armchair.

"So how's it going," he asked after we'd Happy New Year-ed
and tilted our beers at each other. "Reckon you're getting the
stories and pictures you wanted?"

Closing my eyes, I took a long swallow of the ice-cold brew
and sighed contentedly. Pure heaven. "I think so, but you never
really have enough, I guess."

"Is it what you expected?"

"I don't really think I knew what to expect," I admitted, kicking
off the flip-flops and wriggling my toes. The thick shag carpet
under my feet felt splendidly luxurious and sybaritic after ten
days in the bush. "When I left here last year, I thought I was the
world's expert on this war. Looking back, I guess the only thing
those two weeks did was give me a little background to build on.
The mistake I made after my first trip here—and the one I think

most journalists tend to make—was seeing the war itself as the
story. But that's only the backdrop, the setting. The real story is
the people: what they think, why they're here, how they handle the
whole thing."

"So why do you think they're here?"

"For a lot of reasons, not the least of which is the ego trip of
being with Koevoet. Which isn't as superficial as it sounds, I
hasten to add. I mean, it's something that's awfully easy to fall
into. Hell," I admitted, shaking my head in open confession,
"whenever we stop at an army base, I enjoy the looks we get from
those kids. It's silly, and I should be old enough to know better,
but I find myself swaggering right along with the rest of them, trying to look tough and wearing my dirt like some kind of badge.
I know I'm supposed to keep myself detached, but it's damned
difficult when you get to know them."

"How do they strike you so far?"

"Tough, competitive, reasonably bright; not many dummies
among them. And, for the most part—ego aside—they're here
because they love the action. In psychological terms, they're
what's known as 'high-level stress seekers.' These boys are addicts,
adrenaline junkies, pure and simple. They get off on the high that
combat gives them. Not very fashionable these days, but it's certainly not an unknown personality type. And I suspect that in the
end—when this thing is all over—a lot of them are going to be
terribly disappointed and bitter."

"Why do you say that?"

"I remember a somewhat drunken conversation with an old
friend a few years ago. He'd spent twenty years in the American special forces and a fair amount of time in Vietnam: three
thirteen-months tours, and all of it special ops. In retrospect, it's
curious that he should have used the word he did to describe himself and others in the same line of work. Care to guess what it
was?"

He shook his head.

"You're not going to believe this, but it was 'crowbar.' Honest
to God. I remember him saying, 'We're society's crowbar. They
hate us, they never want to acknowledge the dirty jobs they give
us to do, but when the job is done they never throw us away—they
just slip us back in the toolbox until they need us the next time.

And there will always be a next time.' I suppose he was a little bitter. He'd seen a lot of shit, probably killed a lot of people, seen friends die. And when he finally came home to the society he thought he'd been doing it all for, you know what? — he was an embarrassment to it. It didn't want to know him anymore. It certainly didn't want to publicly acknowledge what he had done at its request. I sometimes wonder if these guys here aren't going to have the same thing happen to them when this is over.

"Still, it's a two-way street: society gives them the opportunity to go off and do what they want. It says, 'Okay, there's the bad guys and here's the equipment and here are the rules; do what you have to do within these rules to stop them.' It gives them the most extraordinary freedom of action they'll ever know. It gives them a reputation which sets them apart from the rest of society. And they're so red hot to go off and live at kill-or-be-killed that they accept the terms. What society never explains is what becomes of them when it's all over and they have to come back to the real world. Where they're suddenly expected to live like Joe Shit the Rag Man next door rather than part of 'the most ruthless killing machine in the world.'"

"Where did you hear that?" he asked.

"Well," I allowed, looking at my bare feet and deciding it was time to broach it, "I did a bit of reading up on this bunch before coming back, you know, and there was a lot that was pretty disturbing. I hadn't realized last year that Koevoet was so famous — if you want to use that word. Notorious would be more apt. And for good reason, if I can believe even half of the clippings from your own South African papers. You haven't exactly had what you might call a positive press. I'm a little confused."

"About what?"

"Most of what I've read paints an entirely different picture from what I've seen so far. Everyone here's supposed to be a murderer, a torturer or a rapist. You name it, and they're guilty of it, according to SWAPO, the churches and some of the press back in South Africa. Okay, I've seen that they're no bunch of choirboys, but they hardly fit their popular image of cold-blooded psychopaths, either."

"So what is it that's bothering you?"

"Look: where there's smoke, there's got to be at least a little fire somewhere, right? Only I haven't seen any of it yet. What'd you do, hide all the bad ones before I got here? Transfer them all out to Rundu or Opuwa? Ship 'em back to South Africa? Where do all the stories come from?"

"How long have you been here now?"

"I don't know. Counting last year, I guess about six weeks, maybe a little less."

"And? Seen anyone beaten or tortured so far? Seen any civvie bodies left in the dust? And for God's sake, don't leave out any rapes you might have witnessed, either."

I balanced the beer on my stomach and pointedly raised an eyebrow at him. "You know as well as I do that having a journalist around can do wonders for people's manners."

"Sure, but you've gotten to know some of these people by now. Do they fit the image you've read about? You think they're all closet baby killers just waiting for you to leave so they can get back to what they really enjoy?"

"No, I don't. And that's what puzzles me. Where do all the atrocity stories come from?"

"No, I can tell you that some of them did happen. I'll also tell you that some of them were the products of overly imaginative journalists who've never been here. Or journalists whose sympathies lie with SWAPO. Not all, I will admit, but some."

"When I interviewed the SWAPO representative in London before coming back here, he got pretty excited when he started talking about Koevoet. Just hold on," I said as Ley started smirking and shaking his head, "I accept that a lot of what he told me was bullshit. They haven't destroyed Oshakati or any of the other places he claimed. That I've seen. I mean, I've been to those places. And unless the army is awfully clever at hiding them, there sure as hell aren't '100,000 racist troops' around here. But he was pretty definite about a massacre he claimed Koevoet committed at a place called Oshikuku. What was the story there? *Did* your boys wipe it out?"

"How much Afrikaans can you read?"

"Not much."

"Never mind; I've got a copy of the official inquiry back at the office. Get yourself another beer out of the fridge, and I'll be back just now."

Fifteen minutes later, I heard his car pull into the driveway. Ley padded barefoot through the door, carrying a thick brown folder.

"I told the general before you got here that you'd probably want to know about some of this," he explained, dropping the folder in my lap and heading for the refrigerator to get another beer. I heard the door open as he raised his voice from the kitchen. "In case you're interested, he said to give you whatever information you asked for."

He returned and stretched out on the couch. His beer snapped open with a hiss. "Got a cigarette?" I tossed the pack over and waited as he lit one and drew deeply. "Thanks. I'm supposed to be quitting, but once in a while . . . ," he paused to take another drag. "Okay, let me give you a little background on the Oshikuku massacre. Your pal in London told you that an entire village was wiped out, right?"

"Something like that," I nodded.

"Well, that's the popular story put out by SWAPO, but like most of their propaganda, it's a bit exaggerated. The truth of it is that in March '82, ten Ovambos were dragged from their kraal in the middle of the night and butchered. Not an entire village, but bad enough. Actually, there were three survivors, which was fortunate for us, I guess, but seven innocent civilians died that night. That happened; that's a fact, and maybe the only one everyone agrees on.

"SWAPO claimed that we did it, and one of our esteemed newspaper editors jumped on it. The official magistrate's inquiry determined that there was absolutely no evidence to implicate Koevoet or any other security force unit. Naturally, some people said it was all a cover-up. Standard thing, right? But I'll tell you officially and unofficially that our people had nothing to do with it." He stubbed out the cigarette and pointed to the report in my hands. "Have a look at the first page and tell me how much you can understand."

I opened the brown cover and struggled through the first few lines before giving up and shaking my head. "At a guess, I'd say it's a witness's statement."

He put his hand out, and I passed it over. "This is an eye-witness account of the incident by one of the three survivors. You can make of it what you want." He wet his throat with a swallow of beer, shifted to a more comfortable position, and began to read.

"This is the official statement of one Jolidye Nauyoma, a twenty-two-year-old Ovambo from the Oshipanda ward—area—of the Kwambi tribal district. The Kwambi, by the way, are one of the Ovambo subtribes. Anyway, he starts off by saying that he and the others in the kraal went to sleep on the night of March 9, 1982, at about 10 p.m. Then he says—and I'm translating directly from the statement: 'At about 2 a.m., I woke up. I saw that there were two strange black men in the room. There was a full moon and I noticed that the two men were wearing camouflage clothes and each of them had a rifle. With me in the room were the other people who slept there, Benedikus Nepolo and Shivute Kengaye. We were all forced with a bayonet to leave the room.

'We left the room, and the strangers made us stand against the outside of the kraal wall. I noticed two more strange black men who were wearing camouflage clothes and carrying the same rifles as the others. I and the other people from the kraal were forced to stand against the kraal wall.'"

He paused in the translation. "The nine people he names here who were with him that night ranged from eight years old to sixty-one. Four of them were thirteen or younger. Anyway, he goes on to say, 'I noticed that a fifth man appeared who was dressed in camouflage and had a gun like the others. Then three of the men started shooting at us. I fell on the ground with the others. I was not shot, but at first I thought I was.

'After the strangers shot at us, I heard them shooting and breaking windows of a lorry near the kraal. I lay still on the ground for about an hour. I stood up and saw that the woman, Penehafo Angula, and her eight-year-old son Erasmus, also stood up. I and Penehafo and her son went to another kraal nearby. In the morning, Penehafo and her son were taken to the Oshikuku Hospital, and I saw they had bullet wounds.

'I went to the kraal where the shooting took place and saw that all the other people from the kraal were still lying on the ground where the strange men shot at us—they were all dead.'"

He closed the folder and handed it back to me. "There are other statements in there from people in neighboring kraals who were woken up by the five gentlemen in question. Seems they were looking for that particular kraal—the one where they ended up chopping those seven. All five wore SWAPO uniforms, or at least they weren't wearing the camouflage uniforms we used to have, and all five carried AK-47s, and those the survivors heard spoke Oshivambo with a Kwanyama dialect. Of course, that doesn't mean anything; we've got lots of AKs and captured uniforms and most of our Ovambos are from the Kwanyama subtribe. If you want to believe SWAPO, it was a cold-blooded Koevoet plan to discredit them, just like they say we plant land mines to blow up civvies so we can say they did it. You can believe what you want, but I'm telling you that it wasn't us."

"Then why? Why did they go to that kraal with the intention of blowing away ten people? That's not what you might call a positive hearts-and-minds approach."

"You're wrong. It's an excellent hearts and minds, whichever way you look at it."

"Yeah? Well, you might try to explain that one to me. It doesn't make much sense to this boy."

"No, genuine: if they can convince the PBs that we did it, it makes them more sympathetic to SWAPO. Make no mistake, if the local pops know it was SWAPO—and I think those five went in there to kill someone they suspected of being an informer and didn't want any witnesses—then there aren't going to be many people prepared to give us info. Put yourself in their shoes: 'Man, if I talk to the police the terrs are going to come in and kill me and my whole family.' The same thing happened in Rhodesia, in Kenya during the Mau Mau, in Angola, Mozambique, it's happening in South Africa against pro-government blacks—in fact it's happened in every African country where Russian-backed 'liberation movements' have operated. Believe me, it works."

"Why couldn't it work just as well from your side? If you turn that reasoning around, couldn't it be just as effective an operation?"

"No," he said. "And the simple reason why it couldn't is because people talk. Someone would have spilled it by now. Another reason—something people are too quick to overlook—is that we still suffer from that old Calvinist thinking. We just can't seem to lay the Bible down when the situation calls for it and pick it up again when the dust settles. If we could have, blacks would prob-

ably be in a minority in South Africa today; we'd have extermi-
nated them like you did to your American Red Indians. Don't get
me wrong: we'll go in and floor someone who insists on trying to
hurt us, but—and I'd say unfortunately—the old idea of an eye for
an eye usually gets in the way of a no-holds-barred approach to
the problem."

"So what other things have happened to give Koevoet such a
bad name?"

"I guess the most publicized incident was when two of our
special constables, Jonas Paulus and Paulus Mateus, went on a
private spree one night. They were off duty—but still had their
weapons—and they got drunk and killed one person, raped two
women and stole everything they could lay their hands on that
wasn't red-hot or nailed down. No question about it. We arrested
both of them ourselves and turned them over to the regular police.
They were tried, convicted and sentenced; one was executed, the
other got twelve years.

"And, yeah, we've had other incidents of murder, and most—
but not all—were off duty. But in each case, the people involved
were arrested, tried and convicted if the evidence supported the
charges. At the moment, there are eight ex-Koevoet members
serving sentences for murder and one other being tried for murder. You might compare that with Vietnam. With the exception
of your famous Lieutenant Calley, I don't remember ever reading
about GIs being convicted of murdering civilians in Vietnam,
though dozens have admitted doing so since, and quite often with
the approval of their commanding officers.

"Make no mistake, we've had some very bad boys in this unit,
white and black. But that situation is hardly unique to Koevoet.
There's probably not an elite force anywhere in the world which
has seen extensive combat that hasn't been accused of atrocities.
How many of the accusations are based on truth and how many
are propaganda from the other side is the big question. During
the First World War, the Germans were accused by the British
press of raping nuns and killing babies with pitchforks. I don't
think any of those accusations were ever proved, but people still
remember them."

"Okay, but we're talking about Koevoet," I interrupted. "Some
of the incidents your own press in South Africa have reported did

happen. You've said so yourself. And it appears they've happened more frequently with Koevoet than with other units up here. Why?"

"Look, nothing justifies murder or beatings. In a perfect world, nothing even justifies threats. But the world isn't perfect yet and neither are people; you're going to find bad apples everywhere. We do our best to weed those out, but we're not perfect, either. What pisses me off is that it's happened in every war in history, it's happening right now in other places around the world, but when one of our people does something stupid or brutal, suddenly it's worse because the leadership element, for the most part, is South African.

"These men, blacks and whites, are the most effective counter-insurgency force up here. They see ten, twenty, maybe a hundred times the combat most other units do, which may account for some of the things that have happened. They know, they've seen what the terrs do. You want to talk about atrocities? Try talking about SWAPO atrocities. The very worst we've been accused of doesn't touch what those bastards have done to their own people. And I can guarantee you that SWAPO has never convened a court to try any of its 'freedom fighters' for atrocities against the civilian population.

"And again, I'm not saying that justifies any kind of brutality on our part. But you can't fight terrorism by the Queensberry rules. It's easy to be idealistic, but try it after seeing a few examples of what the terrs do to someone they think has given us info; try it right after you've seen what's left of a black kid who's stepped on a land mine meant for his policeman father.

"I really love those people who say: Well, SWAPO atrocities, that's to be expected; they've placed themselves outside the law, they're fighting a terrorist war against the system. They're *revolutionaries*, for Christ's sake, so it's okay. But you guys — Koevoet — don't you touch a hair on a suspected terr's head to protect the innocent. Those fucking people won't lose a minute's sleep over a civvie the terrs kill, and certainly not over the death of one of our people who are trying to protect the locals from the terrs, but watch them heat up their typewriters if they suspect one of our boys got out of hand!"

"I hear what you're saying, but those people . . . "

"Never see the blood, or a leg blown off, or hear the screams."

"Okay, you're right . . . most of them seldom see the reality of what they write about. It's easy to be judgmental when you never come face-to-face with it, I guess. And maybe I'm being idealistic too, but I just can't imagine seeing or experiencing anything that would make me lose a basic sense of humanity."

He rose and selected a tape, dropped it in and pressed the play button. As the sounds of Vivaldi filled the room, he raised his beer and toasted me. "And I hope you never do," he said quietly, "because it's something you'll never forget.

16

Harbinger of War

January 8, 1987 . . . 2200 . . . Oshakati Base

Dear Jones,

It's raining. For days now, the skies to the north over Angola have been gray and threatening, the gray moving a little further south each day. And last night the first of it finally arrived, rain heralded by sudden wind and the dim clash of muted thunder. Tonight again, harder: glistening, thrashing trees caught in the blue-white—fst!—of lightning flashes, the sudden crack! shaking my room, the rumbling aftermath drowned by the roaring downpour.

Gone now for a moment, the eaves of the tin roof cascading in silver sheets until slowing and slowing and finally dripping plaintively to the contented croaking of newly awakened frogs. Back again, wind and rain hammering the walls and fine spray driven through the screenless window. Outside, between rolling waves of deafening showers, muddied water and torn leaves rush along eroding gullies to disappear somewhere outside my circle of light.

The question on everyone's mind: Is this it, the beginning of the rains, what we've all been waiting for? Or will they slip coyly back as last month, the sky cloudless day after day once more? There's been frustration, a tenseness here, waiting for the real rains, the harbinger of war. And now they've come, carrying inside their darkness the sounds of destruction.

After six weeks, the days had started to take on a sameness, one blurring into another. You awoke under the wet bivi before dawn to unzip the clammy sleeping bag and dress by feel, swearing silently if you'd forgotten to draw socks and canvas boots well inside the cover and found them soaked with the night's rain. You crawled out, brushing sand from your hands and stumbling over tent pegs in the dark. *Goddammit,* as you tripped over something else you didn't remember being there and barked a shin, leaning down to rub it. Regaining your balance, you stood silently for a moment, imprisoned by the black vegetation spreading outward to a hidden horizon.

Here and there inside the TB others were beginning to move. A brief, racking cough broke the thick silence. Orange glows flickered as fuel tablets were lit, and piles of damp twigs grudgingly took fire. You sleepily took in the familiar scene, yawning and forgetting that only weeks before it would have been beyond imagining. This was your world—closer to the bone than anything you had ever encountered. So close that the once sharply defined edge between here and before was becoming less and less distinct; perhaps this had been forever and memories of other times and places were only illusions. *Don't be stupid. No? Then which is the illusion? Both. It's only where you are at the moment that matters.*

Going down on one knee, you reached under the edge of the poncho, patting the sand in search of the roll, then stood and tried to remember the layout of the new camp from the afternoon before. Making your way through the dripping wet bush outside the perimeter, you bumped into one of the Ovambos returning.

"Goeiemôre, meneer."

"Môre, tati."

By the time you returned, more men were moving around the camp. Water was drawn from the spigot at the back of the Casspir into an encrusted kettle which was balanced atop a struggling fire. There was the squeak of a tin provision box opening and the hollow clatter of enameled mugs before the top squeaked shut again. Sleepy sighs were the extent of the conversation as you untied your make-shift tent from its two trees and rolled up the sleeping bag, shoving it all into a diesel-stained duffel bag and making a mental note to pull it out during the day to allow it to dry. It was a morning reminder promptly forgotten until the end of the day, when the damp and sour-smelling bag was pulled out once more. As the sky lightened imperceptibly, the armored cars slowly took form around the camp, bulking silently like scarred war horses patiently awaiting battle.

The Ovambo special warrant officers joined the whites, sitting on the provision boxes or squatting round the fire. Someone set the stained collection of chipped mugs in the sand. A piece of cardboard torn from a ration pack was wrapped around the handle of the kettle and the mugs poured full of scalding coffee. They were passed from hand to hand and slowly sipped as sleep drained from exhausted bodies. A stick was poked into the formless lump of someone still in his sleeping bag. There was another persistent jab, and a tired voice growled a muffled oath as the cocoon began to move. The stubbled and dirt-streaked face of a twenty-one-year-old finally appeared to the quiet laughter of the coffee drinkers. A filthy arm slowly worked its way out of the bag and took an offered cup, drawing it unsteadily toward sunblistered lips.

The group leader detached himself from the group and climbed into his idling, warming car. Switching on the radios, he sipped his coffee and waited for them to warm up before keying the microphone.

"Zulu Twee, Zulu Twee; Zulu Quebec."

"Zulu Quebec; Zulu Twee. Goeiemôre, Toit. Hoe gaan dit?"

Zulu Two, the ops room at Eenhana, was advised in which direction we'd be moving and in return passed on the latest information about insurgent activity and any special instructions. As the group leader jotted down what was coming over the radio, fires were scattered and killed while bedding and stores were thrown into the Blesbok. The day's individual ration packs were handed out to each man. Guns were checked and sprayed with lubricant, ammunition belts examined. Finally, a loose parade was formed. Bush hats were removed in unison at a barked command and heads lowered as the senior Ovambo warrant officer led the group in prayer. On the back of a T-shirt worn by one of the most devout constables, chin tucked down in close communion with his Maker, were the words Kill Them All. Another crisp command, and hats were returned to heads, the parade formation dissolving as the men moved to their cars. The sun had almost reached the tops of the trees when the group leader's car belched dark smoke and bucked forward. Another day had begun.

Less than five miles away, other young men had also awakened. Of the seven, only two had undertaken previous infiltrations.

Both were skilled anti-trackers, as evidenced by their continued survival. The others, in their teens and early twenties, were fresh out of the training camp at Lubango. Their group of forty had been at the FAPLA base at Namakunde for the last two weeks, waiting for the rains to begin.

The group had received its orders and set out the day before, separating into smaller units of five to ten men each before reaching the border. As they split off from the others, the two veterans began badgering the five unblooded boys about using the anti-tracking techniques they'd been taught at Lubango. Better and safer not to leave tracks the racists and their lackeys might see, they harped, than have to anti-track to escape. Further, they must not again approach any kraals other than those already known to the two older men. For the youngsters, the unexpected warnings from the veteran combatants about hiding their spoor did little to quell their excitement. Why should they be concerned about anti-tracking? Hadn't their Cuban and PLAN instructors told them that the South African soldiers and their few Ovambo puppets were no match for the Cuban training they had received and the Soviet arms they carried? Not even the Ovambo traitors and white racists of the hated Koevoet stood a chance against them.

The scolding the two had received for taking a goat from a nearby kraal was accepted with good humor. What had been wrong? As soon as the farmer had seen their Kalashnikovs and realized who they were, he had made no attempt to stop them. As an oppressed Namibian, surely he must support their fight against the Boers. It was for him and others like him that the struggle went on. No, he would not inform on them, they confidently told the two older men.

They laughed and joked about how many racist soldiers they would kill before returning to Angola and a hero's welcome from Sam Nujoma himself. They were the vanguard of the People's Liberation Army of Namibia, come to free their brothers from oppression. Chests swelled with pride at the thought of carrying the struggle forward. For theirs was more than a standard attempt to penetrate to the white-owned farms east of the Etosha game reserve. Before leaving Lubango, they had been given orders to cut across the eastern corner of Ovambo into the Kavango, where no PLAN unit had operated for more than two years. They would recruit guerrillas from the Kavango population and conduct ambushes against the South Africans until recalled. The heavy loads of extra ammunition, medical supplies and uniforms in their backpacks provided for an extended stay far from normal supply routes. It would be a difficult and dangerous trek along the Odilla, an ancient, dry riverbed overgrown with trees that would provide an easy navigational reference for the first part of their infiltration.

The ashes of last night's fire were carefully scattered. The men picked up the blackened remains of the young goat, stripping the last bits of cold, undercooked flesh from the bones before tossing them into the bush. Wiping hands on damp camouflage trousers, they buckled on their uncomfortable web gear and shouldered Soviet assault rifles. The leader waved his men forward, and the group began making its way through the wet bush. The stiffness they felt from sleeping on the cold, wet ground would soon be worked out as they continued their ordered infiltration deeper into Namibia.

I had been with Zulu Quebec for two days. Quebec and its bush partner, Zulu Uniform, were the rising stars in Koevoet. Stephanus Francois du Toit was Quebec's group leader. Six foot, blond and muscular, Toit (pronounced *Toy* in Afrikaans) at first meeting came across as quietly self-assured. His outwardly calm manner was deceptive. Under the surface, this twenty-five-year-old with the film-star looks was an unpredictable and dangerous man with a hair-trigger temper and lightning-fast fists.

Simon, who rode in Toit's car, was Zulu Quebec's Ovambo medic. Small and slender, he looked about fifteen but was ten years older. He introduced himself, taking great pride in practicing his few words of English with me.

Ryno was the group's white ops medic. Like all white ops medics with Koevoet, he was not a policeman, but a member of the South African Medical Service, a separate branch of the South African Defense Force. Baby-faced and twenty, he seemed almost out of place among the scarred Koevoet veterans.

Toit's opposite number was Attie Hattingh, group leader of Zulu Uniform. Short, dark-haired and well-built, his masculine good looks were complemented by a quick intellect and infectious laugh. He had left Koevoet at one point at the insistence of his wife, returning to orthodox police duties in South Africa. But the quiet routine and an agonizing sense of having deserted led to the inevitable divorce. He had immediately requested assignment back to Ops K. Four years with the unit had made him another of those good operators.

Attie's younger brother Adriaan commanded one of Zulu Uniform's four Casspirs. Though quieter, more slightly built, and somewhat overshadowed by his older brother, Adriaan was otherwise almost a carbon copy of Attie. His courage, aggressiveness and ability to think on his feet in a rapidly changing tactical situation marked him as a "natural." More than one old-timer in the unit had already remarked on his quiet leadership and professionalism. It was only a matter of time before he would be given his own group.

In a private moment, Attie confided how much he hated sending Adriaan ahead to do voorsny during a follow-up, knowing that the voorsny cars were invariably the first targets for the desperate insurgents. When I pressed him about it, Attie paused for a moment to look across the camp at his brother. "We both understand the risks," he said quietly. "This is where we belong."

Paul, another of Zulu Uniform's car commanders, seemed never to smile, keeping to himself more than anyone else I met in the unit. His private, somehow sad countenance often made me wonder if he were constantly suffering from some great, unspoken tragedy.

The group's army ops medic, Frikkie, was just the opposite. Invariably good-humored and talkative with an easy command of English, he was always a source of unsolicited advice and bad jokes. Although his steadiness in combat was already admired by his peers, within weeks an act of courage would set even hardened members of Koevoet to shaking their heads and earn him one of the highest SADF awards for valor.

The day had started like most, stopping at one kraal after another, questioning the local population about the presence of any insurgents, back into the Casspirs and on again to the next, climbing down from the cars, questioning all over again. Hours of hard, slogging work, made more uncomfortable with the onset of the rains. Now there was not only the heat, but the oppressive close-ness of humidity as well. Tempers were frayed. Everyone knew that large groups of insurgents were starting to cross the border from Angola. The infiltration had begun in earnest. Digging them out was the tough part.

We had stopped at one more kraal that morning. Children peeked from behind their mothers' ragged dresses at the men and the angular armored monsters bristling with guns. Some of the trackers opened ration packs and held out candies and chewing gum. The children advanced shyly, grabbed the offerings and raced back to the protection of their mothers before stuffing the sweets into mouths.

Three of the constables walked to the kraal fence and began questioning the head of the family. The conversation became ani-mated, the farmer gesturing angrily from inside the enclosure. Looking at the three as he talked, he lifted his arm and pointed behind him, fingers snapping. Suddenly excited, one of the police-men turned around and shouted back to Toit, who immediately left the car to join them. Two SWAPO insurgents had been to this kraal the night before and taken a goat. The farmer had seen only two men, but Toit and the tracker both agreed that it had to mean a group of at least four or five insurgents were in the area. The farmer wasn't sure which way the SWAPO took his goat, but he thought that way, to the east, he said, pointing loose-jointedly and snapping his fingers again.

The men ran back to the car and were climbing through the rear doors when Attie's voice crackled over the radio. His Ovambo constables had just found seven spoor less than half a mile to the east of us. The tracks were definitely from this morning, he emphasized, not more than two or three hours old.

The change in everyone was immediate, an electric energy sparking through the group. Minutes later, we rendezvoused with Zulu Uniform. The trackers jumped off the cars with their stubby weapons, paused to chamber rounds, then ran to join those already on the trail. The hunt had started.

Two hours later, the footprints were down to five, but these five, said the trackers grimly, didn't know their anti-tracking. They showed me spoor so clear even I could see it as I walked alongside them. Toit carried a portable radio to stay in contact with his car commanders as well as with Attie and Adriaan, who were working voorsny. Even on difficult terrain, we followed the insurgents at a fast walk, Casspirs flanking us. The trackers were leaning over and pointing out each footprint with branches they'd stripped from trees.

There, tap, *there,* tap, *there,* tap.

Zulu Uniform disappeared into the bush. Within ten minutes, they had picked up the spoor 300 or 400 meters forward. As soon as Attie relayed the information to Toit, we scrambled through the hydraulically operated doors and the Casspirs raced to the position he had marked with a smoke grenade. We jumped out and Zulu Quebec's trackers took the trail again. *There,* tap, *there,* and *there!* Zulu Uniform had already fanned out, cutting ahead to find it further on.

Reports from two other groups began coming in on the radio. "Zulu November has at least ten spoor south of us," Toit said as we kept pace with the Ovambo constables. "They think they're about an hour behind them. Zulu Poppa has four more east of Nkongo. Shit, we've got some activity today!"

There was another radio call from Attie, and again billowing smoke marked the location of fresher spoor. The trackers, sweating and excited, dived back into the Casspirs, and we accelerated, crashing through the bush to where the smoke still lingered. We were closing faster and faster. In all probability, the insurgents we were chasing could hear the growls of diesel engines growing steadily louder. The changing direction of their tracks showed they had swung north, heading toward the border and Angola. For the pursuing policemen, the 100-meter-wide strip between the two countries had become irrelevant. The insurgents had crossed the border to kill; their flight back into Angola would ensure no escape.

Then it was a running spoor, the Ovambo special constables sprinting through the thick bush, slowing only when they lost the tracks for a moment, milling, then taking off again at a dead run. The insurgents had given up any attempt to anti-track. With the sounds of approaching death reaching them through the bush, they were running flat out and desperately, their spoor a finger pointing directly after them. The rest of their lives now depended solely on luck and how fast they could run.

Toit, running with the trackers, ordered me into his car. Knowing we were behind them, chances were good the insurgents would start setting POM-Z antipersonnel mines along the trail. The squat, pineapple-sectioned bombs seldom killed, but the shrapnel could inflict terrible wounds. In a fast-moving chase like this, an exploding pom-zed invariably slowed down all the trackers as they began looking cautiously for trip wires. Neither Toit nor any of the trackers could trust my inexperience in spotting one. Although his first concern was for the safety of his men, I also suspected he didn't want to be responsible for my getting blown up. I protested only a little, for form's sake.

"Come on, let me stay on the ground with you guys," I asked, hands on knees and gasping for breath.

"Okay, but you stay fifty meters behind us," he said firmly, giving me an out.

There was no way I would get any photos that far back, and he knew it. Considerably relieved, I climbed into the Casspir. As fast as we were moving now, there was no way I could keep up. As we neared the border, the pace picked up even more.

On the car's second radio I heard the word "casevac" and saw Toit listening as he ran. "Zulu November's just had a contact about ten klicks from here," he shouted at me from the ground. "They took out seven terrs, but one of their cars was hit with an RPG. They've got six casevacs and at least one dead. Boesman's scrambling the Pumas!"

I dropped into one of the seats and quickly checked over the cameras. One had only a dozen shots left on the roll. I rewound it and loaded a fresh roll, swearing as the film tail kept slipping out with each jarring bump and sway of the Casspir. I finally managed to thread it, shook out the debris and snapped the back closed. I listened for the automatic advance, gave the lenses another wipe and stood again as we neared the border.

Hot pursuit. We hit the yati and roared without hesitation across the wide, cleared strip into Angola. We came out of the bush and into glaring, sand-reflected sunlight and back into the shadowed bush. Once across the divide, there was no visible difference between the two countries. Toit immediately advised Zulu Two by radio that we had gone "external" and put the helicopters on standby.

Groups Zulu Tango and Zulu Echo had joined us. Half the cars were working voorsny now. The bush around me was full of roaring cars and running policemen.

When the Casspirs and running policemen started going around to pass over their own tracks it was clear we had to be right on top of the insurgents. But only three spoor were still clear. They had bombshelled, each taking off in a separate direction and trying to confuse the trackers by going in circles, hoping their spoor would be lost in the torn-up bush and ground behind the cars. Toit, sweating heavily through the caked dirt on his face and torso, waved the Casspir to a halt. He climbed over the side and dropped through the hatch behind the machine gun mount as we started moving again.

"They're here," he yelled between chest-heaving gasps, quickly checking the guns and pulling the locking pin from the mount. "They're right here!" Cutting along the edge of a kraal complex, we heard a loud, dull bang somewhere off to the side. I jerked around to look in the direction of the sound but saw only thick bush. I turned back to Toit.

"What the hell was that?" I shouted at him.

"Pom-zed!"

A chill went through me. People had to be hurt; people I knew.

The commander of Zulu Echo called on the radio. Toit took the handset away from his ear and looked back as we reentered the bush, one hand still gripping the handle of the .50 caliber Browning. "Jack says he's got five wounded from the pom-zed! None of them are too serious, but he's scrambling the choppers to casevac them out! We can't get gunships till they're finished!"

By now, any semblance of organized control had disappeared as the cars and trackers crisscrossed through the bush, chasing individual spoor. Suddenly faced with an impenetrable wall of bush, Toit's driver turned the wheel hard and took us between two closely spaced trees. We came to a crashing stop, all of us in the back losing our footing and stumbling forward. Weapons, equipment and ration pack tins went clattering across the floor. The driver threw the gearshift into reverse, but the wheels spun uselessly. We picked ourselves up and looked over the side. The bumper had pushed through the gap, but the Casspir's body was too wide to follow. We were jammed.

The two trackers still in the Casspir hit the ground with their machetes and started chopping at the tree trunk while Toit quickly checked the guns again and pulled leaves and twigs from the ammunition belts. A few minutes later, the tree toppled over and the car was free. As we began to move, I heard a burst of machine gun fire ahead of us. Over the radio came the inevitable, "Contact!"

Toit drew his pistol, snapped the slide back to chamber a round, eased the hammer forward and reholstered the weapon. Looking over his shoulder to check that his men were on board, he shouted "Komesho!" and the car lurched ahead, everyone holding on and scanning the bush. With the opening shots of a contact, the trackers on the ground had pulled back or taken cover. Now it was up to the cars.

Somewhere in the recesses of my mind, I suddenly wondered what the insurgents were carrying. Heatstrims? RPG-7s or the new -75s? Who had been killed with Boesman's group? How badly wounded were the others? *Is this the day it happens to you?* But the fear that tingled just below the surface was insulated by the adrenaline coursing through the body. It was a consciousness-raising drug, heightening all the senses—imprinting picture, audio and touch on the mind and body with the speed of light and sound, yet perceived in surrealistic slow motion; that primeval corner of the cortex responding to the most primitive urge to survive. *See it! Hear it! Feel it and react faster than the other so that you will live! Live!*

Another explosion of firing broke out to our left front, and we swung toward it, Toit gripping the spade handles of the .50 caliber Browning, his eyes darting back and forth. The two trackers still with us were down inside now, the muzzles of their assault rifles jammed through the gun ports.

The radio was screeching, crackling "CONTACT! CONTACT!" I stood at the back of the Casspir, eyes trying to penetrate the bush, ears assailed by engine, guns, and radios, nose absorbing dust and cordite. Two cars—Attie's and Adriaan's—appeared, disappeared, in and out of bush and shadow 40 meters to the left, angling toward us. Heavy firing again, the shadows ahead filled with the blue-gray haze of gun smoke. The incandescent sparkles of tracers blazed through the trees to disappear abruptly, one ricocheting off at an impossible angle, cutting a split-second, red-orange streak through the haze. Toit was firing, aiming to the right of the brothers' two converging Casspirs, streams of bullets from the machine guns chopping down brush and raising exploding geysers of dust and sand. And always the chaotic roar enveloping everything around us!

Where are they? I can't see them!

Camera poised, others swinging around my neck in the shaking, swaying Casspir, I was trying to hold on and see while dodging the branches that scraped over the top of the car. I jumped to the left just in time to avoid one branch, only to be hit by another from the side I'd moved to. It caught me solidly across the side of the head, knocking my glasses askew and numbing my ear. With something bordering on panic, I quickly resettled them and saw the two cars to the left had swung further toward us, firing, firing, dust from the impact of their guns ahead adding to the thickening haze.

There was a sudden, bass-like explosion and one of the cars stumbled 20 meters away, hit with something. The Casspir swerved and shuddered to a stop. The firing reached another crescendo, overwhelming even the sounds of the cars and radios. Toit dropped inside, and I followed suit, ducking below the protective armor at the rear of the Casspir. Then he was up again and firing into the gloom of shadows, gun smoke and dust.

There! I saw one running and diving down to disappear into a thicket. We drove directly at the spot, Toit screaming at the driver, "KOLODIO! KOLODIO!" [RIGHT! RIGHT!], then, "STOP! STOP! DON'T RUN OVER HIM! FUCK, MAN, STOP!"

The car swerved, and we braked to a shuddering halt alongside the thicket, dust rolling over us from behind. Toit went over the side of the Casspir, and I dove through the rear doors, hitting the ground hard, canvas boots tangling in broken saplings to send me sprawling full-length into the sand. As I scrambled frantically to my feet and turned to follow, I saw the insurgent roll over, trying to cock his SKS assault rifle. Bent low, Toit ran at him, pistol held forward, everything happening in slow motion: one running, the other jerking at the rifle in his hands; one, his legs driving him slowly through the bush toward the other on the ground; the other looking up, then down, struggling so slowly to draw back the bolt on the rifle; the pistol in the hand coming up, only feet away and the extremes of all their youthful existence concentrated here and now, now, *now!*

Move! For God's sake, move!

A shot, the muzzle jerking; another shot, and then a third. The weapon slipped from fingers that slowly opened. Then Toit, eyes bulging and white lips drawn back from dirt-blackened teeth, was standing over him, the pistol at his side.

Attie and Adriaan came running from their cars. Both were wide eyed and breathing heavily, stoked to their fingertips on adrenaline. The windscreen on Adriaan's car was starred from AK-47 fire. Attie's car had been hit with a heatstrim.

"There's at least one more over there that we took out!" Attie pointed, talking in quick bursts between shuddering breaths. "He was the one that hit us with the heatstrim! Shit! I didn't see him until just before he fired!"

From the thick bush around us, the trackers who had taken cover when the contact started slowly emerged, out of breath from the chase. I saw Frikkie helping Phillip, Zulu Uniform's senior black warrant officer, out of one of the cars. He had been hit across his upper back and through one ear with a dozen or more small pieces of shrapnel. Settling him as comfortably as possible under a tree, Frikkie ran back for his medical kit.

Toit ran to his Casspir and called for a casevac, then sent two cars to clear a landing zone by knocking the bush down. Frikkie carefully and gently cleaned Phillip's wounds, then injected him with a tetanus booster and Sosegon pain killer. As soon as the chopper appeared above the rough clearing, Toit and Attie carried Phillip out to it, settled him next to the pilot and waved him off. As the helicopter rose, they turned away from the stinging sand and I was chilled by the fixed, almost maniacal grins on their faces — until the stunned realization that my own face was a mirror image.

What's the matter with you? Stop it! For God's sake, stop it!

Four of the SWAPO insurgents had died in the contact. Their poor training and inexperience had sentenced them to death the moment they crossed the border. The others escaped into the

Angolan bush, their confidence undoubtedly shattered at being discovered and hunted down so soon after crossing the border. I couldn't help despising their commander for sending them across, knowing full well what their chances of survival had been.

Two of the special constables, both ex-SWAPO fighters, took cardboard packs of bullets from the bodies to reload the ammunition belt for one's Soviet-made RPD light machine gun, still his favorite weapon. Watching as they joked and slipped rounds into the belt loops, I tried to fathom what they were feeling. They'd come from the same background, gone through the same training, shared the same language and customs as the young men they had just had a hand in killing. I'd watched them kick sand in the face of each body after the contact. ("It's what they do to show their contempt," someone told me.) What emotions did they feel at the killing of men whose beliefs they once shared? Was there no sense of paradox at being in the service of those they'd been taught to hate as racist oppressors? Or were my questions irrelevant here, merely the result of my own background and culture, which expected me to question everything in terms of Western morality?

My eyes swung to the nearest body as one of the older Ovambo warrant officers approached it. He stopped and looked at the naked corpse for a moment, staring sadly before leaning over to pick up and throw a bloody camouflage shirt over the body's private parts. In the midst of so much viciousness and blood lust, there was something oddly touching about the gesture.

The tension of the last few hours began to ease. Aside from the damage to Attie's and Adriaan's cars, one other had a tire shot out. As the wheel was being changed, everyone found a shady spot to relax and discuss the chase. Fresh ammunition belts were loaded into the Casspirs' machine guns and coffee brewed while the bodies were searched, their weapons collected and recorded. Toit and Attie examined a set of documents that spelled out the mission that had been given to the boys who lay in the sand.

"What a bonus!" exclaimed Attie. "We've got the locations of the caches the terrs left in the Kavango a couple of years ago. It also names the only two Kavangos in their assigned op area who are known SWAPO sympathizers. Army intelligence is going to love this." He scanned another page of the typewritten orders. "These gooks were expected to stay there until the war was over. They wouldn't have lasted long—not right out of training. What the hell are they smoking up there?"

Soviet and Cuban-supplied equipment was itemized, to include rifle serial numbers; magazines; anti-personnel mines; blocks of TNT; plastic explosive; fuses, and detonators; number of anti-armor heatstrim and anti-personnel pencilstrim rifle grenades; old British-made 2-inch mortar rounds (undoubtedly from stocks left behind in Kenya or Nigeria); Yugoslavian water bottles; and sets of Nicaraguan camouflage uniforms. Sorting through a medical kit taken from one of the bodies, I noticed most of the drugs came from Holland. Others had been supplied by the United Nations International Children's Emergency Fund.

Toit collected the mortar rounds and rifle grenades into a pile. Kneading a handful of the Soviet-manufactured plastic explosive into a sausage-shaped lump, he laid it over the pile, crimped a detonator onto a five-minute fuse with his teeth and pushed the detonator into the oily explosive. He lit the fuse, and we trotted to the idling cars. We were a few hundred meters away when it went off, the explosion muffled by the thick bush.

I imagined the debris settling on the bodies that had been left where they had fallen, wondering what dreams and futures had been abruptly ended for the sake of this backward and little-known land. Of what or whom were their last thoughts? Would anyone cry for them? Would anyone even care?

Another day finished as we rumbled south back across the cutline.

17

Myth and Reality

B Y now, I'd already been in half a dozen contacts where I'd stood head and shoulders above the protective armor of the cars, snapping away with my cameras and totally disregarding the possibility of injury. More than once, the Ovambo policemen had tried to drag me down inside the steel hull to safety, but I'd shake off their concerned hands and stay where I was, looking for that Robert Capa shot. And after each contact, I would be even more convinced that I was charmed, that I could stand up and wave if I wanted to and they still couldn't put one into me. The bullet with *my* name on it hadn't been made. "Cosmic protection," I smiled each time at their shaking heads. And I believed it.

"Look," I'd tell each car commander I found myself with, "If we hit a contact, tell your people back here not to pull me down if I'm standing and taking pictures, okay? I can't get my pictures if I'm inside, right?" Tough, see. Like saying, I got it all together. No way *I'm* going to be hit. And they'd look at me for a moment, shrug as if to say, It's your ass, pal, and pass the word.

January 17, 1987

The trackers had stumbled on fresh spoor not more than an hour after leaving Eenhana that morning. The ground was not only soft, but washed clean by heavy rain the night before. There was no problem following these tracks; the Ovambo policemen had them in the bag. We stopped briefly at a kraal, and a young woman with a baby on her hip pointed north and shook her hand rapidly. She had seen them pass not more than an hour earlier. From that point on, the outcome was inevitable—signed, sealed and delivered.

The tracks led us past Ovambo farmers preparing mohango fields for planting. Oxen pulling plowshares snorted and shied, shaking their heads when the cars roared by, the farmers ignoring us as they tried to control the animals. We crossed old fields, the cars shuddering over last year's furrows, then entered scattered bush that grew steadily denser. The cars spread out in battle line abreast, each leaving flattened thickets and uprooted trees in its wake. Between the green Casspirs, black constables, assault rifles held waist level at the end of shoulder slings, zigzagged through the bush as the men in the cars shouted encouragement. The spoor was growing fresher and fresher.

I watched the constables running hard, dodging between the thin trees, ducking under branches as the Casspirs kept pace alongside. One of them, his face streaming with sweat, shouted breathlessly to Toit: "Gunship! Kontact kom now-now!" It was time to scramble the choppers from Eenhana; we weren't more than ten minutes behind and closing fast. The call went out.

Toit had already pulled the locking pin from the gun mount and swung the guns left and right as we crashed through the bush. The constables inside the car drew back the bolts on their weapons to double-check that rounds were chambered. Their encouraging shouts of a moment ago were gone; faces tightened as the tension became almost palpable, ratcheting pulses higher and higher. There were clicks as safeties snapped down and muzzles were pushed through the spring-loaded gun ports. By now the insurgents could certainly hear the growls of pursuing Casspirs. How experienced were they? Would they stop to set an ambush? Would the next moment stop forever in the blazing, flesh-shredding explosion of a heatstrim burning through the thin steel? Muscles flexed under sweat-darkened shirts as hands tightened on weapons and eyes scanned the terrain through the thick glass. At the chattering whine of a helicopter, I looked up and saw an Alouette pass diagonally above us. The trackers on the ground slowed and dropped back. Any minute now . . . a-n-y minute.

The hell with it! I hoisted myself onto the flat deck above the rear doors, dropping my right foot over the spare tire bracket on the side of the Casspir and tucking the left leg under me. Riding through the thickening bush, I held a camera in one hand and used the other arm to deflect the branches that threatened to sweep me off my place.

Now — with the sudden, staccato explosions of gunfire as Attie's cars hit the contact less than 30 meters ahead of us. As we rolled into it, I could see the familiar haze of gray gun smoke through the thick bush. I'd raised a camera to my eye, looking for something to snap, when sudden automatic-weapon fire started coming from our left.

One bullet clipped the edge of the camera vest over my chest; another struck the beveled top of the Casspir and ricocheted upward. It was as though I'd been punched by a huge fist, the blow knocking the right arm sideways from my body and the camera falling to the end of its sling around my neck. The arm dropped, immediately paralyzed, as everything went into slow motion. I jerked my left hand across to pull up the sleeve of the green T-shirt as my head came down, eyes staring unbelievingly at a red hole in the side of my biceps — a biceps suddenly gone completely flaccid, hanging loose and formless as though it belonged to an old woman. My head twisted away from the wound as my mouth opened and I let out a piercing scream — not from the pain, there wasn't any — but from the shocking realization that I'd been hit! *I'd been hit!*

My head dropped again — and again in slow motion, it seemed — this time to look stupidly into the car to see if anyone had noted my outcry. It was probably no more than one or two seconds after being hit when I realized that if I had caught one bullet while sitting on top of the Casspir, then the possibility of another wasn't entirely out of the question. With that brilliant piece of deductive reasoning solidly in place, I swung my legs over the edge and dropped through the open top of the car with no thought but to get out of the way of what was filling the air around me.

I landed in a sprawl on the floor between the seats. The sounds of screaming radios, blaring engine, shouting men, and assault rifles spitting bursts of automatic fire were deafening. Getting my feet under me, I pushed myself up to a crouch and caught Simon's eye. Leaning forward well below the open top of the car, cameras swinging from my neck, I made my way through the trackers and gun smoke, slipping on the empty casings that were already beginning to cover the floor. The arm hung limply and totally numb at my side. The car swerved and I toppled sideways across two men, one of whom straight-armed me to the floor without a backward glance.

Simon had put aside his weapon as soon as he had seen me and was already ripping open a field dressing when I reached him. He threw a rucksack out of the seat across from him and curtly motioned me to sit, then took the place at my side and carefully eased the sleeve up and over my shoulder. He was working on the wound when Toit took a quick break from his Browning and dropped inside to ask what the hell had happened. Unable to move the arm and not understanding that the nerves were only momentarily stunned, I was sure the bullet had broken the bone.

"ARM'S BROKEN!" I yelled over the roar of the firing. He gave me an angry look, grabbed the radio handset and spoke briefly. I caught the word "casevac." Another withering look in my direction, and he returned to the chaotic firefight still going on around us.

After a few more bursts he poked his head back down and shouted, "ARE YOU SURE?"

I looked up at him and nodded violently. "ARM'S BROKEN!"

"WHAT HAPPENED? YOU FALL OFF THE CAR?"

It was a reasonable assumption, having last seen me on my precarious seat at the back of the Casspir, but not even close to the script I had imagined for this scene.

"NO, GODAMMIT! I'M SHOT! I'M SHOT!"

"NO SHIT?" he yelled back over the firing, an expression of infinite relief spreading across his face as he went back to his guns once more.

I watched Simon working on the arm. As he circled the biceps with white gauze, I concentrated on moving it. Nothing. I tried to open or close the hand. Nothing. It was like trying to move an arm belonging to someone else.

Breathing heavily, I leaned back and closed my eyes for a moment. Then it struck me: what I had worked toward for the last year was finished. I knew the arm was broken. It would be months healing, months before I could use it again. The project was over. I sat forward.

"FUCK!" I bellowed at the top of my lungs, smashing the good hand against the water tank next to me in fury. Simon jerked his hands away. The slender black medic looked at me questioningly. "Sorry, Tati," I said, shaking my head. "It's okay. Sorry." I leaned back and closed my eyes again. *Dammit!*

As quickly as it had started, the contact was over and three of the cars were driving back and forth, knocking down the bush to clear a landing zone for the casevac chopper. Frikkie ran up to the Casspir and clambered through the rear door with his first-aid kit. He unzipped the canvas case and laid it open as Simon scrubbed my shoulder with an alcohol swab. Quickly tapping the syringe he had drawn with Sosegon, Frikkie reversed it and with a downward flip of the wrist drove the needle into the shoulder muscle. Withdrawing it, he smashed the needle against the inside of the car and tossed it out the top. An Alouette passed slowly overhead.

Frikkie pointed toward the open doors at the back of the car. "Let's go!" he shouted. I followed him out of the Casspir and toward the helicopter that was sinking slowly out of the air into the cleared landing zone. Heads down and eyes narrowed to slits, we entered the maelstrom of stinging sand.

As we neared the shrieking machine, I realized I could move the arm. I tried again. It was working; not very well, but I could definitely raise it a little. I tried the hand. The two little fingers moved slightly, curling inwards.

"IT'S NOT BROKEN! IT'S NOT BROKEN!" I yelled over the scream of the engine and flat thudding of helicopter rotor blades. I stopped and turned away from the howling sandstorm to show him the movement.

He grabbed my left arm and got me going again, yelling something in Afrikaans. I didn't understand it, but the look on his face said he wanted me on the chopper and out of his hair. As I settled on the floor next to the pilot, Frikkie latched the door from outside, gave me a grin and thumbs-up through the Plexiglas, then turned and ran low under the blur of the blades. The pilot drew up on the collective control, and we lifted off. When the nose came down and we began the transition to horizontal flight, I looked across the pilot and saw the bodies of the insurgents being dragged together.

The flight engineer placed a set of earphones over my head as we climbed away from the scene. "How's it?" the heavy-set pilot hissed over the intercom. I recognized him as the one I'd been drinking with in the air force compound the night before. "You okay?" he pressed. I nodded, vastly relieved that I could move the arm.

"What happened?"

"Fucker shot me!"

"Genuine? Shit, we heard you'd broken your arm!" He released the intercom switch for a moment, but his lips still moved against the microphone. I heard the hiss again in my earphones as he glanced at me. "Okay, we'll have you back to Eenhana now-now. I've just told them you're hit and that we're on the way. They'll have a medic waiting for us. Relax."

I stared with fascination at the blood soaking through the bandage. The wound didn't hurt at all, but the hand was burning and aching badly. And in spite of the cool wind whipping through the flight engineer's door, I was beginning to perspire heavily. Beads of sweat trickled down my face and neck. It must have hit a nerve, I decided. I couldn't believe it. I'd been shot!

Fifteen minutes later, we were landing behind the revetments at Eenhana. Waiting for me were the rest of the pilots, an army medic and Chris Pieterse, the Koevoet ops officer. The serious, concerned looks gave way to relief when they saw I was intact and mobile. I climbed gingerly out of the helicopter onto the tarmac, expecting a certain amount of sympathetic attention.

Pieterse walked up to me, shaking his head in disgust. He stopped and jammed his fists on his hips. "Well, well, if it isn't Mister Jim 'If I'm Standing Up Taking Pictures Don't Pull Me Down' Hooper," he said without a hint of sympathy in his voice. "Tell me, Dumbshit, how's it feel to get shot?"

"Not too hot," I grimaced, knowing full well whose fault it was.

"Okay, give me your kit and go with this guy. The doctor's waiting for you."

Shrugging off the camera vest, I handed everything to Pieterse and followed the medic to the sick bay. The doctor unwrapped the bandage, noting cheerfully that there was no exit wound. "Looks like it's still in there," he said with an insouciance that was quite inappropriate from my point of view.

The doctor explained that the burning sensation in my hand was referred pain, the result of damage to the median nerve in the upper arm. After my arm was rebandaged, I persuaded him to give me another shot of Sosegon and walked over to the air force compound. On the way, I passed small groups of pink-cheeked national servicemen in brown uniforms who fell silent on seeing me. The blood-stained white gauze stood out starkly against my dirt-streaked tan.

"Koevoet," I heard one whisper in confirmation to another. With considerable effort, I relaxed my hunched shoulders and scowled, looking straight ahead until I'd left them behind. Rounding the corner of the air force area, I sagged in relief and drew the forearm up, cradling it with my left hand. *Goddamn, this hurts,* I thought, my face and eyes screwing up in pain.

Feeling dizzy and nauseous, I sat heavily in a chair under the camouflage net. My shirt was completely soaked with sweat. Dave Atkinson, the chopper pilot who had picked me up, came out of the ops room and pinned something to the front of my T-shirt. I looked down at a piece of canvas cut in the shape of a stylized heart, colored dark blue with a ballpoint pen and edged with red pencil. He stood back, saluted and gave a stirring, if somewhat inaccurate, rendition of the "Star Spangled Banner." I had to grin. My first purple heart.

The doctor arrived to advise Brooks that he should scramble a Puma from Ondangwa to pick me up. I shook my head, imagining the flap and signals going back and forth between various commands about committing a Puma to casevac one lightly wounded man—and a foreign journalist at that. I did my best to dissuade him. The last thing I wanted to do was call attention to myself by receiving special treatment. I could just imagine some staff officer going through the ceiling and urging higher ups to have my access curtailed or canceled altogether. It would not only make things awkward and embarrassing for the people I was with, but would also drag my name across the desks of senior army and air force officers. Knowing that it was always easier and safer for someone to say no than yes, I said I'd wait for the first Casspir driving back.

After a little thought, Brooks came up with the perfect compromise. A Bosbok two-seater spotter plane was already scheduled to make a road reconnaissance from Eenhana to Ondangwa. I could take the back seat. At the end of the mission the pilot would deliver me to Ondangwa Air Force Base, where the primary trauma center was located.

By now in some pain and feeling extremely nauseous, I followed the pilot, who looked about fourteen years old and bore a startling resemblance to my brother Bill, himself a spotter plane pilot in Vietnam. It struck me that when Bill had been hit while flying near the demilitarized zone in late 1968, his wound was in almost exactly the same place as mine. The difference was he had very nearly lost his arm.

It was something I drew little consolation from as I pulled myself awkwardly into the Bosbok and settled into the back seat. My major concern at that point was not embarrassing myself by puking all over the inside of the airplane.

Less than an hour later, we were landing at Ondangwa. We taxied up to the deserted flight line and stopped not more than 50 meters from where I'd stepped off the Namibair flight seven weeks earlier. The pilot shut down the engine and opened the top-hinged door. I climbed out behind him. He walked off in one direction. I walked off in another, looking for the bevy of nurses who had undoubtedly been advised of my pending arrival and who would descend on me with soothing hands and words.

After wandering about for some fifteen minutes, unable to find the sick bay, I spotted Bernie Ley scanning the flight line. His relief at seeing me intact and ambulatory was obvious. I smiled bravely.

Hustling me up the ramp into the sick bay, he delivered me into the hands of a medic. The doctor had gone down to the flight line right after the Bosbok landed but had missed me because I had wandered off in the wrong direction. He was still down there, Bernie said, looking for me. Somehow, this wasn't quite what I had expected.

An ambulance finally pulled up, and a trim, young fellow climbed out dressed in jogging shorts, flip-flops and a T-shirt advertising some bar in Durban. He strolled casually up the ramp. This had to be the doctor.

"Hi. You the doctor?"

"Yeah," he said, getting his ear round the accent and taking in the bandage. "You the American journalist that's been shot?" I nodded vigorously, keeping a keen lookout for the bevy from the corner of my eye. This hand was hurting like a *bastard.*

"Well, he said, yawning, "let's see if we can find someone to X-ray that arm."

Right away I could see I'd walked into the wrong script again. Here I was, wounded in combat, begrimed and reeking of cordite, in substantial pain—and this doctor was yawning!

What I didn't appreciate at the moment was that he and his staff were used to dealing with serious trauma; by comparison, my less than life-threatening wound had all the urgency of a hang-nail. All I knew was that I had been shot for the first time in my life, that it hurt a lot, and that no one seemed to be affording the situation the importance I thought it demanded. I wanted them to fix it. Right now.

I was tempted to affect a thousand yard stare, but gave it up as a bad idea. A blank stare off toward the horizon might make me miss the bevy, hope for which was already fading with depressing rapidity.

The X rays showed a slightly larger than pea-sized object lodged against the median nerve and artery. The bullet had broken up when it hit the edge of the Casspir, and only half of it had ricocheted into me. After snipping away the damaged tissue around the entry wound, the doctor probed the enlarged hole with his little finger. It disappeared down to the second knuckle before he stopped. I saw Bernie turn slightly pale.

"Looks like you're probably going to need neurosurgery to get that out," the doc said, "and we don't have the facilities here."

Five days later I hied myself to Cape Town where the offending object was removed. Didn't have any bevies down there, either.

18

Too Young for Death

February 10, 1987 . . . Oshakati Base

Dear Jones,

Returned a few days ago from Cape Town and a spot of microneuro-surgery. The damage to the nerve has left me with only half a hand that can feel anything. The other half, while outwardly numb, still aches like hell. I must say that I find the whole thing quite extraordinary: it's so seldom one gets shot these days.

There have been two deaths since I've been away; both South Africans, both long-serving good operators. They died in a head-on collision while driving a pickup truck between Ondangwa and Oshakati. The vagaries of fate.

The worst thing (I think) about my enforced absence is that I've missed a lot of stories and combat photo opportunities. Things have been very active here. Yet, there's something niggling at the back of my mind that tells me I would have been damaged far more seriously had I not been away for the last three weeks. Superstitious? Not me. But at Eenhana the night before I was hit, a gushing thunderstorm passed over and not long thereafter, a full moon threw a rainbow into the retreating edge of the rain. (I swear to God. We all stood there and marveled, none of us ever having seen a rainbow in the middle of the night, making silly, giggling comments about "what it meant.") And prior to being hit, part of my singing-in-the-shower repertoire was "Swing Low Sweet Chariot" and "Bury Me Not on the Lone Prairie." You can bet your bottom dollar I haven't sung either since. But don't ever accuse me of being superstitious.

We all know the infiltration is here seriously now. The fighting is the heaviest people have seen in some years. Contacts have become everyday events across the length and breadth of Ovamboland, especially in the central and eastern regions. Intelligence reports say that SWAPO's Typhoon Detachment is preparing to come across. They haven't been seen since 1985, when they crossed the border and withdrew in tatters after being badly mauled by Ops K and 101 Battalion. Still, by SWAPO standards, they are the elite, trained especially for base attacks and ambushes.

A captured insurgent admitted there were more than a hundred of them at the FAPLA base at Namakunde, eight miles north of the Oshikango border post, waiting for orders to come down. It's likely some of them are already on this side of the border. Even the men here admit Typhoon is better and more aggressive than any of the other SWAPO detachments.

"Yes! These will stand and fight," the guys here tell me, rubbing their hands together. "What a pleasure."

February 14, 1987

I had ridden up to Eenhana to spend the week working on my notes and sorting through the first batch of photographs the lab had sent back. I didn't feel up to spending seven days riding through the bush in a Casspir. If something were to happen, I would try to catch a lift out to the scene with one of the helicopters and join the follow-up from there. In the meantime, I had more than enough backlogged tapes and scribbled notes to type out one-handed on my battered Olivetti. And at night I'd be able to throw my sleeping bag on the floor of the air-conditioned ops room, kept cool for the sake of the radios. A rare treat.

On the afternoon I arrived at Eenhana, half a dozen groups had rolled in to rebunker with diesel and water and set up camp outside the base. Aside from fuel and water, Eenhana offered fresh meat and beer. A braai was always the order of the evening, followed by a few beers with the air force. That night, about twenty men sat on either side of a row of expanded metal tables. For some of them, it was the first time they'd seen me since I'd returned from the hospital.

"How's the arm?" Betoger asked.

"Arm's fine, but the hand still hurts," I admitted and took a swallow from my can of beer.

"So where did it hit you?"

I lifted my arm and pulled up the short sleeve.

Betoger leaned forward and peered closely at the bright red scar on the inside of the biceps. "Hell, how did you get hit there?"

"Well, I had the camera up like this," I started to explain, holding an imaginary camera at eye level, "looking for a shot and . . . "

"You must have been surrendering!" he butted in. "You weren't looking for a picture, you must have had your arms raised. Hey," he said, looking around at the others, "we've got a hands-upper here. What kind of journalist did we get? A surrendering journalist!" Everyone started laughing as I reddened. Surrendering, indeed.

I bit my tongue and waited for the laughter to subside. Since my return from Cape Town, there had been a subtle change in the attitude toward me from the men in the unit. The laid-back, albeit heavy, humor and the ease with which it was directed was a welcome change from the earlier aloofness I'd experienced from some of them. The relaxed banter was, I realized, a sign of at least partial acceptance. Although I would forever be an outsider, the injury and my subsequent return to operations represented a rite of passage—an honorary initiation into an exclusive society.

"You really disappointed us for a few minutes, though," someone said.

"Why's that?" I asked.

"No, when the word first came over the radio, we heard that you'd broken your arm."

"Yeah, well, that's what I . . . "

"And all of us were saying what a clumsy fuck you were. *No* one breaks his arm in the middle of a contact, man."

"Yeah, but . . . "

"And then we heard Toit say that you had been hit, and all of us said, 'All right! He's not such a clumsy fuck after all!'" An appreciative wave of guffaws rolled through the group. The speaker slapped a knee and looked around at his audience. "Toit . . . ," he mimicked, pitching his voice high, "Toit said he kept shouting, 'I'm shot, I'm shot!'" He doubled over as everyone dissolved into paroxysms of hysterical laughter, a couple of them choking on their beers.

I waited for it to subside. "Thanks a lot, you bastards. That's great. I really appreciate the concern."

"But you want to take it easy, man," gasped another, trying to keep a straight face. "You're not as young as you used to be, you know."

I glowered for effect and took another pull at the beer. Some took enormous delight in reminding me that I had at least twenty years on most of them. I stared at the braai and pretended I hadn't heard.

"By the way, you got any daughters old enough for me?"

"Bastards," I hissed, still concentrating on the barbecue while they fell about laughing again at their marvelous senses of humor. Comedians. Exactly what I needed.

"So what did you think when you got hit?" asked Attie, wiping his eyes.

"Surprised the hell out of me. Really. I just never thought it was going to happen," I answered, a little mollified that someone was taking my wound seriously for a change. At least Attie was all right. Someone you could always count on.

"Listen," Attie continued, "it's not the one with your name on it that you have to worry about—it's the one that says 'To whom it may concern.'" There was a brief rise at the old joke. "But, man, you can ride on the back of my car anytime," he added.

I smiled with genuine embarrassment and shook my head. "Okay, okay, you don't have to rub it in. Everyone told me it was stupid. You were right. I've got no one to blame but myself. So if you don't mind, I think I'll take my pictures from inside next time."

"No, no," he said. A grin split his face. "Genuine. You can ride on the back of my car anytime you want to. In fact, I'd really appreciate it."

"Why's that?" I asked, eyeing him suspiciously.

"No, if they see an old and easy target like you, maybe they won't shoot at me!" he roared, ducking as I threw my beer at him.

In the morning, the group leaders and car commanders came in to plan the day's movements and get the latest intelligence. Sitting around the outdoor tables, they sipped coffee and gnawed on dry rusks while discussing where they would be operating for the next two or three days. Toit and Attie were planning on working to the west, between Eenhana and Ohangwena. Three other groups, none of whom I knew well, would be heading east. Info from the local population, confirmed by an attempted ambush against a civilian pickup truck late yesterday, placed at least one group of seven to ten insurgents between Eenhana and Nkongo.

Laying out my cameras and cleaning equipment, I started on the thrice-daily routine of blowing out dust, polishing the lenses and checking batteries. Porky, the tall, cropped-headed teenager I'd met during my two-week introduction to Koevoet ten months earlier, sat down next to me with his cup of coffee. The cameras continued to be a popular topic of conversation.

Although more comfortable now using English with me, he was still as gawky and quiet and painfully shy as when I'd first met him the year before. Clearing his throat, he finally asked why I carried three cameras, each with a different lens. With a few minutes remaining before his group pulled out, I passed them over. He carefully held up each in turn and looked through the viewfinder. As he was examining them, big, jovial Betoger ambled over to watch, a rusk in one hand, a chipped enameled coffee mug in the other.

Porky gently placed the last camera back on the table, looking at it enviously. He asked shyly if perhaps I would be interested in selling one to him before I left. I said that I'd gotten such a good deal I really couldn't afford to sell them, but that I'd think about it. Before I could reach for the camera, Betoger put down his mug, shoved the rusk in his mouth and picked it up. Clowning, he sighted through the viewfinder and pretended to take a picture an inch from Porky's nose.

I really didn't know Betoger more than to say hello to, but I'd heard enough stories about him. The most widely told tale—invariably related with great hilarity—concerned the time he and a friend demolished a bottle of brandy and decided to set off two small blocks of Soviet TNT they'd "forgotten" to turn in from a contact. They slightly miscalculated the charge and placement. When the smoke and dust settled, a goodly portion of their barracks was gone. The next morning, they were standing rigidly at attention in front of Brigadier Dreyer's desk.

"What the hell did you think you were doing?" Dreyer shouted at them. The boss was no man to be trifled with at the best of times. The boss in a temper quickly reduced the bravest to quivering jelly. It was commonly held that suffering the wrath of the Almighty might be infinitely preferable to facing the "Brig" when he was seriously outraged.

"Sir, we didn't mean to . . ."

"You're fired! Pack your bags," Dreyer snarled. "I'm sending you back to SA."

"But, sir, you can't do that!" said Betoger, drawing on heretofore untapped courage. "*Please* don't send us back," he blinked, trying to hold back the tears already puddling on his lower lashes. "I promise I'll never do anything like it again. Never. I swear it. But please don't send us back." The pleading and groveling went on until Dreyer relented and banned them to the Koevoet satellite base at Ongwediva. Before they could draw a sigh of relief, he pointed a finger at them and sighted down it. "If I see either of you, or even *hear* anything about you, you're fired, and that's a promise. Now get the hell out of my sight!" Their exile lasted three months before Dreyer allowed them back on the base in Oshakati.

Someone who blew up his own barracks—however innocently—was not the sort I was keen to see handling one of my cameras. I held my breath until it was safely back on the table, then snatched it up and slipped the sling over my neck. I cradled it protectively. These guys were nice enough, but their exuberance tended to get out of hand at times.

Finally, everyone stood and headed to their Casspirs and Wolf Turbos parked outside the base. Attie, always a little impatient to get started, had already left with his group. Toit, still waiting for his cars to finish with their rebunkering, walked over to the ops room with Riaan de la Rosa, one of his car commanders, who had been on leave when I'd been wounded. They would rendezvous with Zulu Uniform somewhere in the bush. I poured another cup of coffee and went back to working on the cameras. Half an hour later, the cleaning done, I roused myself and walked to the ops room.

It was early for a group to radio the Koevoet ops room at Eenhana to put the helicopters on standby; they had found where a group of insurgents had set up an ambush the day before. The site was less than ten miles east of us along the Chandelier Road to Elundu. The ambush team had either tired of waiting for a target or had changed their minds and abandoned the position. Their spoor, moving south, was no more than thirty minutes old.

Toit almost knocked me over as he and de la Rosa charged out of the ops radio room. "Zulu Sierra found a fresh ambush site the terrs left this morning. Lieutenant Ronne's picked up seven to ten spoor just fifteen minutes from here. They've already put the choppers on stand by. You coming with us?"

Something I'd never felt before held me motionless for a second. *What was that?* I wondered, as whatever it was slipped away. I blinked and looked at Toit, who was waiting impatiently for an answer. I shook my head and told him that I'd be riding out with the choppers if they were scrambled.

"Okay, see you later," and they went pounding down the muddy road to get their group saddled up and moving.

So what the hell's the matter with you? I thought. *You afraid or something? Oh right, sure,* I smirked in denial. *I just don't feel like it, is all.*

I ducked into the radio room to check the grid reference of the team that had called in, then strolled over to the air force ops room and communications center. The pilots had already plotted the same position and were pulling on flight suits and shoulder holsters. The flight engineers were out on the hardpan, preflighting the helicopters. I grabbed another cup of coffee and moved outside. There was nothing to do now but wait for the word to go.

Captain Rick Dooley gave me a thumbs-up when I asked if I could catch a ride out with him. I'd flown on a casevac mission with Dooley the day before. An army patrol from 701 Battalion had tripped a POM-Z anti-personnel mine along the road between Eenhana and the army base at Elundu. Two soldiers, one Caprivian and one South African, had been seriously wounded in the legs and feet by shrapnel from the Soviet-made booby trap.

When we landed at the scene, the platoon was spread out in the bush on either side of the road, weapons ready. Although it was unlikely the insurgents were still nearby, no one was taking any chances with the precious helicopters. I hopped out, and the Caprivian soldier, the more seriously wounded of the two, was loaded into the Alouette. Dooley lifted off for the nearest army sick bay at Nkongo.

Being in the middle of the bush without the reassuring rumble of Casspirs or Wolf Turbos and minus the blatant, swaggering cockiness of the men I knew was a fresh experience. It was also more than slightly discomfiting. I had become accustomed to the bearded, scarred faces and loud, irreverent voices of Koevoet.

The smooth-faced lieutenant showed me the spot where the POM-Z had exploded. Looking at the torn up ground and bush, I was surprised the injuries they had taken hadn't been more serious. He explained that they had been trying to find the spoor of a group of insurgents who had fired a heatstrim at a civilian truck earlier that day. I followed him down the road, where he showed me the ambush site, pointing out the slight depression in the sand where at least half a dozen insurgents had lain in wait. Continuing our walk, I saw the anti-armor rifle grenade, broken in half, lying on the side of the road. I looked from it to him uncomprehendingly.

"It hit the truck," the lieutenant said, "but it didn't go off. Maybe rain last night got inside it. Or maybe it was a dud. Whatever. But it didn't go off. The Ovambo civvies in that truck were very lucky."

Before withdrawing from the scene of their attempted ambush, the insurgents had set the booby trap. As soon as the Ovambo civilians had reported the attack, a Romeo Mike team was dispatched. Moving carefully through the thick bush along the side of the dirt road, the Caprivian soldier simply hadn't seen the thin, green trip wire of the POM-Z. The shrapnel had turned his feet into mush. The two who were being casevaced weren't the only ones wounded when the booby trap exploded. I noticed the twenty-year-old lieutenant was limping. Spots of bright, fresh blood were still soaking through holes in the legs of his brown trousers.

Forty minutes later, Dooley flew back in to pick up the remaining casualty and myself. As we lifted off, I saw the lieutenant, head tucked down and holding on to his bush hat, limping away from the howling sandstorm generated by our takeoff. In spite of his wounds, he wasn't leaving his men. I gave him a silent thumbs-up as we rose and turned toward the army base at Nkongo.

Sitting with the helicopter crews under the ever-present camouflage net, I swapped flying stories and other lies, checking my watch every two minutes and affecting an air of boredom. But feet tapped, crossed legs bounced up and down and hands made constant tiny adjustments to webbing and zippers, all in nervous anticipation of coming action. Or maybe it was only me. No matter how many times I did it, the heart started beating just a little faster, the palms became just a little damper, as the wait began. Only this time it was worse. I couldn't put my finger on it, but — *then what's the matter with you? I don't know, it's just that, I don't know — but I feel something. Something's wrong.*

Of three hand-cranked field telephones inside the air force ops room, only one now had any significance: that one connected to the Koevoet ops room. The word to scramble would come over the Ops K radio net and then be passed to the pilots via that one special phone. To my ear, all the telephones sounded exactly the same. For the air crews, each had its own distinctive and immediately recognizable tone. If the wrong one clattered during a conversation, the speaker would pause almost imperceptibly before smoothly carrying on. I never did get the hang of it. Every ring would have my head swiveling round to stare at the open door to the ops room.

"Army ops," someone would say good-naturedly at my sudden start.

"Right," I'd say, and slide back from the edge of my chair.

One of the pilots was in the middle of a story when it rang. He stopped and heads lifted, waiting. We heard the radio operator answer. He came running out.

"SCRAMBLE! THEY'VE HIT AN AMBUSH! THEY NEED GUNSHIPS AND CASEVACS NOW!"

Chairs screeched backward on the concrete as everything else was forgotten and we sprinted the 100 meters for the choppers, holding on to flapping equipment and struggling with zippers on the run. *It's happened. Whatever it is, it's happened,* as I ran behind Dooley. Then we were there and settling in. Switches were flipped on and the pilots started the engines, waiting impatiently for the turbines to wind up. Transmissions were engaged, and the blades started to swing slowly, then faster and faster, the helicopters coming alive, trembling and shaking. Checklists were completed, and a final thumbs-up from the crew chiefs sent the ungainly machines taxiing one by one out of the revetment and onto the runway. Then the tails came up and we were airborne, noses tucked down and racing southeast just above the trees.

Something *was* wrong. This time it was all different. Terribly different. I knew it, felt it in my bones. What had happened out there? Okay, people were hurt, but how many? How badly? And the worst question of all: did I know them? Some indefinable dark monster had slipped into my chest, unseen claws grabbing and slowly tightening.

Relax. Everything's okay. It's only because it's the first time since you were hit. Take it easy. Do something.

I bent over my cameras and gave the lenses a final wipe, concentrating on remembering which was on which side; opening Velcro pouches on the camera vest to double check which held the color film and which the black and white. I clenched the aching right hand again and again, massaging the numb fingers, trying to will them to feel and work, my breath starting to come in short jerks. Finally, I took the headset, settled it over my ears and reached up to plug in the jack.

Dooley thumbed the mike button, his voice distant and metallic. "Sounds pretty bad," turning his dark visored helmet toward me. "They're saying they hit an ambush and took some casualties."

Whatever had been building in me started to accelerate. "How bad?" wondering at the sound of my voice. *Why was it suddenly an effort to talk?*

"Bad."

The monster I now knew for what it was grabbed hold inside my chest and squeezed. *I'm scared. Oh, Jesus, I'm scared.* My words, even allowing for the distortion of the intercom system, came out strained and tight. "How far out are we?"

"Five minutes."

Sitting on the aft-facing seat next to Dooley, I stared at the flight engineer as he leaned across the door-mounted machine gun, scanning the bush and trees flashing by under us, his face a blank.

How could he look like that? Didn't he feel what I was feeling? Was my own face as blank? Whatever had crawled into my chest was really there now, squeezing harder and climbing into my throat. I pulled my eyes away and twisted around to stare out the Plexiglas nose.

This is part of what you came for, boy, I started telling myself. *This is what you came for.*

We banked sharply, and I saw smoke from a white phosphorus grenade billowing out of the bush a mile or so in front of us. Coming up was an open, grassy pan surrounded by thick bush. There they were, half a dozen Casspirs and Wolf Turbos scattered across it. As we decelerated and began a straight-in approach, the other two choppers broke off to set up top cover orbits. Then dust and grass were blowing away under the downwash of the blades, and we bumped and settled heavily. I opened the door and scrambled out, squinting against the stinging sand. Head tucked down, I latched the door and ran toward the nearest cars. Dooley immediately lifted off behind me.

Toit was standing on top of his car, talking rapidly into a handset, his face set in an expression I had never seen before. As I approached, he pointed with a jerk of his free hand toward the rear of a Casspir at right angles to his own. Gathered around the open doors of the armored personnel carrier, a dozen Ovambo special constables stared inside. They made way for me as I came up.

A body lay on the narrow floor, the top of the head toward me. An ops medic kneeled straight-armed above it, pressing powerfully and rhythmically on the chest. Another medic had the head tilted back and at every fourth push covered the open mouth with his own, filling the lungs, then pressing his fingers frantically against the throat for a carotid pulse.

God, don't let me know him, I thought stupidly, as though it would make it less real, *just don't let me know him.*

The ops medic motioned for help, and two trackers climbed quickly inside. Each took an arm to help lift the unconscious body from the cramped car. Above, two helicopters orbited, their turbines and slapping blades adding to the screech of radios and idling diesel engines on the ground. Only the sound of voices was absent as we all watched silently.

*Take a photo. No. Come on, isn't this part of it? Take your pictures.
I can't. It's too private. I can't do it.* I twisted away, not wanting to see,
feeling for the first time like an intruder, a filthy, horrible voyeur
peeking through a neighbor's curtains. When I turned back, he
was face down and Simon, the black medic, was cutting the shirt
up the back. The shirt came off, and I saw the two small, closely-
spaced bullet holes in his side. As they pulled him back over, his
head rolled to the side, blood smearing at the corner of his mouth.

NO! I wanted to scream, *Oh, God, no, not Porky! Not quiet, skinny
nineteen-year-old Porky. I was just talking with him! No! This isn't what
I came for, I didn't come for this!* And as they kept working on him,
I had to walk away, joining the knot of men who stood stiffly and
quietly to one side.

Ryno knelt at Porky's head, one hand behind the limp neck,
leaning down to fill lungs that refused to work on their own.
Trond, the ops medic from Zulu Sierra, straddled Porky's chest,
crossed hands driving downward over the heart. Simon lifted an
arm to wrap it with a blood-pressure cuff and listened with his
stethoscope for any sign of life, all of them working with silent
desperation in the middle of this insignificant clearing in northern Namibia. Above, helicopters still orbited protectively in the
clear morning sky.

Simon placed his fingertips on Porky's forehead and raised an
eyelid with his thumb. He covered the eye with the other hand,
then quickly removed it. There was no change in the pupils. He
spoke quietly to the other two. Trond lifted his hands from the
thin chest and stood, swinging one leg over the body. Ryno
looked up, his eyes stricken and unbelieving. He looked back at
the body and slowly rose to his feet, still staring and wiping
Porky's blood from his own lips.

Then one of the choppers was descending and seven Ovambos and South Africans reached down to gather the body into a
bier of black and white arms. With Toit cradling Porky's head,
they stumbled toward the machine. I ran after them, camera
snapping in the blur of sound and movement, the body
anonymous. Only a pair of green-stockinged feet protruded from
the cluster of men. As I neared the helicopter, I saw another body
already on the floor, soaked in blood from the waist down, the
head turned away. They laid Porky gently on his back next to
Dooley, his head against the seat I had held on the way in. In the

downwash of sand, dust and grass, I stood and stared at him inside the Plexiglas shroud as the chopper lifted and turned toward Eenhana.

I looked around and saw de la Rosa, shot through both arms, eyes wide and face slack with pain and shock, supported from behind by one of the Ovambos from his car. Trond was kneeling and tying a tourniquet around his upper right arm as he sat dazed and hunched forward. Three Ovambo special constables with minor shrapnel wounds were being treated by Simon and Ryno. The wounded could go out on the next choppers. *What did they hit?*

Toit was still on the radio, talking rapidly with the ops officer at Eenhana. He took a deep breath as he slipped the headset around his neck and glanced at me. "Porky and Betoger are dead," he said coldly. "Three of the Ovambos are wounded. De la Rosa's hit. They rolled right into the fucking ambush. Betoger was hit in the abdomen with an RPG that came through the front of his car. Nothing could have saved him. Another car was shot out with heatstrims. The trackers have found where the terrs set the ambush. We've got at least seven spoor. You staying, or you want out on the next chopper?"

Yes. I want out. "No," I shook my head, "no, I'm coming with you."

Because this isn't the way it happens. Because someone's going to tell me that they'll be okay, that this isn't real. Betoger's the one who pleaded with the boss to stay, he can't be dead. And Porky's not really dead, either. I was talking to him just an hour ago. It's all make-believe. In a minute someone's going to say, hahaha, really fooled you, didn't we?

"Porky called his own casevac," Toit said as we started rolling. "Right after they hit the ambush, I heard him say over the radio that they needed a casevac. I told him I'd already called for it and asked him who'd been hurt, and he said it was himself. I asked him how bad and he said, 'Bad.' Then one of the Ovambos got on the radio and said, 'Hurry! The shirumbu is dying. He needs help.'"

An hour later, Toit looked down at me from his position behind the guns. "You're really quiet today. You okay?" I nodded dumbly. "Are you sure?" Another nod. "Want to go back?"

I shook my head. "No, I'm okay. No sweat," I said, hardly recognizing my own voice.

Thirty minutes later, we hit the first one. Perhaps he knew there would be no surrendering because he came out of the bush with his finger squeezing the trigger of his AK-47, shots going wild and blowing out one of our tires before a dozen shots took him down. His head snapped back as he half twisted and dropped. An RPG-75 rolled away from the body, its shoulder strap shot in two. The head pressed forward into the blood-spattered sand as one leg drew up. I watched it through the armored glass window of the Casspir, unable to make myself stand or even lift a camera until it was over.

I followed the trackers out the door and turned toward the body, flinching badly at the unexpected burst of automatic fire. One of the Ovambo constables, face contorted and eyes narrowed to slits, had begun emptying his fifty-round magazine into the dying man, the high-velocity bullets plucking and lifting the camouflage uniform away from the shivering body like a narrow, concentrated wind rippling across it.

Porky and Betoger had been his friends.

By mid-afternoon, I had forced myself out of the car alongside the trackers. It was the only way. The next day I was back to normal. As normal as you can be, I decided.

Soon after the ambush, Zulu Two radioed Toit to say General Dreyer didn't want any of the seven making it back to Angola. "What the fuck do you think we're doing," Toit snapped, having just watched the chopper taking Porky and Betoger back to Eenhana. There was no question in anyone's mind about these people escaping. For the next three days, the teams threw themselves into their work with an intensity and determination exceeding anything I had seen. The third day after the ambush, the last of the seven ambushers fell under Koevoet's guns. It was rumored that at least one tried to surrender, but in a contact, someone explained patiently, in the *confusion* and everything, well . . . .

Beneath the camouflage net of the air force canteen at Eenhana that night, an exhausted and filthy group of policemen bowed their heads in memory of Porky and Betoger. They would not be spoken of tonight, but as heads and cans of beer lifted to offer a final toast, eyes blinking back what was there, something escaped to trace a furrow down a dust-caked cheek.

19

Questions and Cliches

S o why was I there? I asked myself often enough and was asked over and over when I returned. It seemed such a simple question that there should have been an easy answer. But there wasn't; there really wasn't. Posturing? That's what a lot of it was, I suppose: I'm here, I'm cool. Though, God knew (I hoped), there was far more to it than that. It was convenient to pass off my presence there as a search for the truth of a little-understood African war; that was actual, that I was doing. It wasn't until later that I realized I had gone there to learn the truth of myself as well. All the questions and cliches of "grace under fire" were part of the search, and when I finally thought I had it, had passed my own examination, there was a sense of belonging, with all that went with it. That featureless spot on a world map my eyes would once have passed over without hesitation became the center of my universe.

Acceptance and belonging didn't come easily, but they came. Of course, it helped being a little unique. I was a foreigner and a journalist (or a writer when I was feeling particularly pretentious) who went into the bush with them week after week, unarmed and dripping with cameras; which made me a novelty, and a little special, but special only in a different way from anyone else who was there or passed through. I had come of my own volition to live amongst them, to tell a story from an insider's view, a story that couldn't be told honestly any other way. Or at least that's what I said I believed. I came looking for what I was born to, and that I believed totally.

In my four months there, I saw only one other journalist arrive to take the measure of the war. He came escorted from

Windhoek, inarticulate and posturing with the best of us. It was understandable posturing, but I didn't like it or him.

I'd just been wounded for the second time by then, and he avoided me like I carried the plague, eyeing the bloody bandage distastefully and saying nothing, at least to me. I wanted to know why they let him in: this was my story, my people, he was a trespasser, but I kept my mouth shut, hoping childishly that when they took him out it would be a dry run. Contacts were my province, goddammit, he didn't have the right to one; I'd earned them with my sweat and fear and blood. But the second day in the bush, the group he was with found a single spoor and there was the inevitable conclusion.

When his escort officer, waiting in Oshakati, heard about it over the radio, he decided his boy had seen as much as he needed and sent a chopper to pull him out. The group commander said when he was told there was a helicopter in-bound, that he had his gear stacked in about thirty seconds flat; he was ready to get out of there, no shit. Smart man. When Bez told me that he laughed conspiratorially in a way that made me feel better. Not a lot, but some; I was too greedy, too selfish, too puffed up with my own self-imagined uniqueness to be entirely appeased.

A few days later, we saw the piece he had written. I couldn't read the Afrikaans, but the photos told me more about him than the copy. After the contact, he'd posed on one knee next to the body, holding the dead insurgent's rifle. The photo was there, implicit in its suggestion. It was good for another laugh, and I was perhaps less than charitable, mentioning it more often than was necessary, with all my own implicit suggestions about myself. Just who did he think he was fooling? I wanted to know. Of course, I was too cool: *I* wouldn't have had a photo like that taken of *me*.

Until I thought about it and saw that he was behaving only slightly more obtrusively than I, perhaps. Just who did I think *I* was fooling, I should have asked. It was still *I'm here, I'm cool*, and I guess he had as much right to it as anyone else. But I saw in the photo (would the article have exonerated him?) the pose of white superiority (who did he think were the heart of the unit, did most of the killing *and* dying?) that many within the unit—yes, even here—believed as well, but were too involved, too sensitive, perhaps even too aware of the contradictions to flaunt. Still, he was neither the polarized kaffir-baiting thug nor the hands-thrown-in-the-air moral hypocrite. In fact, he was probably more like all of us, black and white, than I, at least, was prepared to admit at the time.

Out of the bush, you never really thought about dying. Of course, it was possible, but you never thought it could happen to you. Getting hurt?—well, who didn't get hurt occasionally? No big thing, you said pompously after it happened the first time. But even then, you never thought about getting hurt seriously. That and dying just didn't exist. They did, of course, but were so deeply repressed they couldn't touch you. Most of the time, anyway. Sure, there were times you were frightened (frightened? try terrified), and it was okay to mention it—as long as you didn't mention it too often. "Yeah, I'm afraid sometimes," said a group leader; "Heatstrims, those scare me." And that was the only time I heard it, at the end of a drinking session that suddenly turned serious. But in the morning it didn't exist again, and good manners prevented pursuing it further.

"Aren't you scared?" Jackie asked me once not long after we'd met, and I laughed and said, "All the time"; but that was before I understood what he was really talking about, before the naiveté of a schoolboy adventure wore off and it became something else entirely. God, was I dumb. Later, I felt it so badly on two occasions—after Porky and Betoger were killed, then again at Ohangwena—that I was crippled; not by the fear of dying, but by the need to *live*. Yet afterward, I understood that I had never been so aware of being alive. Never. Another cliché, but there it was.

"Violence freak, adrenaline junkie," said an accusing journalist disapprovingly after I'd come out, which wasn't entirely correct, nor completely wrong either, as far as it went, but he would never really know. It was certainly the fashionable thing to say, and I understood why he had to say it. As a political child of the Sixties, though, at least he could have smiled just a little when I agreed by quoting Mick Jagger at him: "Violence gives you a buzz." I was ready to drill him with sharper homilies from his folk heroes of the peace-and-flowers era until I saw it would be wasted effort; he simply wasn't prepared to acknowledge the paradox, and instead glared at me with furious self-righteousness. Had he been more honest, he would have understood that we were co-sinners. It wasn't my covering the war that got to him; it was whom I chose to go with. Real journalists pick their sides more carefully, is what he meant to say. And sides, of course, was what it was all about.

Had he been willing to listen, I would have tried to explain that in some ways, it was all pure fantasy; since when did middle-aged American writers find themselves with unheard-of dispensations that allowed them to go charging through the bush of Namibia and Angola with an elite counterinsurgency unit? But the fantasy was real; sometimes altogether too real. And that was the opiate: the proof of the risk.

And risk, of course, was what it was all about, too.

There is no one who goes into it—chasing war or adventure (war correspondent, if you please)—who doesn't get at least a tingle from being seen as different, as somehow a little special. "Boy, it must take real balls to do that. You wouldn't get *me* out there." And you smile or frown and say, no, it's just a job, you know, denying the image as custom requires. Which of course only plants it all the more securely, convincing them that not only are you insanely brave, but modest too, and wrong on both counts, if they only knew. Sometimes—for those who matter—you try to explain that what they do is what requires the courage: a family, a secure nine to five and all the rest you've run away from all your life. You tell them that what you do requires no courage because it is an obsession over which you have no control. It's not courage, but an overwhelming *need*. And because they haven't the need themselves, cannot conceive of a reason for having it, you're stuck with the image they've conferred. Which is exactly what you wanted all along anyway, however fraudulent.

Every man in the world hugs to himself a secret image of who he is or what he wants to be. It's not given to many to take it out, give it a dusting and look at it critically. In the end, it was everything I'd hoped for, and more, and still not nearly enough.

20

Tale of an Ancient Warrior

P IET and I walked away from where we had pitched camp at the foot of the tall, granite outcropping. We followed the cold, clear stream that gurgled through the rocky, alkaline desert of the Kaokoveld. To the west and north, mountains rose sharp-spined and purple in the fading light. Somewhere among them was the source of the brook that tumbled along the deeply eroded defile. The brutal starkness of the terrain, so unlike the flat, monotonous bush of central and eastern Ovambo 100 miles behind us, was enough to take the breath away: a land designed for awful contemplation.

We stopped alongside a deep pool and stared for a long moment at the darkening moonscape. Piet hunkered down, the rifle that seemed a part of him resting across heavy thighs.

"I worked out here for almost four years," he said, breaking the silence. "Most of it on foot." His mutilated right hand released the rifle for a moment and traced an arc along the horizon. "Good places to get ambushed."

I waited. Piet didn't volunteer a lot. "Were you?" I finally prompted.

He nodded. "Walked into one not so far from here. Nineteen gooks." His eyes moved slowly across the land before he stood and balanced the rifle over his shoulder. "Started shooting right in front of us," he said matter-of-factly, pointing to a stunted bush not more than 50 feet away.

I turned with him and we started back. "So what happened?" I asked, unable to hold back the question.

"No cover, no place to go except forward. We floored seven. I killed four myself. Lost one of my boys, five wounded."

Silence returned. There was only the grate of our boots on loose shale and sand. The stocky figure next to me paused and we looked back at the jagged, silhouetted mountains. "The worst one was right after I started working out here. It was about this time of day, and we were driving along a trail out there." His chin lifted toward the mountains. "There was a dry river bed on our right, a tall kopje — a rocky hill — on the other side. I was at the back of the Casspir when we were hit. Two RPGs went through the front of the car, and two cars behind us were shot out. My car was already burning as we went off the trail and into the riverbed. I thought the driver was doing it, trying to find cover. The rest of us got out and started firing towards the kopje. The driver and gunner didn't come out, so I went back in to get them. I was going to pull the driver out first, but when my hand went halfway through his neck, I knew he was dead. When I pulled the gunner out, his left leg was gone and the right one was hanging on with just a little muscle.

"I put a tourniquet around the stump, then cut off what was left of the right one and tied that off, too, and got a drip into him. The fire in the car made a good target, and the gooks started shooting mortar bombs at us. I had to crawl back to the other cars to treat the wounded and start drips for the ones who needed them. The terrs finally stopped shooting, but we didn't know if they had run away or were moving around to hit us from another direction. We had to wait there all night before the casevac Pumas got to us." He shook his head and looked at me. "The gunner died. I thought I could save him, but he died before the casevacs arrived."

We started back down, loose rocks skittering away under our feet. Scattered across the sand of our oasis camp below, cooking fires glowed red and orange, sparks twisting frantically to disappear into the cold night air. Halfway down the slope, he coughed into his claw of a hand and cleared his throat.

"But that was when I was still a youngster," he said shyly, embarrassed at having talked so much.

"How old are you now, Piet?" I asked, the story still echoing inside my head.

"Twenty-three," he said, shifting the rifle in his arms.

21

Death by Moonlight

March 10, 1987

Dear Sugar Jones,

Still here, though I'm hoping to wind everything up before too long. My plans are to complete two more week-long deployments, which, given the intensity of the fighting, should see me with all the material I'll need. As was forecast, the insurgents are standing and fighting, and according to everyone here, they've changed tactics — more of them carrying anti-armor weapons with orders to concentrate on knocking out the cars. Even the small-arms ammunition they're using now is armor-piercing and easily capable of penetrating the thin steel of the Casspirs and Wolves. Casualties — while nowhere nearly as appalling as SWAPO's — are nonetheless up. I keep remembering Jim Durand telling me last year that people always seem to get hurt or killed just before they leave. Which is silly and illogical, of course, but just between you, me and the fence post, Sugar Jones, I wish I already had the photos I need.

Fate. Had I deployed with Jackie's group as we'd planned, maybe it never would have happened, but he decided to take a break from it for a while. I transferred to group Zulu Whisky, only they were pulling out a day early, and I couldn't make it. Bez, Zulu Whisky's team leader, said, Jim, catch a ride with Lesch and Zulu Juliet on Wednesday; they'll be RV-ing with us in the bush.

Wednesday morning I was ready to go, but one of Lesch's cars had a turbocharger problem, and we waited and waited till early afternoon for it to be repaired. Lesch finally said the hell with it, we'll take our time working up to Ohangwena, TB there and wait for the car, then RV with Bez on Thursday.

So that's what we did, arriving at the small Security Branch base five kilometers south of the Angolan border late that afternoon. An hour before sunset, the fourth car finally appeared and we set up camp under the trees about 150 meters south of the base. Cooking fires were soon going. Waiting for them to burn down to coals, we slipped into the base for a beer and a shower.

Even after four months and all that I had seen and shared, there remained a subtle barrier that kept me truly apart. Although my presence now was considered unremarkable, with rare exception—and understandably—I was still an outsider to these men. Even if I had become part of the furniture, I remained an unarmed piece of the furniture. Another reason, of course, was the language. Among the blacks I met, only Jerry Mbwale knew more than a pinch of English, and of the whites barely a handful were completely comfortable with the language. Often what I perceived as aloofness was shyness and embarrassment about stepping outside the comfort of Afrikaans.

Although I had a nodding acquaintance with most of them after four months, it wasn't until I had deployed with a team that they became more than faces and passing hellos. But even in the relative intimacy of a deployment and the shared danger, questions had a way of drawing lines. So it behooved me to sit on the sidelines and play the role of quintessential listener and quiet observer.

Each group had its own distinct personality. One might enjoy a reputation for aggressiveness and cold-blooded efficiency, another for being laid back and easy going. There were high scorers, usually commanded by grizzled veterans in their mid-twenties who had learned their trade under founder members; there were groups that slogged along, seldom shining but doing the dogsbody work. Each was a unique microculture within the Koevoet subculture; each a fascinating study of men at war. Tonight, I contemplated Zulu Juliet's car commanders as I quietly cleaned my cameras and nursed a beer.

Apie stood inside a nearby wire cage, feeding potato chips to two servet monkeys that sat on his shoulders. Their shrill scoldings when the pack ran empty set him to smiling and opening another as he clucked soothingly to them. Short and round and sporting a goatee that looked as out of place on an otherwise beardless face as the pistol on his hip, his placid nature made him the unlikeliest candidate for Koevoet membership of anyone I had met in the unit.

Zulu Juliet's SADF ops medic was Charles. Of medium height, with curly, black hair, he was the son of an Italian immigrant to South Africa. Six months of his voluntary one year assignment to Koevoet were already completed. When the next six months were over, he told me, he was going back to South Africa to continue his studies. After that, he'd be pleased never to see the operational area again.

The new cop on the beat was Boeta, who had been with the group only a few weeks. The tallest and youngest of the car commanders, he was the prototypical farm boy. Still learning the job and eager to prove himself in the way of new guys everywhere, he seemed the most serious.

Lesch, blond and carrying too much weight from the beer, was one of those with a quick, easy laugh and a joke for almost any occasion. No one could ever really accuse him of being too serious. A four-year Koevoet veteran, he had taken over as Zulu Juliet's group leader only three months earlier when Claasen, the previous commander, had been badly wounded by a POM-Z antipersonnel mine.

(Still convalescing, "Claasie" was always there to meet them when they returned from the bush, leaning on his cane and favoring the leg with the fresh, shiny scar tissue. In spite of a fractured wrist and serious nerve damage that kept both his wrist and lower leg in steel and plastic braces, he was constantly pestering Dreyer for permission to return to ops. I never got to know him well, but he always struck me as a quiet Jackie, genuine, committed and deeply caring about his men and the civilian population. I still remember seeing him standing in front of Zulu Juliet's storeroom that day, watching and waving as we pulled away from the empty parade ground. I kept my eyes on the lone, motionless figure that grew steadily smaller and smaller and finally disappeared as we rolled out of sight.)

Drying off and dressing after our showers, we talked about base attacks. None of those in the group had experienced one, though the shrapnel holes through the thin walls of the toilet and shower block where we stood were mute evidence of an attack on Ohang-wena eight months earlier. No one in the base had been injured, but the existing damage was enough to stir the imagination. Walking back to our camp, Charles wondered aloud what would be the best thing to do in the event of a mortar attack.

"Lie down and don't move," I said seriously, as though I knew what I was talking about. Looking at the large maroela trees spreading over the parked Casspirs, I imagined falling mortar rounds exploding in the branches to shower the ground with shrapnel. "But first get away from trees like those," I added in an off-hand remark.

Lounging around the glowing embers, replete and mellow, we talked of this and that, the conversation always coming back to the intensity of the present infiltration. Lesch admitted there hadn't been anything like it for a few years. Even allowing for the more than two hundred SWAPO already killed or captured since the beginning of the year, Koevoet's losses of fifteen killed and over forty wounded were high.

"We're definitely bleeding this year," he said, "The ratio isn't good."

The talk came around to base attacks again. "You know, the gooks revved this place last year just a couple of days after you left. Two or three mortar bombs landed inside the base, and the water tank was hit with an RPG, but no one was hurt. Fourteen of the Swaps were killed on the follow-up the next day." It was a story I'd heard over and over again from Brand, Viljoen, Nella and a dozen others.

"One mortar bomb landed right behind the toilets and showers," said Lesch, "You see the holes in the walls?"

I grinned and nodded in the firelight. "Yeah. Wouldn't have wanted to be sitting there when that happened."

Lesch sipped his coffee and stirred the coals. "They hit the place right after midnight. When the last mortar bomb landed, they tried a ground assault. Two of 'em were killed outside the walls, and the rest gapped it back into the bush. Their detachment commander probably didn't explain that there'd actually be people shooting back. We found out later that their plans were to capture at least one white, load him in a Casspir, and force him to drive them back to Namakunde. Big ideas, but they got a big surprise instead."

I stared into the coals and tried to imagine it—exploding mortar rounds, streams of tracers crisscrossing in the night, murky figures slipping through the high grass toward the base. *That would really be something,* I thought in blessed ignorance. *That would really be exciting.*

Lesch, Apie, and Charles settled under their mosquito nets around the side and front of the Blesbok. A Casspir was parked parallel to it thirty feet away, and I lay on my cot between the two. Boeta stretched out on his ground sheet between me and the others. The fire slowly died, conversation of contacts and women and contacts and women dwindled with it.

"You know, it's probably about time for another rev here," said Lesch; "full moon, middle of the infiltration. Never know." He laughed.

I zipped up my sleeping bag and looked at the sky. "Anyone know which of those two constellations is the Southern Cross?" I asked, pointing an arm overhead.

"It's that one, the lower one," said Boeta.

"No, it's the higher one," said Charles. We slept.

March 12, 1987 . . . 0330.

I came awake as the first two mortar rounds screamed out of the night, exploding just 20 meters south of us. As I rolled off my cot like a great brown slug in the sleeping bag, I saw streams of tracers flashing overhead from the west and northwest. This really isn't happening, I thought, the guys in the base they're just playing a joke, stupid bastards, and they better stop it right now. But I knew it wasn't any joke.

Then the rounds were dropping right on top of us: **whu-WHUMP! whu-WHUMP!** *so near and closely spaced there was nothing to do but not move and flatten against the ground, head to the side* **whu-WHUMP!UMP!whuWHUMP!** *close enough to feel the solid slap of shock waves through the air, knowing to stand was to die* **whuWHUMP! whuWHUMP!** *and in the moments between explosions hearing the* **crack!** *of bullets and whirr-whine of shrapnel overhead.* **whuWHUMP! whu-WHUMP!WHUMP!** *and screaming silently* JES**whuWHUMP!**IST!

THEY'RE TRYING TO KILL US! **whuWHUMP!whuWHUMP!** *and not knowing if anyone was alive or dead around me and they kept coming* **whuWHUMP!** *and coming* **whuWHUMP!** *and then I hear Lesch* JIM ARE YOU OKAY? *and yelling back* I'M OKAY! *only shit scared* **whu-WHUMP!WHUMP!** *then Lesch again* GET OV**whyWHUMP!**DER THE CAR! *and screaming back* I'M OKAY HE**whuWHUMP!** *knowing if I moved they would find me, kill me, too afraid to move, terrified, more terrified than I ever knew possible, if I move they'll see me, hear me, kill me, eyes squeezed shut, then one so close* **WHWHUMP!** *that everything went orange, the explosion inflating the sleeping bag around me like a balloon for an instant and my left forearm suddenly gone numb in the hot blast and thinking it was from the concussion, just the concussion, no pain, just numb, it'll be all right in a moment* **whuWHUMP!** *then the hiss of tires shot through with shrapnel and behind and over that sound the sound of a steam kettle* **whuWHUMP!** *high pitched and constant* **whu-WHUMP!WHUMP!** *and I think a radiator's been holed* **whuWHUMP! whu-WHUMP!** *but no, the cars are cold it can't be a radiator* **whuWHUMP!UMP!** *oh god it's someone screaming, someone's been hit* **whu-WHUMP!** *and all I can do is try to live, to flatten myself against the ground, feel it, love it, burrow into it* **whu-WHUMP!** *down and thin and tiny, I want to be small, make me small, smaller so they can't find me* **whu-WHUMP!WHUMP!whuWHUMP!** *then above a flare arcs into the sky, bursting into three slowly descending lights, turning everything blood red around us* **whuWHUMP!** *Oh, Christ, it's one of theirs, it's a Russian one* **whu-WHUMP!** *not one of ours* **whu-WHUMP!WHUMP!** *and the mortars start walking away from us toward the base and finally I recognize the sound of return fire from the base and the hollow* thunk *of our mortars leaving their tubes and arcing away in the dark to the north and west and I lizard crawl still in my sleeping bag under the car and in the dark I bump against someone who's not moving and a couple of feet away is another trying to breathe ragged, wet, shuddering breaths, blood bubbling in his chest and throat, and then they're back on us again* **whuWHUMP!whu-WHUMP!** *then moving off again* whu-**whump!** whu-**whump!** IS ANYONE HURT THERE ARE TWO BAD ONES HERE! *I scream, and Apie screams back from underneath the engine* LESCH IS HIT I'M HIT LESCH IS HURT BAD! *and Boeta yells* I'M HIT BUT I'M OKAY! *and I yell back* WHERE'S CHARLES IS HE OKAY WE NEED HIM! whu-**whump!whump!** *and Apie,* I DON'T KNOW I CAN'T FIND HIM I DON'T KNOW WHERE HE IS! *and now the incoming is slackening and I start wondering if the terrs are coming* *in on the ground, how many are there, and I think of all the weapons still in the cars and scream* DOES ANYONE HAVE WEAPONS? *and I hear our own people firing back, aiming into the bush and grass to the south and west, yellow-orange muzzle flashes punctuating the dark and finally there's a lull in the explosions and I rise to one knee* whu-**whump!** *Not close but I'm down again, seeing streams of tracer fire coming in, searching, lower and lower, and our own fire going back along the same paths and then there's no more incoming and Lesch is screaming in Afrikaans to stop firing and bit by bit it tapers off and suddenly everything is still.*

We waited. The firing had stopped. Now there were only the moans of the wounded. I looked at my watch; the face was gray with cordite. Wetting a thumb, I wiped some of it off and saw the time was just after 0400. The attack had lasted almost half an hour. Johannes, the Ovambo I had nudged under the Blesbok, was dead, the other, Stephanus, was badly wounded and unconscious.

"Where's Charles?" I asked slowly, wondering at the calmness in my voice. "We need him." I looked around, my movements slow and liquid. An afterglow-like lassitude washed over me.

"Maybe he's already gone over to the sick-bay," said Apie quietly.

We stood and looked toward the base, where something was burning, flames reaching high above the protective berm. The smell and smoke of cordite hung everywhere in the moonlight. All around us were the shallow, frosty-white depressions left by exploding mortar rounds. The tires on the Casspir and Blesbok were flat, and the Casspir's windows starred from shrapnel. Bright gouges showed on the armored sides.

"Careful where you walk," said Boeta, flashing a dim torch over the ground around us.

The plastic tail fins of three unexploded rifle grenades protruded from the hard ground; the insurgents had forgotten to remove the safety pins. Within 20 meters of where we'd lain, at least five mortar rounds, half buried, had also failed to detonate.

Christ.

I tried to help move Stephanus from under the car and realized my left hand wouldn't open. Looking around at the back of the numb forearm, I saw a puckered and bloody hole three inches below the elbow. Hours later, an X ray would show that a piece of shrapnel had torn through six inches of muscle and lodged above the elbow. In spite of the surface numbness, the arm was starting to ache from internal bleeding. I could close the fingers, but they refused to open without assistance from the other hand.

Shit, more nerve damage.

Dragging the camera vest from the duffel bag next to my cot, I managed to fit the flash to one of the cameras. The filter on one lens was shattered: a piece of shrapnel had clipped the metal rim. (Later, I'd find five holes through the duffel bag. My cot and the shirt I'd laid over my filthy, caseless pillow were shredded. It took me a long time to understand that what made those holes had passed barely a foot to either side of me.)

Inside the base, one of the Casspirs was blazing; a mortar round had landed inside, setting off white phosporus smoke grenades and rupturing fuel lines. The flames cast a dancing, reddish glow across the compound. The elevated water tank, hit again with an RPG, emptied itself noisily in arcing streams. Groups of uninjured men stood with their weapons, laughing with the brittleness of relief, coming down from fear-induced highs.

The two young servet monkeys, eyes wide and screaming in fear and bewilderment, lay on the floor of their cage. Both their spines had been severed by shrapnel. In the shock of the aftermath, they were ignored. A few hours later, they would be mercifully shot amid the empty potato-chip packs.

The floor of the small sick bay was splashed with blood, the seriously wounded lying side by side, the walking wounded clustered quietly outside in the square of light thrown from the open door. I edged my way through them with my camera. A doctor concentrated on Stephanus, lifting the back of his neck to insert a breathing tube down his throat. A thick field dressing around his head was already soaked through and dripping with blood. Two ops medics, one Ovambo and one South African—the side of his neck streaked with caked blood, worked side by side on the others, putting in drips, splinting shattered limbs, staunching blood from the worst wounds.

Fifteen minutes later, Apie and three trackers, each at the corner of a poncho, carried Charles into the sick bay. An inch or more of blood had pooled at the weighted center.

Dear sweet Jesus, is he alive?

"We found him thirty meters south of the car," said Apie. "He must have run when the rev started. An eighty-two landed right next to him. He was still trying to crawl away when we found him."

But first get away from trees like those, I'd said. Oh, God, did he remember that? Is that why he ran?

Pink and grey intestine bulged from his side, and there were deep shrapnel wounds across his forehead. The frontal lobe was exposed. His body carried another dozen terrible wounds. In spite of it all, he was still quietly conscious. Incredibly, he would live.

Boeta limped from two pieces of shrapnel that had passed through the fleshy part of his thigh. Lesch's back and right side were raw from literally hundreds of tiny fragments of shrapnel and grains of sand driven into him by the blast of the mortar round. Had Stephanus and Johannes not been between him and the blast, Lesch might now be dead. Had I crawled under the car when he called to me, I would certainly be dead. The V-hull of the Blesbok had deflected shrapnel from the exploding mortar round down onto them. Of at least a dozen razor-sharp fragments that hit the duffel bag and cot on either side of me (how many others might have been even closer?), I had a single piece in my arm. Was it fear or the absolute belief I would die if I moved that kept me from scuttling under the car? Whatever, I was lucky. I was lucky, lucky, lucky.

In the radio room, messages had gone out to Ondangwa Air Force Base, reporting the attack and listing the casualties. Three of the wounded required immediate casevacing. The base commander, a young Security Branch lieutenant, set the microphone back in its clip and stood. His ankle was zigzagged with lines of coagulating blood. Limping toward the door, he hesitated, then almost as an afterthought, turned to show me his assault rifle. The lower yoke of the folding steel stock was broken cleanly in two.

"How did that happen?" I asked.

"Shrapnel," he said wonderingly, shaking his head and staring at the break.

In the middle of the attack he had seen the mortar round land inside the Casspir, setting it afire. In an almost fatal gesture, he and another had left their cover and sprinted toward the car to move it away from others parked alongside. As he was crossing the parade ground, another mortar exploded next to him. A single small fragment hit his ankle, a much larger one was stopped by the assault rifle. He looked at the weapon and then at me.

"Knocked it right out of my hands," he said, trying to grin. The corners of his mouth twitched and settled, the effort wasted. He shrugged and limped out the door. More luck.

The officers' mess was turned into a ward for the injured who had already been treated. Mattresses were dragged in. Lesch settled on one, lying on his unwounded side. His senior Ovambo warrant officer squatted at his side and quietly briefed him on the extent of Zulu Juliet's casualties. His hand moved slowly over Lesch's wounds, keeping the flies from settling. The youngest member of the group entered through the screen door, his wrist and hand heavily bandaged. He started to sit on the concrete floor.

"Nee," said Lesch, shifting over and patting the mattress. "Hier, Tati. Kom." The boy lay next to him, staring blankly at the wall. Cups of steaming coffee passed from hand to hand.

An hour and a half later, two Puma helicopters thundered low overhead. But for the risk of men dying, they would not have come until the sun was up and the area around the base secured. The heat signatures from the engines made them especially easy targets at night for a SAM-7 heat-seeking missile. They came out of the darkness, bellies and rotor blades briefly illuminated above the base, then vanished. *Come back!* Our ears followed their low, tight orbits as they came back around to land in the glare of Casspir headlights, a vertical windstorm of dust and sand enveloping them as they settled like giant bumblebees one after the other outside the berm.

Figures rose from the surrounding shadows, bending to lift stretchers, then moved into the stinging sand, their shouts blown away under the stream of turbines and the staccato bass of whirling rotor blades. The stretchers were slid awkwardly through the doors, walking wounded were helped on board and we lifted off for the thirty-minute flight to Ondangwa Air Force Base and the primary trauma center.

Inside the Puma's cavernous hold the high-pitched whine of

engines running flat out made conversation impossible. We sat on the cold aluminum floor, those of us at windows watching the barely visible terrain flashing by just below. Halfway there in the first thin light of dawn, Stephanus went into cardiac arrest. A medic gave him mouth-to-mouth, one of the wounded applied external heart massage as the rest of us watched numbly. The pitch of the blades finally deepened as the nose of the helicopter lifted, and we floated across the long runway at Ondangwa.

We landed in the predawn gray and medical teams were standing by. Stephanus was immediately transferred to a waiting ambulance and rushed to the intensive care unit. The other seriously wounded were carried or helped into the remaining ambulances for the 150-meter trip to the trauma center. As the rest of us climbed tiredly from the decks of the Pumas to the tarmac, there was no outpouring of relief, no laughter to mark our arrival. The cheerful, willing faces of the medics were ignored; the world outside the last three hours had become irrelevant. What we had seen and felt and heard had become the focus of our existence, and for the moment, there was nothing capable of intruding into the experience. Tomorrow something might replace it, but for now it was all there was or ever would be in our lives, and we walked quietly and singly across the tarmac, each lost in his own thoughts.

"All the casevacs are flown into the hospital there," Henk had said as *we passed the base the year before.*

Under a double-layered steel mesh canopy outside the operating rooms, ten triage stretchers had been set up and were quickly filled. The sickly sweet and coppery smell of blood mingled with the hospital odor of disinfectants while doctors and nurses worked over shattered black and white bodies. A team of three concentrated on Charles; still semi-conscious, he grimaced as an incision was made between his ribs and a chest tube inserted. In the middle of it all, I took photos automatically, trance-like.

In the intensive care unit, a medic stood clear of the metal-framed bed and pressed electrodes against Stephanus's chest, stepping back as the unconscious body bucked under the electrical surge. The heart monitor was silent. He stepped in again; there was another buck. Nothing.

Come on, man. Live!

A third time. Stephanus's body seemed to bounce off the stretcher under the jolt of electricity. The heart monitor beeped. Everyone held his breath. Another beep, then another and another. The doctor nodded, and the medical team stepped in to surround the bed, hiding Stephanus from my view.

I returned to the triage area. Gurneys with broken bodies were being rolled from the X ray room into the operating theaters, the surgical teams working nonstop. My own X ray showed a bullet-size piece of Soviet shrapnel lodged a few inches above the elbow. I was told that I would be the last to go under the knife.

Under the mesh canopy, a medic was carefully cleaning Lesch's raw back. His bush shorts were eased off, and we were all suddenly aware of the blood on the front of his underwear. Lesch followed our eyes down and blanched. He reached down quickly to pull the elastic waistband forward and check. The elastic snapped back, and he sighed. The blood was from another of his wounds. As witnesses, we sighed with him, a nervous giggle going around the stretcher.

Half an hour later, I walked back into the ICU to check on Stephanus. The stretcher and white mattress underneath his black torso were soaked in blood. Depressions in the mattress where the feet of the stretcher pressed into it had filled with blood. The screen of the heart monitor peaked and beeped rhythmically. Tubes carrying whole blood and saline snaked from his arms to overhead sachets. His chest rose and fell in concert with the rhythmic hiss of a respirator. A medic, sandwich in hand, sat at his side, keeping check on the life-support systems.

I was standing next to his bed when his heart stopped for the last time, the monitor emitting a steady tone, the screen showing a straight unbroken line. *Help him!* The medic put down the sandwich and wearily began to turn off the machines. *No! they can't stop now. They can't just let him go!* The medic looked at me.

"We couldn't do anything more," he said. "It took us ten minutes to get his heart going when we got him in here. He was already brain dead. We just couldn't do anything more," his voice pleading.

My eyes lingered on Stephanus, then turned to the next bed where a wounded insurgent lay, captured the week before. Here was one who would applaud, who would laugh, at the death of Stephanus and Johannes, both of whom had been wounded and died next to me. And Porky and Betoger. *Remember them, you bastard?* The last of the wall I'd tried to keep around my emotions these four months suddenly fell away. Staring, trembling, I raised a hand and drew the forefinger slowly across my throat, lips drawn back in irrational, animal hatred. Frightened and helpless, he looked away and pulled the starched sheet over his face.

"*. . . maybe I'm being idealistic too, but I can't imagine seeing or experiencing anything that would make me lose a basic sense of humanity. . .*"

"*And I hope you never do,*" he'd said. "*Because it's something you'll never forget.*"

Suddenly ashamed, I walked quickly outside and leaned against the wall, sliding down to sit in the sand. As I cradled my arm, the tears came and I wept silently. For Stephanus and Johannes, whom I didn't know, for the wounded and maimed, and perhaps most of all for me; a loss of innocence.

I didn't come for this. Yes, you did; this is exactly what you came for: the adrenaline, the fear, living on the edge, the image. Just what did you expect? You love it. Don't deny it. Yes, but I didn't come for this. Tell that to someone else. All right! But let me love it tomorrow, please, please, just let me love it tomorrow!

I looked up and Simon, one of the wounded Ovambos, was sitting patiently in front of me. "'Sawright, Tati," he murmured, handing me his Coke, "'Sawright, Tati."

I took a swallow and coughed half of it through my nose, spraying both of us. Embarrassed, I wiped my face against my shoulder.

"Kom, Tati," he said, rising and helping me to my feet. "Kom."

We walked back inside, and I saw Stephanus being rolled out of the ICU. Outside, two medics and a chaplain struggled to slide the tall, lifeless figure into a body bag. I noticed the teeth on the zipper were broken. For some reason, it suddenly became terribly important to me.

"It won't work," I said, pointing. "There's some teeth gone. It won't zip up; it won't *work.*"

The medic, the same who had switched off the machines attached to Stephanus, looked up, his eyes wet. "Then I'll just have to sew it up, won't I," he snapped, standing abruptly and walking away.

As later pieced together, a group of about twenty-five SWAPO had crossed from Angola carrying five mortars, at least one surface-to-air missile to be used against casevac Pumas, plus RPG-7s and medium and light machine guns. They split into two units, one to the northwest, the other to the west. The first was to concentrate on the base, the second group to hit us.

Three of the insurgents were spotted just outside the base immediately before the attack started. They were killed before they could use the rocket launchers two of them were carrying. When the group to the northwest started firing, their mortar bombs went over the top of the base and landed among us, along with those fired from the group to the west. For much of the attack, we were the sole—if unintentional—target of all five mortars and two or more machine guns. Some people said we were getting RPG air bursts as well. It wasn't something I could verify; my eyes were never open long enough.

Later that day, another insurgent was killed by one of 101 Battalion's Romeo Mike teams and the SAM-7 found abandoned. As it turned out, at least half the attackers escaped into Angola and the FAPLA base at Namakunde before the Romeo Mike teams arrived to throw blocker groups along the border. The rest had been forced to turn south.

The day after the attack, groups commanded by Toit, Attie, Bez and Boeta (who, in spite of his wounds, refused to be casevaced) were working southeast of Etale when they found them. In a contact spread out over a square kilometer, eight SWAPO insurgents died, though not without casualties on Koevoet's side. Bez's car was hit with a heavy burst of armor-piercing machine gun fire which wounded three of the Ovambo constables. In the middle of the contact, Frikkie left his car and ran through a hail of SWAPO gunfire to drag another wounded black policeman to safety, an action for which he would ultimately be awarded the Honoris Crux—the equivalent of the Silver Star. Thirty minutes later, another spoor was picked up and a ninth insurgent killed. The score had been balanced.

SWAPO's propaganda radio reported that the People's Liberation Army of Namibia had destroyed Ohangwena and killed dozens of South African racist soldiers. They did not mention dropping two mortar bombs on an Ovambo girls' school dormitory east of the base, killing two young women and wounding another eight.

Which isn't entirely the end of the story. Had I not been hurt during the attack, I would have been riding with Bez, Zulu Whisky's group leader. It was his car that was hit.

Fate.

22

This I Wanted to Say to You

*E*LENGA *Tyu Kwanyama* Gabriel Kautuima was, as his title said, hereditary chief of the Kwanyama, largest of the seven Ovambo tribes. He was a special and frequent target of SWAPO at his kraal near Ohangwena. A spare old man of great dignity, he greeted us courteously as we ducked under the low eaves of the thatched roof. We shook hands in the African way, and he motioned us to sit on the upturned logs around the edge of the circular hut. We sat first; to look down upon such a respected elder would be unseemly. Chief Kautuima spoke English, but out of courtesy to his counselors and the serious young men who were his guards, he politely asked that he speak in Oshivambo.

"Tate'Nkulu" (Grandfather), said Barnabas, the interpreter, pointing at me, "this man is from America and asks that you tell him of Ovambo and Namibia."

Elenga Tyu Kwanyama Kautuima, chief headman of one quarter of the population of Namibia, regarded me seriously for a moment. "We hear many things from the outside world. We hear over the radio that the United Nations says SWAPO is the only voice of Namibia. But I tell you the Namibians did not send them there. They went of their own accord.

"Perhaps some Ovambo person sent these people with a piece of paper saying they came from the people of Namibia. Perhaps it was the kings and headmen of some other place who sent these people with a piece of paper. But I am chief headman of the Kwanyama, and I know the Ovambo nation never sent anyone as a representative to the United Nations with such a piece of paper.

"The United Nations see only one side, and they do with us

as they please, but I do not know what to say about this. The United Nations would take things away from Namibia. If they take petrol away, for example, they are not against the whites— they are against the blacks. If we can find no petrol, how can we go to the markets, which are far, and make our business. These people who say you should not bring this and this to us—these people are working against us."

He stood and took the tail of a Soviet mortar round from where it was hanging on a roof pole. "If the man who bombarded me with this was a representative of the Ovambo nation, why did he come back in the middle of the night and attack my kraal where the children sleep? Is this a man who represents the Ovambo nation? Even on the path to my house, SWAPO has planted six land mines and two have killed my people.

"There was a big water tank and water pump to supply water to the hospital. In the night, they bombarded the tank and water pump. The patients were left without water. Only the patients suffered. Those who made the bombardment had their own brothers and sisters in the hospital. Is this the way to treat your own people? Perhaps the reason for planting these mines and bombarding me is because I am a headman and against them and have guards. But the people in the hospital are defenseless.

"We want peace, to sit around the table and talk. But SWAPO is against this. They say to the United Nations that all they do is for the freedom of Namibia, but if you see what they do to their own people, you know this is not true. SWAPO say they want to free the people, but how will they free the corpses of those they have killed?

"Just as you yourself came to see, I would like the people of the United Nations to come and see for themselves. Perhaps because they have good bread and an easy life, they do not want to leave America and see for themselves. But if I sent a representative to America to speak for me, no one would listen.

"Just as I provide food for my own home, so Namibia—not those from outside—must provide the solutions for the people of Namibia. You can go and write of what I say, but I think it will make no difference. Things will not change. We want freedom, but not the 'freedom' spelled out for us by SWAPO and the United Nations. The United Nations should have brought freedom to Angola and Mozambique—which they recognize—but there is death and poverty, not freedom.

"The United Nations started long ago and made many resolutions that came to nothing. And this Resolution 435 will also be thrown away like other resolutions have been thrown away long ago. All these resolutions will get older and older . . . and mean nothing in the end.

"This I wanted to say to you."

23

A Time to Go

A few days after I was hit, the surgeon examined me again. I could lift the back of the hand, but the fingers wouldn't follow, folding uselessly into the palm. "Radial nerve," he said, "but maybe it's only neurapraxia," he added encouragingly: "shock-wave trauma. Could be the nerve's only temporarily damaged by the shock wave when the shrapnel went through your arm. If the nerve itself wasn't hit, you should start getting recovery pretty soon."

So I stayed on, hoping the hand would recover enough to use the cameras quickly or hold on inside the cars. Of course, to have said that the only thing I wanted was to get back on operations, to record the action, to continue the story, might have sent a polygraph wild. I knew that to climb back into a Casspir and head into the bush would have taken more than I had shown so far. Maybe more than I ever had.

All I knew was that I didn't want to leave.

"Shrapnel Jim," Attie called me, but it wasn't just Attie who kept reminding me: "Left, right . . . center," tapping the middle of their chests on the last one—where the next one was going to connect if I went on. You've used up plenty of your luck, they were telling me; don't squander what you have on balance.

Even newly-promoted General Dreyer shook his head. "I don't think you should go back into the bush," he said. But it was only an excuse left hanging there, one I could pull down and wrap around me if the hand began working and I didn't want to continue. *Yeah, I'd really like to, but the general, he said I couldn't,* if that's what I needed.

Each morning I'd visit the sick bay where one of the medics would massage a cupful of black, jellied blood from the wound. One morning, I looked up to see Kokkie watching the procedure. He caught my eyes and shook his head. "Vasbyt, Jim," he murmured. Hang in there.

By the end of two weeks, the wound had finally closed, but there was no improvement in the hand and I knew I was just spinning my wheels by staying on. The infiltration had reached its peak, and I'd taken to hanging around the ops room, listening to the groups calling in on the radio and following their progress on the map that covered one wall. Every "Contact!" I heard took me back into the bush, images strobe-flashing through my mind, while calls for casevacs twisted and knotted my insides with the newly learned questions and selfish hope: *Who? How bad? And if it's bad, if it's a really bad one, just don't let me know them.*

Then one day: "Ambush!" That was all, nothing more. My eyes darted from the group's last reported position on the map, to the radio and back again, the call taking me breathlessly out-of-body and riveting my feet in place until it was over and they were talking again. But it was all too agonizing. And vicarious. I had become a safe voyeur; non-essential. It was time to leave.

A few days before my departure, I walked into the ops room. It was unusually crowded with grim-faced policemen. Dreyer was talking on the radio. I asked someone what was happening.

"Captain Koch's been hit—hit bad. He was in a gunship when they spotted two terrs. They came in low and didn't see three others. He took five AK rounds, and the flight engineer was killed. Three rounds went through the captain's body, and both legs were hit. He's already on the way to Ondangwa in a chopper. They don't think he's going to live."

The same Klaus Koch whose arm had been torn apart three years earlier when an RPG had exploded against his rifle. He'd been through three years of hospitals and operations to partially repair the damage, returning to Koevoet between each operation. The surgeons still hadn't finished with him when this happened.

Two days later, we heard from the hospital in Pretoria. He was still in critical condition. By the end of the week, word came that he was going to make it, but they'd had to amputate one leg.

When the day finally came to leave, Jackie volunteered to drive me to the air field at Ondangwa. We stopped first at headquarters so I could say good-bye. As we were pulling away, I saw Johnny, the Ovambo warrant officer from Zulu Tango. I had just heard he was getting his own fighting group and was up for promotion to lieutenant. Jackie stopped the car, and I ran over to him. We met in the middle of the empty parade ground.

"Johnny, ek moet nou gaan," holding my hand out. I have to go now. It exhausted most of my Afrikaans.

He flashed a smile and took my hand. We looked at each other for a moment, one of us not knowing enough Afrikaans, the other without English. Still gripping my hand, he fished in his breast pocket and withdrew a small ivory amulet, yellowed with age. He turned the hand over and pressed it into my palm.

"Gaan goed," he said—Go well—closing my fingers on the good-luck charm. Not trusting my voice, I nodded, and turned abruptly for the car.

There wasn't much to say as we sped along the tarmac road. Scrawny cattle grazed placidly on the sides of the road. Those massive, gray anthills jutted from the landscape like silent sentinels among the scattered makalani palms. We passed the bars and Cuca shops with the names already imprinted on my mind. OJ's Mississippi Satisfaction. The Happy Bar. The Sorry Bar.

Ahead of us was a column of green Casspirs. We overtook the first one and I saw Adriaan sitting behind his gun mount. I cranked down the window and leaned out to wave. He punched the air and gave me a thumbs-up. As we came abreast of each car, I was greeted with waving black arms and shouted good-byes. Jackie slowed alongside the lead Casspir. Attie, headset firmly over his bush hat, leaned over with that familiar grin and shouted something that was whipped away in the wind. Jackie accelerated, and I turned to watch the group grow steadily smaller behind us. Before another hour passed, they would be in the thick bush somewhere between Ohangwena and Eenhana, hunting. I wondered where they'd TB tonight. Eenhana, I decided automatically, unless they found spoor that took them into Angola.

It was four and a half months since I arrived, a year almost to the day since my first trip into the bush with Marius Brand, Otto Shivute, and Zulu Alpha. I had seen and experienced more than I'd ever bargained for.

"You know what Johnny said to the general about you?" Jackie said, breaking the silence. I shook my head. "He told him, 'We want to keep that shirumbu here.' You're going to be missed."

The road ahead almost blurred. *All right, goddammit, just take it easy.*

Jackie stopped at the gates of the air force base while new South African conscripts passed mirrors under the car to check for bombs. They stared at Jackie with barely concealed awe. They recognized the olive-green uniform. Their eyes widened as they took in my arm in its sling. They had heard stories about Koevoet.

It was suddenly all too absurd. "It isn't part of your program," Henk had told me. And then: *How was I going to do a first-hand account of counterinsurgency operations by hanging out with a bunch of cops?* Four months in the bush, the scars, the people, the association and now these kids at the gate thinking I was one of the dreaded Koevoet. The only cliché I had missed was the slap across the face and saying, Thanks, sarge, I needed that. *Look, I don't want to go out on some Boy Scout camping trip,* I'd told Bernie Ley on that first day. Had I ever been that green?

"What's so funny?" Jackie asked.

"Nothing," I shook my head. "Really, it's—nothing."

But I don't want to go, Jackie.

We pulled up in front of the dusty air-movements shack. Jackie unloaded my kit bag and typewriter case and checked them onto the flight for Pretoria. High above us, a four-engined C-130 Hercules was in a steep, spiraling descent. Two Alouettes chattered over the thin bush around the base, 20-mm gun barrels projecting from the open left-hand doors.

"I've got to be getting back," he said.

"Sure."

"I wasn't just joking when I said you'd be missed, you know."

"Thanks. Listen. Say good-bye for me to everyone I didn't see this morning, okay?"

"Yeah."

"And keep your head down."

"You too," and he was gone.

Pretoria was like another world; crowded sidewalks full of staid and uninvolved South Africans, all going about their business, their knowledge of the bush war limited to what they read in the newspapers. Like Londoners reading about Northern Ireland. Where I had come from might have been a million miles away. On the moon, anyway.

Bernie Ley arrived in Pretoria for a conference and on my last day there drove me to the airport. On the way we stopped at 1 Military Hospital. We took the elevator up to the orthopedic ward. In the visitors' room was one of the Ovambos from Zulu Tango who'd been wounded by the POM-Z the day I had been with Toit and Attie in Angola, the day before I had been wounded the first time. He was sitting in a wheelchair playing cards with a soldier from 101 Battalion. He flashed a smile of recognition when we entered. We shook hands, and Bernie brought him up to date on what had happened in the unit since he had been away. He listened eagerly, asking about different people. Yes, he knew Captain Koch was here; he had seen him that morning.

A nurse interrupted and motioned us to follow her. Koch brightened when he saw us come in. "Hoe gaan dit?" he whispered hoarsely. The respirator had only been removed from his throat that morning. Below his knee the sheet fell sharply away to the mattress. *So what the hell do you say?*

"How's the arms?" he rasped.

"Hell, it's nothing. I mean, really, no problem. Nothing like—how about you?"

"No, I'll be okay," he whispered. "I guess I'm pretty lucky. Looks like I'll be here a while."

"Shit, you'll be back up there before you know it."

He shook his head slowly. "I'm not going back. My little girl, she told me, 'Daddy, please don't go back again.'" He averted his eyes, then turned his head away from us. "I'm finished with it. I've done my share." He looked back at us, holding on tightly to himself. "I've done my share," he whispered fiercely.

We stood awkwardly next to the bed, trying to ignore the missing leg and making uncomfortable conversation until some of his family arrived and we made our good-byes. Months later, I would hear that he had returned to the unit.

We rode the elevator down to the floor where the intensive care unit was located. A nurse admitted us. Bernie explained what we had come for, and she led us into the stainless steel and glass ward. Another nurse stood at a raised station, where she could monitor the life support systems and see into the five cubicles around her. The first nurse indicated the cubicle directly in front of the station and we walked to the door. A black body lay on the bed, starkly outlined by the crisp, white sheets. A respirator mask was held in place by an elastic strap; dangling tubes and wires led away from him. One leg was gone below the knee.

"He's been in a coma since he arrived," said the nurse. "It's impossible to say when he'll come out of it."

"You recognize him?" Bernie asked.

"Yeah." But I didn't, really. I'd only been with the group one day when it happened. And the respirator, how could I tell with that over his face? All I knew was that he had been sleeping less than fifty feet from me when the first mortar round landed that night at Ohangwena.

I took one last look, then turned and walked away. I was going home.

Epilogue

C OMING back was like I'd never been away. Everything was the same: the people, the places, the mind-sets. Only I had changed, and there wasn't any help for that.

There was an obsession to explain what I'd seen and done and learned; I had to tell them. Everyone. It was part of me now, and I wanted to grab the world by its shoulders and say: *Listen!* But not many really wanted to know, and when a reasonably intelligent and articulate friend interrupted with a whiskey and soda and asked, "But what does it all *mean,* old chap?" I finally slowed down, kept to myself and started writing.

Some asked, "So, how are things down there?"—already knowing the answers they wanted to hear, smug or annoyed when the answers they heard fit or didn't fit the neat compartments they'd built to receive them. Both sides as convinced as if they'd been there, both sides equally unknowing. But experts; they *knew,* they had read it all, according to whichever gospel they chose to believe. They didn't have a clue.

The first couple of months were the worst, trying to come down, trying to put it down on paper; re-adjusting, back in the flow, and listening to stories of what real life was all about: holidays, job frustrations, schools, and spring sales. "And I found the most darling outfit for next to nothing," she said, changing the subject to something more important.

I called Bez, Zulu Whisky's group leader, one night to ask how everyone was doing.

"No, everything's fine here," he said. "Really slow. Oh, yeah,

Flip — you remember Flip? — from Zulu Foxtrot? — yeah, he was hit this morning. He was on the ground during a follow-up and got hit in the leg by a heatstrim."

I remembered Flip being caught on foot during the contact near Ondobe, when all he could do was hug the ground and hope.

"What happened, how'd it happen?" I shouted down the line.

"Nothing special," Bez shouted back, "just a normal contact."

A few weeks after returning to the quiet English countryside, a letter arrived from Claasie. He was still waiting for his wounds to heal enough to return to the bush.

> Hi Jim
>
> I'm writing a short letter just to let you know that everything is still okay.
>
> On 1987/05/07 at 03h00 SWAPO attacked the town with B10's. Only two bombs fell inside the town. No casualties inside the town. By 07h00 the first terr was killed and 11h30 four more. (Zulu Foxtrot + India and Zulu November + Alpha were the groups that got them.) Two were captured.
>
> Excuse my writing. The writing is bad, fractured bone in wrist still hurts a little. Also it's a long time since I'm writing English. One of Z5's cars from the Opuwa base was shot out on the tar road near Concor. The white group leader as well as the black driver were killed. I do not think you knew them.
>
> Attie of Zulu Uniform was hurt by a POM-Z mine as well. Please tell the people overseas what's happening here.
>
> Yours sincerely,
>
> Claasie

Postscript

I T seems so long ago that I walked back across the hot tarmac at Ondangwa. I remember pausing in the line of passengers and staring at the Pumas sitting quietly on the hardpan. At the hospital just beyond the flight line, all was quiet for the moment: no medics rushing wounded into operating rooms. How quickly it had all become a part of me, a part that could never be forgotten. Then it was time, and I ducked through the door and boarded the flight that waited to take me away.

I stared out the window, face pressed against the Plexiglas until long after it all disappeared; another lifetime fallen behind. Gone. When I settled back in the seat my pudgy civilian neighbor—a bureaucrat by the look of him—noted the sling and smiled patronizingly below a narrow mustache.

"Going home?"

"Yeah," I answered, not much wanting to talk.

"Defense force?"

"Uh-uh, just passing through; journalist."

"Is it? So who do you write for?"

I told him, but he hadn't heard of them. I could see he was disappointed. I closed my eyes and leaned back, hoping he would shut up or disappear.

"So, what happened to your arm there?" he insisted, which was what he was really interested in.

"Shrapnel," I said, the tone suggesting he mind his own business. *Leave me alone.*

"Genuine?" he said, raising his eyebrows, no longer disappointed. He'd met someone who'd been wounded in the operational area. "What happened? Kaffirs get you?"

Suddenly, there was nothing about him I liked; not his narrow mustache, nor his safari suit, not his double chin or soft hands or pale skin. Damned if I'd explain anything.

"Just kidding," I said. "Tennis elbow."

His eyes and nostrils narrowed. Lips pressed together, he returned to his girlie magazine. So much for South African-American relations on this flight.

It's hard to believe how much time has come and gone since then. Adriaan, Attie's brother, is dead, killed only days after taking over as Zulu Quebec's group leader. Bennie, Jackie's right-hand man and soul mate, and Daniel Taiko who saved Zulu Foxtrot from the ambush were both killed during the April '89 fighting. Herman, who experienced his first contact the day Daniel saved us, lost a leg to a heatstrim the same day Daniel died, and won a place in Koevoet legend: after the contact, he amputated what was left of his own leg with a penknife. Otto Shivute, the twenty-four-year-old with more contacts than he could remember, has died of kidney disease at a private clinic in Walvis Bay.

On a happier note, when last heard of, Jerry Mbwale was selling insurance in Oshakati. Toit, married and a father, is doing the same in Pretoria. Marius Brand, Boats, Flip, Ryno, Paul, Claasie and Frikkie all survived and have left Namibia, some still in uniform, others into civilian life. The unit, of course, was disbanded, and — save those Southwesters who elected to remain in the country of their birth — almost everyone else is gone; even many of Koevoet's Ovambos, their lives forfeit under a SWAPO government, are moving to South Africa.

And did they leave embittered? you might well ask. And I would try to look wise and say: yes, some, and predictably so; the rest simply philosophical about the years they lived through. I beg your pardon? Oh, yes, yes, I do hear from a few of them from time to time; just quick notes to tell me where they are and what they're doing now.

And yes, I still think about it — hard not to, really — that fractured mirror of moments and people: snatches of conversations, and the early morning smell of wet bush mingling with blue diesel exhausts; hours of mind-numbing boredom inside a Casspir as it nosed its way through the undergrowth; the sudden, heart-pounding rush at the first shots of a contact. Everything seems so clear still. Especially the people. The people. As if I could step through the mirror's frame and they would all be there: just the way they were.

If broken glass and shattered bodies could be put back together again.

When you leave somewhere it is gone forever; what you remember will never be the same again. People leave, others arrive to take their place, and even those who endure have changed, grown or diminished, from what you remember. So let them all remain as I have described.

It was a war in another life beneath a visiting moon.

> *Forebear to judge, for we are sinners all.*
> *Close up his eyes, and draw the curtain*
> *close;*
> *And let us all to meditation.*
> —*Henry VI, Part 3, iii.31*

Glossary

AK-47	Soviet-designed assault rifle.
AKM	Version of AK-47 with folding stock.
B-10	Soviet-designed recoilless gun firing a projectile with approximately the same destructive power as an 82-mm mortar bomb.
BAKKIE	Pickup truck; literally, a bucket.
BLESBOK	A mine-protected supply vehicle built on the same chassis and V-hull as the Casspir. Each Ops K group of four Casspirs was accompanied by one Blesbok.
BOSBOK	Tandem-seat, light-observation aircraft used by the South African Air Force.
BRAAI	Barbecue.
C-130	Hercules four-engined transport and cargo aircraft.
CANU	Caprivi African National Union, a liberation movement formed in 1962 and allied with SWAPO. Dedicated to the independence of South West Africa/Namibia, many of its members who crossed into Angola and Zambia eventually were imprisoned by SWAPO for tribal reasons.
CAPRIVI	(Or Caprivi Strip.) A strip of land once claimed by imperial Germany with an eye to connecting German West Africa with German East Africa (now Tanzania) via the Zambezi River.
CASEVAC	Casualty evacuation.
CASSPIR	A mine-protected armored personnel carrier originally designed for the South African Police (SAP) and used by both Koevoet and the SWATF 101 Battalion on counterinsurgency operations in Namibia. The name is an acronym derived from the Casspir's

	designers—the Council for Scientific and Industrial Research (CSIR)—and SAP.
CCN	Council of Churches of Namibia, which supported SWAPO's efforts to liberate South West Africa/Namibia.
COIN	Counterinsurgency.
COMOPS	Communications Operations, a "hearts-and-minds" program designed to draw the local population away from SWAPO and to engender support for the government and security forces.
Cuca shop	A small shop selling a limited selection of such items as canned goods and beer. Named after a legendary but no longer available Portuguese-Angolan beer.
Cutline	A cleared strip that separates South West Africa/Namibia from Angola. *See* Yati.
Eenhana	A company-sized permanent base occupied by 53 Battalion, an SAAF helicopter detachment, and a Koevoet communications center.
Goeiemôre	Afrikaans for "Good morning."
FAPLA	Popular Armed Forces for the Liberation of Angola, the Angolan army of the Soviet and Cuban-backed MPLA government.
Heatstrim	South Africa security forces' nickname for the Soviet-designed M-60 high-explosive antitank rifle-launched grenade.
Hoe gaan dit?	Afrikaans for "How goes it?"
Kaokoveld	A dry and mountainous desert lying west of Ovambo, bordered on the north by Angola and to the east by the Atlantic Ocean.
Katima Mulilo	A small town at the end of the Eastern Caprivi and Sector 70 headquarters.
Kavango	Tribal area of the Kavango tribe, lying east of Ovamboland and south of Angola.
Koevoet	Afrikaans for "crowbar." When the unit was first formed, it was nicknamed Koevoet, to signify prying loose the SWAPO insurgents from the thick bush. Koevoet became known as Ops K. The official name was South West African Police Counterinsurgency unit (SWAPOL COIN), though Koevoet remained the popular name.
Kolodio	Oshivambo for "right."
Kolomosho	Oshivambo for "left."

KOMESHO	Oshivambo for "forward."
KRAAL	An enclosure of sharpened logs set on end surrounding the branch and woven-grass huts of an Ovambo family.
MPLA	Popular Movement for the Liberation of Angola, the Angolan Marxist government supported by the Soviet Union, East Germany, and Cuba.
MOHANGO	The Ovambo staple crop of grain sorghum.
OHANGWENA	Kwanyama tribal headquarters and location of 21D, a permanent police security branch base.
OMEGA BASE	Headquarters for the SWATF 201 "Bushman" Battalion.
ONDANGWA	The second-largest town in Ovamboland and the location of the major South African air force base in the operational area. It was also the location of the primary trauma center.
OPERATIONAL AREA	The northern area of South West Africa/Namibia that bordered on Angola. This included the Kaokoveld and Ovamboland of Sector 10, the Kavango and Western Caprivi of Sector 20, and the Eastern Caprivi of Sector 70.
OPUWA	Western-most Koevoet base, located in Kaokoveld.
OPS K	*See* KOEVOET.
OSHAKATI	The largest town in Ovamboland and the location of Koevoet and SWATF headquarters.
OSHONA	A low area that fills with water during the rainy season. The pronunciation is corrupted to *shona*.
OSHIVAMBO	Language of the Ovambo people.
OVAMBO	The largest ethnic group in Namibia, comprising over 55 percent of the country's population. The Ovambo people are made up of seven distinct sub-tribes: Kwanyama, Ndonga, Kwambi, Ngandjera, Mbalantu, Kwaluudhi, and Nkolonkhadi-Eunda, each with its own dialect.
OVAMBOLAND	(Or Ovambo.) That area of South West Africa/Namibia that traditionally has been the home of the Ovambo people. Part of Sector 10, together with the Kaokoveld.
PENCILSTRIM	South African security forces' nickname for the anti-personnel version of the Soviet M-60 rifle grenade.
PB	*Plaaslike bevolking*, Afrikaans for "local population."
PKM	Soviet-designed, general purpose machine gun.

PLAN	People's Liberation Army of Namibia, the official armed wing of SWAPO.
POM-Z	"Pom-zed," Soviet-designed anti-personnel mine/booby trap.
R5	Short-barreled version of the Armscor R4, the 5.56-mm automatic rifle based on the Israeli Galil, based in turn on the AK-47.
Rev	An attack on a base.
Romeo Mike	*Reaksiemag,* Afrikaans for "reaction force." Used to designate 101 Battalion's teams using Casspirs in Ovamboland.
RPD	Soviet-designed light machine gun.
RPG-7	Rocket-propelled grenade launcher capable of penetrating up to 6 inches of steel armor.
RPG-75	Telescoping, one-shot rocket launcher. The first one seen outside the East bloc was in Ovamboland.
Rundu	Small town in the Kavango located 7 kilometers south of Angola. It was headquarters for Sector 20 as well as the easternmost Koevoet base.
RV	Rendezvous, "romeo victor," used to designate a grid reference.
SAAF	South African Air Force.
SACC	South African Cape Corps, a unit within the SADF, manned by Colored South Africans.
SADF	South African Defense Force.
Shirumbu	Oshivambo for "white man."
SKS	Soviet-designed semiautomatic rifle. Obsolete by modern standards, but still in common use by SWAPO during the bush war.
Spoor	In the context of this account, tracks left by SWAPO insurgents.
SWAPO	South West Africa People's Organization, the Soviet-backed liberation movement dedicated to wresting control of South West Africa/Namibia from the South Africans.
SWAPOL	South West African Police.
SWAPOL COIN	South West African Police Counterinsurgency, the official name for Koevoet.
Strandwolf	Mine-protected supply vehicle based on same basic design as Wolf Turbo. Used exclusively by Ops K.
SWATF	South West Africa Territory Force.

TATE'NKULU	Oshivambo for "grandfather," used as polite form of address for an elder.
TATI	Oshivambo for "father," used as a polite form of address between men of similar age and station.
TB	*Tydelike basis,* Afrikaans for "temporary base."
TGNU	Transitional Government of National Unity, a black majority government in South West Africa/Namibia appointed by the South Africans.
TRACKER	Usually an Ovambo special constable highly skilled in following the spoor of SWAPO insurgents.
UNR 435	United Nations Resolution 435, which called for United Nations-supervised elections in South West Africa/Namibia.
VOORSNY	"Ahead cutting" in Afrikaans.
WINDHOEK	Capital of Namibia and overall army and police headquarters.
WOLF TURBO	Mine-protected armored personnel carrier, designed and built by Windhoek Maschinen Fabrik in South West Africa/Namibia. It was used exclusively by Koevoet.
YATI	Cleared strip of border between Namibia and Angola. Also referred to as cutline.
ZULU	SWAPOL COIN headquarters in Oshakati.
ZULU TWO	SWAPOL COIN communications center in Eenhana.
ZULU THREE	SWAPOL COIN investigation center adjacent to Zulu..
ZULU FOUR	SWAPOL COIN base at Rundu in the Kavango.
ZULU FIVE	SWAPOL COIN base at Opuwa in the Kaokoveld.

About the Author

JIM HOOPER is a free-lance defense photo-journalist specializing in Africa. He first took up writing as a television documentary writer. He deserted T.V. in 1976 to become a professional skydiver, amassing over 3,000 jumps as owner of the world's most prestigious sport parachuting center in Zephyrhills, Florida. In 1984 he sold his home and business and left the United States to resume writing.

Since then, he has covered conflicts in Chad, Sudan, Uganda, South Africa, Namibia, and Angola. His articles and photographs have appeared in a wide range of publications, including The *Economist, International Defense Review, Jane's Defence Weekly,* and *Armed Forces.* His photographs are syndicated by the Paris-based Gamma agency.

Mr. Hooper graduated from the University of South Florida with a degree in Russian. He is divorced, and divides his time between areas of low-intensity conflict in Africa and his home in an ancient Saxon village in Hampshire, England, where he carries on a torrid love affair with his Morgan 4 + 4 motorcar.

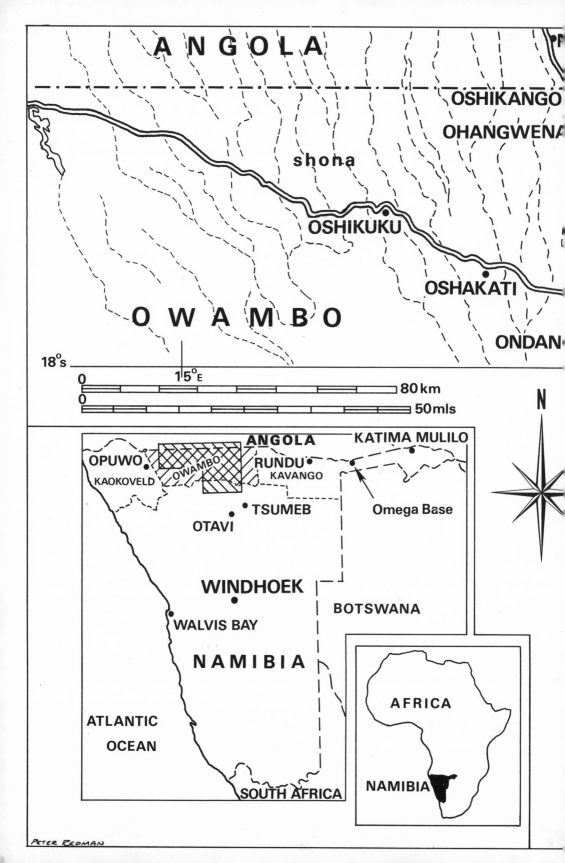